Eat Dust

Hartman de Souza has a background in theatre, education and journalism. He has been associated with several theatre groups in the country and was, till September 2015, the artistic director of the Space Theatre Ensemble, Goa.

Eat Dust

Mining and Greed in Goa

HARTMAN DE SOUZA

HARPER LITMUS

First published in India in 2015 by Harper Litmus
An imprint of HarperCollins *Publishers* India

Building 10, Tower A, 4th Floor, DLF Cyber City, Phase II,
Gurugram Haryana – 122002, India
www.harpercollins.co.in

P-ISBN: 978-93-5136-484-9
E-ISBN: 978-93-5136-485-6

2 4 6 8 10 9 7 5 3 1

Typeset in 11/14 Adobe Jenson Pro (OTF) at
Manipal Digital Systems, Manipal

Printed and bound at
MicroPrints India, New Delhi

To Justice Santosh Hegde, former Lokayukta, Karnataka, and his investigating officers, for uncovering the rot in Bellary; and the Justice M.B. Shah Commission and its investigating officers who uncovered the rot in Goa.

For Aki, and for Cheryl, who growled with conviction and refused the money that would take away the trees; for Peter who sowed in our heads the seeds of rebellion, and Dora, who understood as far back as 2008, that it was only civil disobedience that would save the earth. For our cousin, Sister Lisa Pires of the Presentation Sisters Convent and her colleagues for taking a firm stand against the mining.

And Hugo de Souza, damn you, you should have been alive to read the first draft, and you too Shyamsundar, why did you let that creep mess with your head?

For Beena Sorab, who was an integral part of that gang. Specially for the man who messed with Hugo's and my head, Reverend Dr Albert de Mendonça, Head of the Philosophy Department, St. Xavier's College, Goa.

Also Brij Raj Singh and Praful Bidwai, both of whom gave due encouragement to this manuscript, but passed away before they could read the final draft.

Mario Pinto-Almeida, old warhorse, cynical but honest advocate, I can't leave you out, can I?

And for Steve Siqueira, jazz musician, and Dr Eddie Rodrigues, sociologist, my Goan soul-brothers from East Africa and close friends and collaborators all these many years. And Godfrey Pereira, my East Indian friend and writer from wilder Mumbai days, who visited the farm twice, saw the mining and urged me to write. Also Valentino Gasper, crazy potter/sculptor/artist for many kinds of support and collaboration over many, many years; and also Olinda Fernandes, ex-Nairobi, now in Toronto, who painted Carmel College, Goa, a bright red.

Especially for Javed Anand and Teesta Setalvad, old friends from even wilder Mumbai days, who continue to inspire me in their fight for those killed in the Gujarat massacre. Your fight is our fight too. As is that of the late Bharati Roy Chowdhury, and now Ashok Chaudhary and Roma Mallick of the National Forum for Forest Peoples and Forest Workers, who, in spite of state-sponsored repression, have unswervingly supported the cause of the forests and those who live and work there.

For every Indian below the age of thirty who believes that forests and mud and water have more value than the ore.

And last, but certainly not the least, humbly placed at the feet of the other more prominent members of the BUZZ household, Ujwala Samarth, and Zuri and Zaeen (and not to forget Koko). And of course Ramesh and Prabha Samarth and their extended and very crazy family. Without such unstinting love coming my sorry way, this book would never have seen the light of day.

Only when the last tree has been cut; only when the last fish has been eaten; only when the last river has been poisoned; only then will they know you cannot eat money...

— A saying of the Native American Cree people

Contents

A MAP OF THE MINES

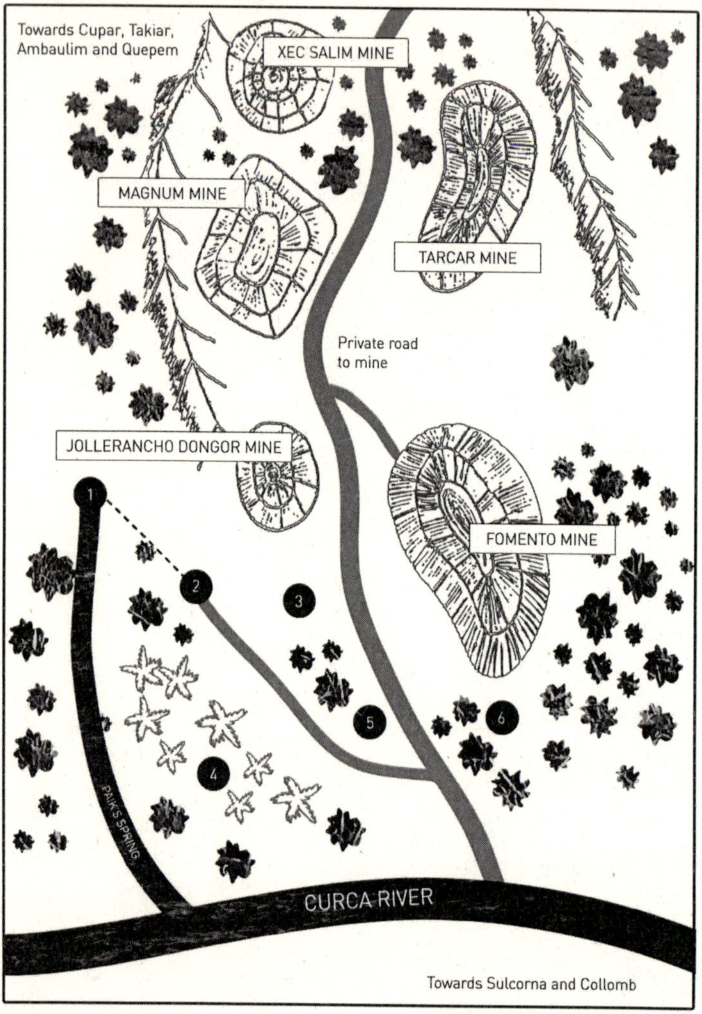

KEY

1 PAIK'S SPRING
2 PAIK'S TEMPLE
3 FREEDOM FIGHTER'S HOME
4 THE FARM
5 GAONKAR HOUSE
6 GOVERNMENT HIGH SCHOOL-MAINA

A Bird's Eye View

It is likely that a crested serpent eagle flying at its highest can see the whole of Goa – a little more than a hundred kilometres from the north to the south at its longest, and some forty or so from the east to the west at its widest – with just one of its eyes.

It is actually the easiest thing in the world to circle Goa, although one should attempt this only on a Sunday – given the chaos and congestion that prevails on its roads anytime between 8 a.m. and 7 p.m. on other days of the week.

I made that journey four times while writing these chronicles, thinking that I needed to see Goa the way a crested serpent eagle would.

You could begin like me, with an early breakfast at the local chai shop in Gaundongrem, close to Goa's southern borders and the rivers Galgibaga and Talpona, dipping bits of crusty village bread into a bowl of spicy coconut gravy with soft diced potatoes and peas swimming in it. If the meal is had during the rains, the prized wild mushrooms picked from the surrounding hills will find their way into the curry. Breakfast is just a stone's throw away from the temple of Mallikarjun, and Gaundongrem is the last village as the ribs of the ghats slowly unravel eastwards. The road then climbs past the entrance to the Cotigao Wildlife Sanctuary, snaking its way through several valleys, each delightful, beautiful.

This canopy of hills breaks just before Neturlim, the last watch between the plains and the human settlements westwards, and the huge spine of the ghats that towers beyond it to the east, reducing Gaundongrem to a mere speck on the landscape.

Beyond, perhaps around prehistoric shrines dedicated to deities of centuries past and never discovered till now, lies the source of the river Kushawati, a series of hills that lets out the water needed to make this river majestic as it tumbles down through the valleys below, taking with it smaller brooks, springs and tributaries.

North from Neturlim, the drive runs adjacent to these magnificent ghats that line the eastern borders of Goa, coming in from Karnataka and going north towards Maharashtra, bringing with them corridors of wildlife that existed thousands of years before the area was taken over by human beings. At regular stages along the road, past the towns of Sanguem and Sanvordem as well as the Selaulim dam that allows south Goa to quench its thirst, you get ample evidence that precious water sources are now under siege.

Past Sanvordem, perhaps near the entrance to the Bondla Wildlife Sanctuary, one could stop for a light lunch. That depends, however, on how much of an appetite you still retain after witnessing first-hand the ravages of mining.

If you are stupid enough to make this journey on a weekday at the height of the mining season – as I was – you would do well to drive with the windows closed to keep the dust out – baking slowly under the blazing sun as you inch your way through a never-ending line of trucks. Ahead of you are trucks going empty towards the mines, and the ones coming from the other side are overloaded with ore meant to be dumped into the barges that line the deep and easily navigable rivers Zuari and Mandovi.

One crosses smaller rivers, creeks and brooks – dwindling away in a silent display of the destruction caused by mining. Probably the saddest sight of all is that of trucks being washed at the edge of these water bodies, turning their crystal clear water a dirty brown.

During the three months when the monsoon breaks and mining is forced to a halt, a drive through this corridor is all one needs to witness the destruction that humankind is capable of. For close to ninety kilometres of potholed road, you find yourself surrounded by hills shorn of trees and earth. The trucks responsible for this carnage are queued on either side of the road – washed, gleaming and waiting for the mining season to start again.

On this mission to encircle Goa, past the skeletons of the hills and forests that once used to grow between Sanquelim and Bicholim, one bends northwards in a long westerly curve towards the old Portuguese fort (now a tourist resort) at Tiracol overlooking the sea. A break for some late tea, perhaps, or even a couple of tall whiskies with ice and soda to wash away memories of the unpleasant sights you witnessed along the way.

When you finally reach the sea, it's with a heavy heart. The plateaus leading to it have already fallen to several consortiums, including Goa's duly elected representatives of the people. The press reports this in detail. Lionel Messias is perhaps Goa's first investigative journalist and a fellow black sheep because he cannot be bought. Everybody at the helm of power hates him because he has nailed them all with facts, figures and names complete with documentation showing which Goan politician has hooked up with which businessmen to colonize the area. But nothing really happens. He continues to batter them on his website[1] and they continue to broker deals. Goa is just a pimple on the pretty face of India.

The lawyers will come out, link hands with environmentalists, make little attempt to work on the ground and move the courts instead. Until those protesting block the roads, and resist till the bitter end, are there really any guarantees that justice will prevail?

So close your eyes then, because when you open them again you will see plush golf courses[2] enclosed by fences with razor-sharp wire; more gated resorts for high-end tourists; plush housing colonies for the rich and famous; even a new airport for Goa[3] that everyone here admits is not needed. Everyone, except the precious few with a big stake in bringing in tourists by the horde, and the ones that see beauty only in structures made of cement, concrete and steel.

No thought has been given to the families that inhabit the plateau where the airport seems near destined to come – the people who lived there even before the Portuguese invaded Goa. These are the traditional custodians of some fourteen perennial springs that break in the plains from this same plateau. The plateau has thriving flocks of huge hornbill that, stupidly, have not learnt to fear people yet. They will have to find a new home – which will not be easy, given the fact that just south of the plateau, in Asniye and some seven other villages in Maharashtra's ghats, Goa's Dempo family mined contentedly.[4]

An hour spent at the northern border, brooding dark thoughts and seeking solace in staring at the sea as it readies to welcome the sun for the evening ahead, gives one enough time to drive southwards along the coast to return to the Agonda or Palolem beaches (a few kilometres from the starting point that morning) for a drink before sitting down to a late dinner at about nine.

No drink will hide the grief of knowing that an otherwise idyllic journey has been marred by this damning evidence.

Goa is so tiny, older Goans used to refer to it as their 'mandkulem', a Konkani word lovingly used to denote a baby crawling on the floor and beginning to discover its world. That term has acquired a cruel twist these days. Over the years, they have helplessly watched this baby attacked by three wolves.

On the one side is an industry that refuses to rein in its government-sanctioned excessiveness. This middle-aged wolf goes by three names – Tourism, Real Estate and that magical term, Infrastructure, and turns every Goan politician (and their cronies and well-wishers) into wealthy contractors, businessmen and industrialists before your very eyes.

It prowls around coastal Goa, the twenty kilometres from beach into land, where you witness this from the fort at Tiracol and the majestic and deep river before it in Goa's northern end to the last hill where the Galgibaga and Talpona rivers come in at the southern borders. From north to south, Goa's industry takes as much as it can get, moving ever further inland, grabbing as much as it can take and as fast as it can take it. The greed of those who sell and buy knows no measure.

The second is an old, wiser wolf who sits back until it is time to eat. This is the Mining Industry and its home is the magnificent Western Ghats – where sacred groves play host to ancient trees and mountain springs. But it is also a place where this industry's greed[5] has been the strongest in recent years, putting entire forests and hills to the sword.

The last wolf, possibly the most vicious, is the youngest. He is plain, simple Consumerism, and all that this phenomenon brings with it – the blind promises of gratification that will eventually lay Goa (and the rest of the country) to waste.

It was an undeniable fact, something anybody at the window seat of a plane flying into Goa could see, that the forests and hills and water bodies on the eastern borders of Goa were being steadily annihilated.

And along the coast, the towns and cities-in-making on Goa's plains and plateaus are chockfull of garbage dumps. Where once were tilled fields, roads flanked by greenery and a thriving water source, today you see man-made swamps and roads bordered with refuse. Village business establishments, hotels and even restaurants make surreptitious trips late at night to dump waste in a field, often right under a board put up by the local panchayat expressly forbidding such practices.

On one of these mornings, when the sun has just peeped out and the children are being dropped off at school, it is not uncommon to see a Honda Civic or some such limousine slow to a crawl. One of its windows will whirr down to let out a hand – elegant and covered with gold bangles – holding out a neatly knotted plastic bag full of garbage. Moments later, you find the bag in a rice field bordering the road, and the car gradually receding into the horizon.

South Goa's largest city Margao has a garbage dump, the famed Sonsoddo,[6] on the outskirts of its eastern side that should have rightfully been a tourist destination. Sonsoddo was once a beautiful hill that both hid and announced beauty. Leaving Margao eastwards, if you take the road left after Sonsoddo, you move towards the outskirts of Raia, into Santimol, and onto Rachol, the site of Asia's oldest Catholic seminary. Just beyond it is the magnificent expanse of the Zuari, itself under threat from both mining and the 'infrastructure' industry.

Hidden behind Sonsoddo is the entrance to Curtorim, a village still standing largely idyllic in the midst of lakes and tilled fields and water channels. But now, as with a hundred other villages in Goa that have ostentatious dwellings intended to proclaim success and happiness, numerous fields are lying in disuse, many even buried in mining waste to aid the construction of more buildings.

There is a heady cocktail at work in Goa. On the one hand is the ambition, greed and almost vicious quest for wealth and power shown by at least two generations of Goan politicians (as well as the men and women they have carefully moulded in their own image), and on the other is a palpable public apathy. So Goans complain long and hard, but always stop short of actually taking a stand on an issue and pursuing it to its logical conclusion.

A mixture of inefficiency, ignorance and delaying tactics ensured that the once-scenic Sonsoddo hillside degenerated into a garbage dump so huge, unattended and fecund, it is now a major source of information on how *not* to approach the vexed problem of human-generated waste.

This vulture and crow-infested dump is right next to one of Goa's best schools, Manovikas, whose former director and founder, Therese Almeida, a respected educationist and the author of a textbook on environmental issues, unsuccessfully battled the political skulduggery behind this shameful sight for more than ten years before the century ended.

However, the real irony isn't that Sonsoddo was not brought to a halt, but the fact that the contract to rectify this mess was awarded to the same Goan family business establishment that destroyed the hills and forests with their mining operations.[7]

The Timblo family also own a well-known hotel on the southern outskirts of Panjim, overlooking the many barges hauling ore from their mines down the Zuari river, into the bay and onto the ore carriers that line the sea's horizon. Some five or six years ago, the same family had successfully procured a willing state government's compliance to shamelessly whitewash a Supreme Court order asking them to demolish an illegal construction at the resort.[8] Nothing happened. Because this is Goa, and life must go on.

In Sonsoddo, they did to accumulated, unsorted garbage what they did to ore stacked in their mines for the monsoons. They covered it with metres and metres of thick jute, which – apparently – lessened the stench, trapped the leach so that it could fester better, kept scavenging birds away, and gave passing motorists the surreal sight of bare hillocks that were the colour of faded denim. Now, as these chronicles head to the press, this 'green' company has constructed a huge shed as big as their hotel to simply hide everything.

It just got worse in Goa in the Age of Greed: 2005–2012. If one turned due left when facing Sonsoddo, spinning on one's heel to look the other way and fly some forty or so kilometres as a gull, one would cross the Zuari, cross Panjim and the river Mandovi, and reach the long stretch of beach in north Goa that begins past the rocky outcropping at Aguada and goes northward from the villages of Candolim to Calangute and Baga. Just where the beach first breaks at Candolim lies the twisted, rusted wreck of the ill-named *River Princess*, an iron ore carrier.[9]

It lay on its side, unattended for more than ten years, creating unnatural eddies and currents that have drowned several unsuspecting tourists. One among them was a brilliant young college student of whom I expected great things. I roundly curse the mining industry for his death. This wreck has eroded an entire stretch of beach that, in all likelihood, will never return to its original state. One cannot ignore the fact that with every passing year that the sea chooses to show her fury, a significant part of the village of Candolim may just disappear. It's another matter that not even a few hundred metres away from it is Goa's garbage-free version of Monte Carlo, home to tycoons ranging from airline owners to TV magnates.

Like Sonsoddo, Goa's famed garbage dump, there was no action taken – even though the wreck was widely and consistently covered in the local media. Successive governments as well as the mining magnate (an independent MLA to boot) responsible for the ore carrier cloaked the heinousness of this ecological disaster under government-appointed panels, discussions and legal wrangling.[10] Now, even though the bulk of the wreck has finally been removed, a substantial portion still lies below the water. This is Goa. Life goes on. Tomorrow, they will get the necessary permissions to build a marina over it to provide anchorage to private yachts.

As it welcomes its showrooms and malls, a new generation of Goans (and other Indians) – armed with education and the firm belief that it is only money that can make the monkey jump – allow greed to take over. They are willing to set aside the norms of decency, turn their back on justice, fairness and compassion, so they can shop, eat and celebrate.

Field after field has been covered with concrete for the construction of resorts, luxurious housing complexes and holiday homes. They have cut into entire hills to construct industrial estates, bridges and broader roads. Goa has totally disrupted its traditional water patterns and then, almost wilfully, created swamps that mix with sewage and run wild with foreign undergrowth and weed. India's wandering poor have made inroads into the state, earning their daily pittances as they join the ranks of urban Goa's 'service industry'. And in the hinterland, mining companies were eating around the ghats to get at the ore.

Reacting to Portugal's hold on her colony, Jawaharlal Nehru was supposed to have famously referred to Goa as a pimple on the face of India. Now look at how the pimple has been squeezed.

Japanese prospectors discovered the first traces of iron and manganese ore in Goa in 1905, around the same time that the Belgians started digging into the mud in Karnataka. A fledgling mining industry developed in the next forty years and today's Goan magnates – supporting the fascist cause back then – exported as much as 100 tonnes of ore. By 1954, cashing in on the post-War boom, the same families shifted allegiance to the Allies and raised this to 1 million tonnes. Given their new nationality, things only got better. The figure rose to 10 million tonnes by 1971 and close to 15 million tonnes in the 1980s, ensuring the rapid growth of a hegemonic industry that – long before the dawn of the Bellary cowboys – was raising its own sun in Goa and getting set to pull the strings.[11]

In the 1990s, both price and tonnage rose further. In the new century, they went through the roof.

A public petition urged the Ministry of Environment and Forests to uphold the moratorium on clearing new mining leases, pending a comprehensive social and scientific audit being undertaken in Goa.[12] As the petition duly noted, Goa had less than 1 per cent of India's landmass, but contributed to more than 40 per cent of India's iron ore exports. The petition brought to the ministry's attention that Goa itself would cease to exist at the current pace of mineral extraction. It said there was no effective monitoring mechanism in place either from the Central or state government to ensure that mining was not done in violation of environmental norms.

Our high-growth-rate pundits in Delhi knew well that more than 85 billion tonnes[13] of mineral reserves lay in the ghats off both our shores, just waiting to be 'exploited'. While the looting was on in Goa, they had pledged to increase foreign investment to $20 billion as the new century took off.[14]

There are those inside the government and outside it who remain adamant that 'theology' should not colour the debate over the chopping of trees and destruction of water sources. This is also a coterie that preaches 'pragmatism' – a view of the world where truth, tragically, is defined by what 'succeeds'. The belief that the environment is the only social wealth we all truly have in common is seen as nothing more than unnecessary intransigence.

In the 1970s, when traditional Goan fishermen with their 'Rampons'[15] (cooperatives named after the type of fishing boat used and owned by many of them) complained that mechanized trawlers were systematically eradicating traditional breeding grounds, nobody was listening. Politicians[16] entering the trawler business ensured that the Rampons had no choice but to adopt the new technology themselves. In north Goa, it is doubtful if more than one small Rampon of four or five boats exists. In south Goa, there are two, maybe three.

While this debate raged, once even culminating in huge padyatras from the four sides of Goa that many of us actively helped converge in Panjim, a majority of the Goans chose the more pragmatic option of eating fish from their plates without being overly concerned about how it reached there.

In 1967, mackerels were available in Mapusa at one rupee a hundred, and landlords of the time ordered a couple of bullock carts full at ten rupees a cart. They would use it as manure, carefully burying lines of rotten fish in pits they dug around their coconut trees. Today, hundred rupees may just get you a measly few. And then again, the size of the fish seems to be getting smaller, a sign perhaps that Goans don't care that they are eating catch that has not had a chance to achieve adulthood.

Village lore on the southern coastline will tell you that right through the 1980s, when gold was hard to come by and India salivated at the sight of this accursed mineral, cargo ships and even dhows would smuggle gold and silver bars from souks in the Gulf and would be met at sea by Goan trawlers who brought the loot to shore to be ferried by road to Mumbai. Issues such as these, while not debated in the legislative assembly either then or now, reside as common village knowledge stifled even at that local level by silence and acquiescence.

In all fairness, most Goans probably realize only too well how the rest of India sees their 'amchem mandkulem Goen'. The famous and wealthy, Bollywood stars, well-heeled day-trippers and tired executives desperately enact their versions of cool as they traipse on the grounds of a luxurious hotel.

Not too many sunning themselves by the pool in such a resort would know that the bulk of Goan waiters there are paid as little as 800 rupees and designated as 'trainee waiters'. If at all they are made permanent, they could hope to get something close to 3,000 rupees. Most enhance their incomes from tips, and patiently wait for their recruitment agents to process their papers so that they can join one of the cruise liners, where, perversely, they are greatly valued for their skills in hospitality.

The latest trend of course, is to dig out the old family papers and apply for Portuguese citizenship and then head to the UK, where many young Goans now compete with poorer East Europeans.

Goa has changed rapidly. Given the huge prices that old Goan villas command, these are now owned and it must be said, beautifully restored and maintained by prematurely retired investment bankers, high-end executives and rich businessmen who've settled in Goa in some luxury to reconnect with a stress-free life. Goa is now the official residence of highly qualified and experienced professionals from various parts of the country who have moved here to connect with their more creative side. And that's the irony. If you have the means – and too many younger Goans don't – then Goa is a great place to live in. Even now.

Have those who have bought into Goa integrated themselves into the Goan villages where they now live? A very small minority do, but those tend to be past the age of forty and living in Goa for some fifteen to twenty years. Those younger and well-heeled – artists, designers, writers, dancers, scholars – are here for the ride. Make the bucks slaving elsewhere, then come to Goa to chill out, do yoga, walk the beach, play with and care for the stray dogs, turn organic, reconnect with one's inner self.

Maybe they are just quintessential tourists: when the going gets tough in Goa, they'll move to Gokarna or points further south and leave their footprints there instead.

For 'hip' urban wannabes, well-heeled or not, Goa is the clandestine chance to break out of the conformity of college, junking bras for a halter and puffing marijuana to live dangerously – if only for a week. For a certain sort of Indian man, it provides the chance to see a white woman in a bikini up close and real. For the government in New Delhi, given that Goa brings just two seats to the elections at the national level, it is useful for the partial royalties its rich mining families diligently provide by way of exporting ore.

Goans with money and drive, who make it to Page 3 news articles with photographs showing them exchanging smiles with the rich and famous from Mumbai or Gurgaon, are often shocked by just how many 'outsiders' have bought a piece of their pie. Yet, they too are, for all intents and purposes, neutral outsiders. They have the luxury of sitting on the sidelines; an apathy common to those who have lots of comfort, and want far more.

The sad truth is that Goa, which has a long history of welcoming and even trading with its invaders, has been ensnared once again – and this time for good.

Like they say in the village bar: when this beautiful woman that was once Goa dies, and she is reduced to looking no different from a decrepit suburb of Mumbai or Kolhapur, even God will not be able to identify her carcass.

1

THE MINING PIT

We are in the village of Maina, home to the foothills of the Western Ghats as they fall on the eastern borders of south Goa. Behind our backs, the sun breaks to give us a morning that is clean, fresh and magical.

To your right, like a large chunk of flayed meat laid out in the rising sun to dry, is the Fomento Resources mining pit. The Timblo family owns it. This is your first evidence of how a thickly forested hill can literally disappear, leaving in its wake a huge pit, some two-three acres in width and deep enough to swallow a seven-storey building.

This mining operation was the one that first caught my attention. I used to drive past it every morning to drop my niece Aki to school, leaving my sister Cheryl's farm on the dot of six-thirty every morning. Morning, noon or midnight, to me it felt as if the mine pit was screaming in pain. Had it not been for Thelonious Monk playing on the car stereo, I may never have survived.

This was only the first of the *five* mines that lined this three-kilometre stretch of winding road from the farm to the village of Cawrem ahead. The next ten kilometres or so led us through three other villages affected by mining to the rapidly urbanizing town of Quepem.

This is what the book really is about. It's a chronicle born out of the morning trips I would make with Aki to school in Margao, then returning on some days to pick her up again. On each such journey over a period of six years, I bore witness to the sheer monstrosity of the mining operations between the farm in Maina and the growing town of Quepem. It just seemed to worsen with time and distance.

By 2010, the misshapen town of Quepem had become Goa's third mining town – after Bicholim to the north, and Sanvordem to the east. The three made up a squalid triumvirate in the infamous 90-kilometre mining belt that destroyed the eastern slopes of the Western Ghats as they broke into Goa. Almost overnight, we started seeing men who had made their money from mining zoom up the road to Sanvordem on swish bikes and cars.

In the 1990s, there was a thickly forested hill where the Fomento mine now stands. The tree cover and undergrowth had once been so thick on this now-vanished hill that you could not have made even an eighth of the way up. This holds true for any of the hills here. In the 1980s, I managed the trek only with the help of Pauto, who worked on Cheryl's farm. He was my ageing storyteller, and a man who knew all the steep hills here like the back of his hand.

If you do not find the traditional paths, you cannot climb these hills. Between the thick trees, you could find thorny shrubs and grass that grows well over your knees. The way ahead is often blocked by vines thicker than your wrist, and there was every chance that you may come face-to-face with anthills bigger than four basketballs put together or be pulverised with fear as snakes slither swiftly across your path. You may even be forced to retreat in the face of a thick web, big enough to cover a dining table, hosting a spider as big as a child's palm. Yet, when you take a path that was carved over the years by the steady treading of bare feet and cattle hooves, climbing becomes as easy as it would be on a well-designed staircase. If your rhythm is right, you could do it in forty-five minutes or an hour.

The idea that a hill just disappeared left me fuzzy-headed. How does one come to terms with the deliberate destruction, in peacetime, of agricultural practices and the everyday life of people whose only crime is that they live here? Or the wasteful hacking of trees, the seismic upheaval of mud, the conscienceless blasting of aquifers? All of the forest's original inhabitants – the fish, otter, crabs, spiders, beetles, butterflies, moths, lizards, frogs, birds, hares, porcupines, deer, wild cats, wild boars, leopards, bison and even tigers turned refugees.

Every time I drove through this dusty road back in 2006, I could feel the bile rising up my throat even as my hand moved desperately to change gears and speed away from the scene of carnage. And as the sun rose, the sight of the scars and the devastation that greeted us was enough to make a few in our midst wish that we were young enough to pick up a couple of guns and go, as the dacoits in the Chambal ravines say, faraar, turn into an outlaw.

In 2008, even as we were informed of a centrally-appointed panel that was being set up to investigate the plundering of the country's resources by private mining companies, you could still hear the culprits at work on this very road – the harsh sound of metal pounding the earth, followed by the sharp hiss of thick, dark exhaust fumes being let off into the air.

Now, thanks to a September 2012 Supreme Court order, there's greenery afoot.[1] It is as if Ganesha himself had appeared and spread wisdom. In the more thickly wooded hills further south, you see tiny yellow blossoms in the open ground, which the local children pluck to place at the god's chubby feet.

When I finally left the farm in Goa, the ban had kicked in and the mining had come to a dead halt. Now, a good three years later, as I return and see what cures the monsoons have brought, it is humbling.

Today, I can only hope that these hills between Maina and Cawrem, so stunning and painful in their beauty, are never clawed into again.

As I try to bring this chronicle up to date, I recall how they used to launch the mining season by pumping out the sparkling rain water that had accumulated in the mining pit during the monsoons – caring little for the fact that the copious amount of muddy water being expelled was destroying the low-lying agricultural lands north and east of the mining pit.

When they were done pumping the water out, there was still a small amount left in the pit. That water would, like a festering sore, turn rancid and green with slime after a few days in the sun.

In September, as the last vestiges of rainclouds disappeared from the sky and the pit dried out, they would bring in giant earth-moving machinery and start widening the sides of the pit. By October, when the heat levels in the pit had become hellish and the stagnant water in the centre dried to a wrinkled scab, they would set about deepening it. Concerns about mining below the water table or destroying underground aquifers figured nowhere in this scenario.

Standing in front of the Fomento mining pit at that moment, any young visitor from Karnataka could have drawn parallels with the infamous mines of Bellary. If you Photoshopped the picture to remove the still-existent greenery in the surroundings (that would eventually go anyway), all you would have been left with was a huge dark crater surrounded by acres of orange-red desert.

It is difficult to understand how the respectable Timblo family business systematically took away an entire hill and its forest over a period of twelve years. If the grim sequence of events were to be reconstructed now, we can see that they first began to dig and hack behind the hill – a place where nobody could see what they were up to for quite a few years because of the height and girth of the natural formation.

That was way back, before the new century came along. The mining companies in the area weren't yet sending out ore-filled trucks in those days, just preparing the ground while they worked out their deals with iron-hungry China. The low-grade hematite ores found in Goa can only be used when blended with high-grade magnetite concentrate found plentifully in China, and in 2007, backed by that country's appetite, the price for Goa's ore – low-grade as it was – jumped from around 65 dollars a tonne to 170 in just a year. The miners were not going to ignore that.

They got rid of the trees first, taking away the topsoil and dumping it outside their lease area. Then they separated the low-grade ore that had been dug out and stockpiled it in huge mounds. Later, as if those mounds were under their lease, the miners went back to where they had dumped the topsoil and started digging there too. China wanted our low-grade ore, and there was a lot of that in these dumps.

In the 1990s, the front of the hill that you saw then was like the set for a Cecil de Mille movie – a prop. Behind it, Fomento Resources had left a burnt orange-red wasteland in their wake. If you drove your bike into this area behind the hill at night to see just what they were up to, it could get pretty scary. You would inevitably lose your bearings between the dunes of low-grade ore and the maze of dusty truck-tyre marked roads. Your high beam would eventually meet your own narrow bike tracks, and then you would stop, switch off the lights and look up at the stars for help.

In 2007, the mine was about 500 metres from the school. Today, it is less than a hundred metres away. By 2010, there were 15,000 mining trucks in Goa and many more on the way. It got so bad that the superintendent of traffic wrote a letter to the chief of police in April 2011, saying that the number of trucks driving through the mining zone should be reduced by fifty per cent. The letter was ignored because the trucks had created prosperity almost overnight, for the locals who owned them as well as the state, which earned Rs 1,000 crore as royalty in 2010.[2]

However, through 2008–11, at the height of Goa's Age of Greed, it was better if you didn't have to look that way as you drove past. Everyone knew, and the mining barons themselves admitted it, that the mining would last barely fifteen years at the rate at which it was going.

This translated into: 'Let's take it out as fast as we can.'

In the mining season of 2008-09, it was as if the mining barons, always a close consortium of rogues, had received inside information about a Central inquiry (later to be better known the Shah Commission) to probe illegalities in their trade. Before such an inquiry was actually instituted and then tabled, the mine owners had already set about preparing for its arrival – and any strictures it may put into place.

They seemed to have calculated that they had about two years and a bit to loot the place. Almost overnight, they brought in even bigger machinery, doled out even more loans for trucks and worked in relentless shifts.

At night, three of the mines here were still working. With powerful generators and bright arc lamps lighting up the pit, huge shovels piled mud into trucks manned by a skeleton staff through the night. A little after dawn, the truck drivers would come in on their motorcycles and park them between the trees before getting onto the overloaded trucks and setting off for Sanvordem, where the barges waited, at a reckless speed.

Two simultaneous operations were taken up even as the day shift gave way to the night. On the one hand, the trucks went out with even more loads and even more trips were made. On the other, the digging continued unabated, with one pile of ore going into the trucks for immediate export while another – unable to be transported immediately because even over a thousand trucks were not sufficient – was covered with a bright blue plastic sheet for protection from the rains. The mine owners planned to uncover the piles and export the ore once the storm of the investigation had passed.

The rapaciousness of what the mining companies did appears to be directly proportionate to their growth rate. Goa's second-largest mining company, the Fomento group, for instance, had exported only around 1 to 2 million tonnes of ore in 2005, and far less in the years before. Newspaper reports say this figure doubled in 2007–08.[3] According to the data on the company website, their production went up from over 6 to 16 million tonnes of ore in just a year.[4]

These were the only figures that were 'officially' recorded. Only God and the mining companies in Goa know how much was actually sent out 'unofficially', and how much of the brunt was borne by the state exchequer.

The monstrous scale of mining in Goa during this period can be understood from the figures released by the Controller General of the Indian Bureau of Mines, who admitted in 2013 that Goa had iron ore stockpiles of about 700 million tonnes.[5] Given that Goa's ore has always been low grade, this quantity may actually have been much higher. They began piling the ore from the 1960s, when there was neither an export nor domestic market for it. Even if one followed the minimalist guidelines laid down by the Ministry of Environment and Forests, mining companies were supposed to plant trees in these low-grade ore dumps, which also contained mud and clay, as they had faithfully promised to do so when they sought so-called 'environment clearances. They did not.

This may have been just the tip of the illegally mined stockpiled ore because, in September 2011, an RTI request filed with Goa's department of mines found that the department had only fifteen plots registered to stock ore. What it did not reveal as activist Ramesh Gauns found out and later told the press, was that mining companies had taken up plots at some distance from the mines in Bicholim, Sanquelim, Navelim and Usgao in north Goa.[6] In the worst case, they had encroached on about 20 kilometres of the banks of the river Mandovi, and even installed illegal crushers to turn lumps of ore into fines. It took the Goa State Pollution Control Board until April 2012 to actually rap the mining companies on their knuckles.[7]

Even as they killed more hills and forests to further widen and deepen their mining pit, the Timblo family gifted the children of the Government High School, Maina, with exercise books and pencils and umbrellas for the rains. Later, they added plastic shoes, money for new uniforms and made promises of providing educational stipends to parents – depending on how much land they held. Several meetings were held between mining officials and local leaders at the school itself. Many of us knew that as soon as they wangled the necessary permissions to extend the scope of their mining, the Timblos would shift the school into a new building elsewhere, all the better to extend the mine without fear of criticism over endangering the lives of children. In north Goa's mining corridor, at least two schools were completely surrounded by the mining operations.

Two visits in 2011 by the Justice M.B. Shah Commission – the Centrally appointed body to look into illegal mining and exports in Goa, Karnataka, Orissa, Jharkhand, Andhra Pradesh and Chhattisgarh – made the mine owners hot behind their collars.[8] Before both the visits, Fomento launched a corporate social responsibility programme, brought in another clinic, tried to appease the youth of Cawrem by giving them jobs at the mine, opened a ramshackle centre with a few computers in the village, refurbished temples and shrines, and threw promises and coin all over the place.[9]

By the time the Shah Commission team came visiting, mining companies in the area had done everything short of getting signed affidavits from the people of Maina and Cawrem testifying to their contributions to the two villages.

By 2010–11, the company's prospecting drill had come a stone's throw from the edge of the school's football ground, barely fifty metres from the road we drive on. Just before the

Shah Commission's visits, Fomento laid down concrete stakes painted in red – complete with numbers, letters and symbols that bordered on gibberish – to supposedly demarcate the mining territory.

Not too far away stood four or five security guards in black uniforms, each armed with mobile phones that they would whip out whenever anybody unfamiliar approached the pit. They would photograph the visitors before calling in the managers.

Here too, there was money to be made on the chain. The security guard, like the migrant truck-driver or cleaner, held far less value than the ore meant for export. Lawyer Nandita Haksar, who has studied human rights violations in the Northeast for decades, documented how men from that region ended up in Goan mines as security guards. It was nothing short of an organized slave trade.

Labour contractors, an invention of India's Second Industrial Revolution, lured young, well-built males from the Northeast to Goa. While the better-looking, 'smarter' ones were sent to resorts and gated colonies as 'security guards', the ones who didn't know any English ended up at the mines. In the more forested south of Goa, adjacent to the sanctuaries, one would find these sorry figures – deprived of their documents and (at times) even their pay – sweating it out under the hot sun in black uniforms to guard the mines from curious journalists or the occasional villager bringing cattle to graze at the edges.

To their employers, it was enough that the young men *looked* 'Nepali' and brought with them, therefore, all the attendant attributes – wizardry, kukri skills, an endemic knowledge of kung fu, or whatever.

Lisa Monteiro and Kimberly Collaço, two young journalists from the *Herald* in Panjim, visited Maina after Justice Shah's report had been tabled. They were stopped at the Fomento pit by guards from the Northeast who barely spoke Hindi but seemed friendly enough. The men were actually frightened, because almost overnight, they had seen the mining stop, the machines come to a halt and their owners disappear. They let the journalists through to view the pit but, at the same time, followed instructions and called the managers on their mobiles. By the time the two women got back into their car, a mining jeep had arrived with the managers. They parked at a distance and filmed the journalists walking into the school and later getting back into their car.

The two women came back from the visit to the Government High School shaking their heads.

'Did you know about this?' Lisa asked. 'The teachers there think the world of Fomento! They say it's only because the company came to this area that their lives have improved, that the government did *nothing* for them.'

'Yeah,' added Kimberly, 'they behaved like guides taking us on a tour, showing us everything that Fomento had given to the school – computers, uniforms, books, pencils, pens, chalk ... A teacher even asked the students in one of the classes, "Do all of you like mining?" and they answered in chorus: "*Yes* teacher!"'

Later, as all of us knew, they had plans to shift the school further east on the road to Pirla because this would allow two mine owners and their politician-contractors to extend operations all the way to the Curca, the river that runs past the farm. Of course, the mining company readily agreed to finance the construction of a new building.

Many of the drilling points to test for ore are still dotted around the old school building, and all the way up to the hill leading to Cheryl's farm. They knew exactly how much ore lay beneath. In those days, two barren dumps of dirty brown waste towering well above the 26-degree slopes legally specified for such heaps formed the skyline in that neighbourhood.

I still remember a scene from 2009, where a solitary tree – far more gigantic than the ones that had fallen around it – stood at the edge of the pit with its head unbowed and its bark still fresh. The tree, now leafless, had once stood at the base of a hill that was eventually razed to the ground by miners. On the slopes of this gigantic pit, with its sheer walls and torpid water, it was strangely heartening to see the tree continue to stand its ground in a last-ditch act of defiance against the bulldozers.

Not for long. It fell a few months later. I wonder if the miners bulldozed it or blasted it into oblivion. The pit continued to get bigger – in width as well as depth – because they were working round the clock.

As you pass the Fomento pit to your right, the road out of Maina becomes straighter. Not that the view will get any better.

Ahead of you, just past the mining pit, is a patch of forested land that the Fomento Group has already bought. If mining were to resume, it will surely disappear.

The road that leads from Maina to Cawrem past the school, twisting like a snake, also shows signs of changing. Six years ago, it was just broad enough for two mining trucks to pass at the same time – slowing down to a crawl while doing it, much to the drivers' chagrin. However, after the ban on mining kicked in, the road showed signs of being 'worked on', and on its edges were the ramshackle dwellings of the people brought in to do the laying.

The sheer volume of trucks coming into the mines at the height of the mining, put together with the heavy rains and a local contractor who cared only to have another contract come his way soon enough, ensured that this road was ridden with potholes wide enough to swallow a small car.

After the ban on mining, the BJP government – which came to power in the 2012 elections – and its coterie of contractors brought in landless labourers from the drought lands of Karnataka and Maharashtra to work on the road. The funds for this had already been sanctioned by the earlier Congress government's Churchill Alemao, minister for the Public Works Department (or, as some refer to it, the Public Waste Department).[10]

The new contractors used their mining trucks to transport men, women and children and their meagre belongings here, and dropped them – as literally as one can imagine – in a clearing at the side of the road. Later, these same trucks hauled broken laterite stone (probably from the closed mines) and dumped it in piles along the road. It might as well have been a scene from an old Hollywood film, depicting black American prisoners breaking rock in a chain gang.

Early every morning, every able-bodied person, whether old or young, would either start breaking stones into small bits or carrying it in plastic basins on their scarf-covered heads, while their infants – swaddled in old clothes for protection from the morning chill – sat happily sucking their thumbs.

Back then, Alemao did not sanction any money to the poor villagers of Maina and Cawrem, or even to assist drought-stricken refugees from the neighbouring states. He did spend a lot to extend the mining corridor for the convenience of his brother, Joaquim Alemao, though. In fact, as far as Churchill Alemao goes, the chickens alas, are coming home to roost.[11]

The sugarcane fields adjacent to the new road were once the largest between the villages of Pirla and Maina, and were owned by Anand Gaonkar, a prosperous award-winning farmer who lived at the bottom of the hill.

People say that around 2005, or perhaps even earlier, Gaonkar sold all his land near the Government High School and all the way to the border of the farm, to Joaquim. Incidentally, Joaquim was the minister for Urban Development in the earlier Congress government.

In the local bar, everyone marvelled at Gaonkar's good fortune. They say he pocketed at least a few crores in a simple cash-for-land transaction that made everyone in the picture, from the peon to the clerk of the panchayat considerably richer. However, Joaquim seemed to think that he had got himself a very good deal anyway, given how the price of ore was heading for the ceiling.

At any rate, almost overnight, Gaonkar turned into a role model for other landowners in the area. He discarded the old sloping-roofed laterite brick-and-plaster house, and built a large two-storied house nearby, painting it an alarming shade of blue with gleaming white trimmings. He constructed a wall around the house and installed a huge gate, though, thankfully, he hasn't chained a pedigreed dog in front of it yet. Inside the compound, Gaonkar built a small family temple and painted it bright pink with blue borders. He made a driveway and bought a Sumo, hiring a local driver from Cawrem who once worked at the farm. His daughter, a recently practising lawyer, was presented a bright-red Indica.

By the time he bought the land from Gaonkar, Joaquim – like a few other Goan politicians and their kin – was well on his way to becoming the mining magnate he so desired to be. He was a 'raising contractor' for mines in Keri and Adavpal in the already devastated hills and forests of central and north Goa. The term 'raising contractor' was invented by the Digambar Kamat government to ensure that political detractors could float their own mining companies and start making money instead of becoming a hindrance. Joaquim had begun digging for his mining bosses on private forestland at Rivona in the northeast, and planned to reopen an old mine in Pirla barely ten kilometres east of the farm.

Now, let us return to the road we were on, just past the Fomento mining pit on your right. Since late 2006, Joaquim's heavy machinery had started digging into the spine of the last and highest hill just as soon as the rains abated. He had a lease that extended from this disused mine that was eating away at the side of a hill known as Jollerancho Dongor to the edge of the last valley before Paik's temple, almost parallel to the traditional path that pilgrims took to visit the adivasi deity's spring.

Nobody seemed to know who really operated this lease. The signage at the mine, which was hastily painted and put up when the Shah Commission came visiting, declared that it belonged to Anil Salgaocar. This gentleman was the head of Salgaocar Mining Industries, a smaller but equally important member of the five mining families that ruled Goa in those days. Anil set up his new company after he broke away from his two younger brothers, Shivanand and Dattaraj, and the V.M. Salgaocar Group founded by their father, the late Vasudev Salgaocar, in the fifties.

Anil Salgaocar was also the independently elected MLA from the Sanvordem constituency, the second mining town in Goa after Bicholim in the north. At least one newspaper carried a photograph of him taking his afternoon siesta in the assembly.

He was there to get a first-hand account of what was being discussed about mining during the proceedings.

We can gauge how small a player Anil Salgaocar was from the fact that when he contested the elections in 2007, his declared assets amounted to only some 70-odd crore rupees. This is not bad at all, when you consider that this small family company exported 2 million tonnes of iron ore in 2010-11.[12]

Prior to the first visit of the Shah Commission, *none* of the five mines between Maina and Cawrem had the requisite boards providing the names of their companies, details of the mining operation listing lease area and the date of official environment clearance. We saw this first hand. They simply felt no compulsion to do so.

Apart from smaller mining companies owned by Goans who were not unrelated to the mining families, there were a few magnates from Rajasthan and Gujarat in the business. They had probably migrated to Goa in the period following World War II – when the US strongly supported Portugal's decision to keep Goa as its entry point to combat the influence of the then Soviet Union. And then there were the ones who came in from Mumbai and the other metros in the 1960s and the '70s, either signing up old leases to mine, or just sit on until the time was right to sell.

So Joaquim's mine was actually under a lease belonging to Shantilal Kushaldas, a migrant from Gujarat long settled in Goa. Kushaldas happened to be a close associate of the larger undivided Salgaocar family till the mid-1960s, and was now embroiled in litigation to ascertain who the real owners of the assets were. None of this was actually very clear because while the roughly painted signage outside the mine said it belonged to Anil Salgaocar, the so-called 'public hearing' to accord clearances to this operation – which began work even before they were handed out – was held in the name of Kushaldas.

Just after the Shah Commission's report was made public, NDTV's Srinivasan Jain asked Joaquim Alemao about the allegations made against him in the Commission's report. 'I did not know it was illegal. I was only doing business ... it is my constitutional right to do business,' he told Srinivasan in a sing-song affront. 'Do you want to take that right away from me? Then what I will do, *starve?*'

On his land you would find shabby-looking security guards keeping vigil through night and day. Go a little further, and you would find a barrier among other sure-fire signs of a mining operation. There was a road leading into the mine that was not yet broad enough to let two trucks pass.

While Joaquim, as we will see, had made a wise investment by buying the land from Gaonkar, because of the ban, he turned out to be one of the more unlucky ones from that time.

Unlike the Magnum Mine, which lay on the other side of the same giant hill, he did not outsource the job to highly competent professionals in the industry. Instead, Joaquim chose to hand the job over to locals loyal to him, and they worked at their own leisurely pace.

So, when the Shah Commission came visiting, his company, Raisa Mining, was still preparing the ground for the operations to come. This meant clearing the tree cover, digging out ancient topsoil from the side of the hill, penetrating an aquifer or two, and opening out the ground for the riches beneath.

Before the commission visited, about twenty motorcycles were always parked at this entrance every day. They belonged to the supervisors, heavy machinery operators and truck drivers. Inside, one would always find bright orange trucks and a jeep or two. Whenever Joaquim or his managers visited the site, they would be seen driving inside in huge white or black SUVs with dark windows and licence plates showcasing the family's known fetish for the number 9.

As you followed the lines and contours of the hills from south to north, you notice that the very colour of the hills, a kilometre or more on either side, had changed. The misty blue patina that once covered the luxuriant sunlit green cover in the early mornings was now a dull lifeless brown. Every time you drove up, the bright yellow bulldozers near the summit had shaved off another few metres of forest.

Even sadder is the fact that the Old Portuguese mining concessions in the area hold the traditional names for these foothills, which form the cusp between Maina and Cawrem. As each is related to a local tribal deity or legend made manifest in water, the old folk in the area refer to them with reverence.

Joaquim's lease was titled 'Jollerancho Dongor', using the Portuguese variant of the name and not its traditional spoken sound in Konkani – 'Zollarancho Dongor', the Hill of Zollar.

The word 'dongor' for hill connotes a forest. You will not, for instance, find anyone in this area referring to the huge mound of barren waste at mine number one, the Fomento operation behind the school, as a dongor. Moreover, the dongors in this part of Goa are all linked to sacred springs. The shrine, the site of worship and awe, is nothing more than a spring of fresh water.

Tembechem Dongor, therefore, means the hill with the iron pot; Devapan Dongor, the hill with god; and Jollerancho Dongor, the hill of Zollar. On all the hills in the eastern slopes of the Western Ghats, one will find local spring-shrines that are home to ancient pre-Hindu deities propitiated with something as starkly spiritual as a mud pot and a stone from the spring placed in it. Such was the kind of respect that villagers, who practised a shifting cultivation in these hills or tended its many cashew plantations, had for nature's bounty. It was a genuflection to water.

In these villages, the older people stand in awe of Jollerancho Dongor. Some say it was thus called because it had a lot of water, and attracted mosquitoes by the thousands. Older villagers in their seventies say this is the hill on which they spotted tigers coming in from the thicker forests west. And then there are others who say that the steep hill was named so because it was the home of a benevolent demon called Zollar, whose spring – containing water of the sweetest kind – was protected by the denseness of the forest, the steep climb and the demon himself. Stories have it that many ventured to this spring protected by Zollar: young men in search of fat hares; wizened old men hunting wild pig; cocky men in their prime doing it to impress their lovers. Sometimes they were even taken against their will. Everybody was led astray by Zollar, tangled and smothered in the vines of his hair, and made to disappear for a few days at least. Villagers say they would be possessed by Zollar's spirit. Even if the demon did let them return to their homes, it would be after extracting a promise from them. All in the village noticed that they would appear to be in a trance for a few days, and when they finally recovered, would be nicer to their neighbours for fear of what Zollar would do to them.

In 2009, all the mines in the area – following government regulations – audaciously put up flags, banners and buntings to celebrate 'Mines Safety Week', as if the activity could ever be safe for our fragile environment. There was an irony here. Goa's Department of Mines Safety was staffed by professionals who took their job very seriously indeed. And yet, the safety of mining personnel apart, there can be no other way. To get at the ore, you have to hack the trees, upend the earth and do away with the vast aquifers that nurture the springs that provide us with water.

Opposite Jollerancho Dongor is the old entrance that Fomento used in the late 1990s, when they were only hacking the back of the hill and forest. Ore extracted from the mining pit behind the school now takes another road that links the four hills east of this road that you can't see, with more mining operations that have steadily destroyed them as well as their springs. The old Fomento entrance now leads to a kind of service yard–one that contains dilapidated trucks and machinery, barrels of oil and diesel piled against the wall of a typically ramshackle shed stained with the red of mining waste, store rooms, dirty living quarters for menial workers and shabby canteen facilities as well as primitive toilet arrangements.

This was once a small part of the Maina village in the 1980s, comprising three houses and a bar-cum-provision store. However, like the hills, it seems to have become a part and parcel of the Fomento 'mining backyard'. The company has tried its best to mask it, but between the dumps of waste, you can see the expanse of wasteland it has left behind: mining dump leading to mining dump, as far as the pit behind the school. Once the ore is over and the mining contractors leave, yards such as these will turn into shanty towns and slums for Goa's increasing migrant labour force – poorer citizens displaced from their land elsewhere in order to foment growth and industry.

Everywhere along the mining corridor barracks with poor toilet facilities sprouted up to house migrant workers from the mining belts of Karnataka, Jharkhand and Chhattisgarh who drove the trucks or took up menial mining jobs that Goans did not care for. Now, after the Supreme Court ban on mining in Goa, they have had to run away and turn into 'environment refugees' yet again, such being the shabby alternatives we offer them by way of 'creating jobs'.

In such mining-dependent, transient and seasonal habitations, there will always be a ramshackle garage for trucks with its attendant mess and stains, and a few new houses of people who own land there. This has been happening increasingly in the mining corridor after the Supreme Court ban, especially in the days following the 2012 elections, with incomplete buildings on encroached forests or even government-owned land being willingly doled out to buyers by unscrupulous local politicians. All the buildings have been constructed with money made from owning and operating mining trucks.

Nearby, you find other mining-related businesses – one or two smaller huts with tiled roofs that serve as provision stores, eateries, or yet another bar where truck drivers used to tank up for the haul.

There is further evidence of just how insidiously a mining company can encroach, grab and destroy. Had you slowed down your car at this very same spot as the new century broke, you would have heard the distinct sound of water and wondered where it's coming from.

From July to September, thanks to a relentless rainy season when the surrounding hills fill themselves with water and then let it flow down, the sound of gushing streams east of the road used to be well above the low hum of your car engine. And if you let your imagination play as you coasted, you would have heard a low gurgling sound. From October till February, except at night, you would have to stop and switch off the engine to catch the sound of the water from this brook. The sounds were muted but still clear. After that, well into the summer of May, you would only have heard the water late at night, and that too, after you had parked the car and walked to the edge of the road. This time, the water would sound extremely muted, as if women softly weeping.

By 2007–09, there was hint of neither water nor tears on that bend. The brook that flowed through the hill had been covered with mining waste, and the ground levelled to create more space for the service yard. Close to where the spring ran, an orchard of banana trees flopped helplessly in the heat. There were fleets of trucks untidily parked between heaps of dark, oily mud.

As any mining engineer worth his salt will tell you, the worst obstacle to a mine's profit-making motives is the presence of water. The deeper the mining operation goes into the earth at the side a hill, the more aquifers it will burst, drawing water from the surroundings. As this water prevents them from getting to the ore in the pit, it is therefore pumped out and 'diverted' in accordance with the technical specifications. The water goes where it can, or, for reasons known only to the tribal deities who once presided over these hills, simply disappears.

Let us first look at the topography surrounding this spring, as it was before the mine near the school was developed. This spring had its origins in Jollerancho Dongor and flowed under the road through a natural culvert that had survived for at least a few centuries. It went towards the school, skirting the hill where the Fomento pit now stands. Behind the school and a small hillock that still stands at the edge of the slope leading down to the pit was another small settlement of Maina with a few houses and many more trucks. These were villagers who had already sold their land to Fomento by 2010, and were just waiting for another year of mining before moving to new plots that a mining-compliant administration would gratefully give them. Behind them, this same spring joined the Curca, handmaiden to the Kushawati, which flowed some distance east.

Unfortunately, water will not stay silent like the Goan polity. Because of the pressure that builds when water gathers and moves in an enclosed space, you can't choke a spring even if there's a few hundred tonnes of mining waste above it. You merely send it elsewhere, towards soil and sub-structure that will accept the pressure and give way. Therefore, on the slopes of the pit adjacent to the school in 2010, the same spring bubbled and frothed out with rage– probably because it was trapped by the impermeable ore beneath. Given the depth of the pit and the slope towards it, the water would naturally head to the pit.

In a stroke of 'brilliance', Fomento dammed the slope towards the pit with a dyke made of several truckloads of mining waste. The water collected on the grassland in front of the pit. A rough and ready track led to this pond, so that mining trucks could be washed early every morning in the remnants of this once-freely flowing spring.

But flowing water isn't easily quelled. In 2012, after the ban on mining kicked in and everybody thought that the spring had disappeared, it fought its way back with the help of heavy September storms. Soon, the water made its way back from the hill behind Joaquim's lease of Jollerancho Dongor, and cut a path for itself back to the mining pit behind the school.

2

Remembering Paik's Temple

Through the nineties, when the greed of mining was yet to make an appearance in Maina and Cawrem, there was no separate 'community hall' near Paik's temple. A spacious covered porch served that function. The inlaid cement benches were polished through use, and the floor was clean enough to warrant removing your footwear.

Given that the state's first government had hastily ratified old Portuguese mining concessions and Goa's mining families had hastily gobbled them up, a new plan was put in place as the century broke. In retrospect, the plan seems sickeningly familiar.

With one hand, they bought a stake in the devotion to the local deity – Paik, or whomever the villagers in the mining affected belt favoured – and ornately 'refurbished' old, even ancient, temples into garish and graceless quasi-modernistic structures. Even in this largely non-Catholic mining belt, they restored and repainted, or set in ghastly vitreous tile, the occasional village cross, shrine or chapel where the families of Catholic truck drivers and other villagers prayed.

With God on their side, they assumed nothing could go wrong.

With the other hand, showing their concern for the practicalities of the real world, they constructed cheap and unsightly 'community halls' next to the temple. Villagers were told that they could use these 'fruits' of mining for weddings and other social gatherings. Ironically, in village after village in the mining corridor, these very community halls were then used to conduct the sham 'public hearings' to fast-track the earlier Congress government's illegal permissions to mine.

Paik's temple is a barely fifteen-minute trek from the fork of the valley below.

Hills tower above on either side as you walk up, and the slopes are lush with cashew trees, the strong fragrance eddying up from the leaf sap even when they are without flower. It is as if the thick cloying fragrance of leaf rotting and going back to soil brings out the vapours of life itself. Leaving this fork to begin the climb, you find a clump of giant jackfruit trees, heavy with fruit, standing to the left. Below them, in a seemingly dark and foreboding gorge, lies a perennial well.

During the rains, this benign pool of still grey water suddenly hears the call of the wild, roaring and bucking its way madly out of the ground to surge close to half a kilometre into Cheryl's farm where it flows into deep pits dug to harvest what we can of its bounty, before tumbling out again to join the river Curca below. This well is fed by aquifers below the hill, and Paik's temple stands to its right. Located less than a football-kick away is Jollerancho Dongor, an integral part of Paik's pantheon and the very place where Joaquim Alemao launched his mining operations.

Back in the good days, you could trek up the hill to reach a tiny place of worship shielded by a grove of large trees at the summit. Paik would be there, waiting to greet the sun and bowing his head before the Mother Ghats on Goa's eastern borders. The vast range of hills behind the temple blocked the western horizon from sight, and went northwards towards Cawrem, where the other mines were. Behind these hills, the sun would disappear for a good hour and more before it finally set.

It was always unbelievably cool at Paik's feet, even during the height of summer. The old temple was never locked because there was nothing to steal. The open and unassuming sanctum sanctorum was shiny and clean, and the garlands of hibiscus, marigold and jasmine left behind by visiting devotees were rarely even a day old.

The temple was built in the late 1970s on an earlier shrine. As is the case with many a labour of love, it defied convention. It was a simple, pared-to-the-bone laterite structure with a tiled roof, mud-plastered and then whitewashed by villagers once a year. The temple looked and felt like a community hall.

Most villagers, busy with the everyday tasks of tending to their land and crops, didn't even know when the temple committee was bought over by the mining companies. The building contractors in the area, however, were ready to roll, rubbing their hands in glee at the prospect of making some additional money.

So midway through the new century, they did what they do to a hill when they set about creating a mining pit. They brought in the bulldozers and the earth movers, and just scooped out part of the hill where Paikdev stood with his trees – where he stood, mind you, guarding the sanctity of *water*.

By mid-2008, six or seven concrete structures had come up near the spot where the ancient temple had once stood, making up a new mining-inspired mockery for Paik. More than three-quarters of the grove that gave shade to travellers had disappeared. One wondered what they did to the huge mango, tamarind and jackfruit trees. The hill to the side of the old shrine had been gouged out to create an open ground. The ground itself had been levelled with tons of scree, and concrete piled over that. Shorn of tree and shade, Paik's abode was now blisteringly hot and dusty. At the northern edges, where the ground sloped sharply to the base of a valley, more bright orange scree had been unloaded in piles about a few feet high. More of the hill had been taken away to make a wider road to the new 'temple', and a shabby 'community hall' with a corrugated roof had been 'constructed' some distance away.

Where a devotee once struggled up the hill to seek solace amidst greenery now lay an entrance without mystery or promise, wide enough for three cars to pass. The shrines are always gated now, and locked with a chain. Through the bars in the muted gloom within, frayed garlands of dead flowers sway helplessly in the hot wind. The shrines stand in the same position as Paik once did, backs guarding the valleys that lead to Paik's Spring – Paikeachi Zor as it is known here. However, when the morning sun rises, you see coats of dull pink distemper stained with mining waste, instead of the play of shadow and light that once revealed Paik to the eye. This is Paikdev manufactured in a mining company and imprisoned in concrete, then garishly painted into dissonance.

In 2009, there were some sixteen mining leases under process in Maina and Cawrem, and five were in active operation.

One of the leases was shamelessly titled 'Paikeachi Zor'.

Paik is worshipped by the Velip community that inhabits these hills leading in and out of Maina and Cawrem. In his most basic avatar, he sits astride a rugged high pony. In earlier depictions, say the older people of the paintings they had grown up with, he rode bare-chested and wild-bearded with a spear, like the quintessential tribal warrior that he was.

In the more contemporary representations, he no longer rode into battle. He seemed embalmed, armed with a sword and astride a shining white horse, a shawl draped across his chest, his beard tamed into shape, the fire in his eyes dimmed and still.

It is interesting to note that, among some adivasi tribes in Odisha, on the mountains where the mining companies inflicted even more damage than they did here in Goa, the word 'Paik' seems to hold a different meaning. It denotes a kind of representative of the tribe, perhaps even a custodian of the village commons – someone who is respected, almost like a chieftain. They also trace the origins back to a person who was transposed into their everyday world as a deity and protector.

Given that Goan historiography in the main has been largely dominated by upper-caste dispositions, it is a shame that one may never know the reason why the Paik from Maina chose to take to spear and pony and ride out. Who or what was he defending his people from?

There is scattered research to trace the migration patterns of Goa's indigenous peoples. In fact, the *Gazetteer of the Union Territory of Goa, Daman and Diu*, 1979, holds that they have probably migrated to Goa from one of two sides – Assam, Odisha and Bengal, or from Kerala's Malabar area. Some communities, particularly those who inhabit the north-eastern section of the Western Ghats as they break into Goa, maintain that their tribal ancestors migrated here from the forests bordering Karnataka and Maharashtra.

But cultural-historical research into the Goan past bypasses these tribal migrations, bestowing primacy and the hallmark of cultural worth on later migrations – those of the Saraswat Brahmins and others who assumed a higher status on that same casteist ladder, and brought with them the power of the written word and scriptures that were said to be God-given to a chosen few.

Successive Goan governments have kept their indigenous populations dangling at the end of a chain from 1962 – when the more politically conscious, better educated and vocal Gavde community started the first organization asking to be recognized as a Scheduled Tribe – till this very day.[1]

These foothills, the high border areas of forest that separate Goa from Karnataka and Maharashtra, are packed with ore and water – both resources that fuel development. These are also the hills where indigenous people can be found 'squatting' in the middle of the Indian industrialist's road to 'growth'.

Ahead of us, northwards in the village of Ambaulim where the hills flatten and water bodies break free only to be choked by the thirst for urbanization, we find the Gavde community.

One could say that in times past, well into the 1970s, these tribal communities were an integral part of Goa's once-flourishing village economy, growing a wide range of crops and vegetables, fishing, harvesting salt, tending orchards and trading their essentially local produce at regular village markets that still continue to be held.

The state's indigenous communities on four sides surround the villages of Maina and Cawrem. They are found living in the deepest of the forested ghats around Neturlim village, where the Kushawati has its source. This may be the heart of the Netravali Wildlfe Sanctuary.

There too, thanks to the mining lobby's ridiculous insistence that Goa did not require a buffer zone around its wildlife sanctuaries because it was so small, one could find a dozen or so ongoing mining operations. Even as their land and water were taken away, the tribals were told that poverty is a greater evil than pollution. The younger males of the two communities were lured into buying trucks and making money.

These ghats and the ancient communities they shelter come all the way down to Sulcorna, some eight or so kilometres south-east of us, and much closer if you happen to be a bird. They bring with them the Kushawati that flows past the Don Bosco School, an institution that has done stellar service for the children of these communities. At least twenty of the children there, for instance, trek an hour across the hills west of the school from villages that one would be forced to call remote. They love the school, and they consider the walk a lot of fun. They come laughing to the school, and they return laughing.

Situated across a bridge over which the Kushawati gushes in force during the rains, the school dispels the notion that architecture requires hillocks to be levelled into nothingness, and buildings can only be square. The more you see of it, the more you feel that the architect's sense of proportion and structure is derived from the surrounding ghats.

The Salesian priests also run a state-of-the-art polytechnic, a women's centre, a large model farm, and now even conduct courses in organic farming for younger people in the area. They have also been in a long, protracted battle with the mining families that flaunt colonial concessions that cover a large part of the property. These were claims strongly backed by successive mining-driven governments.

Midway up the huge hill that overlooks the school, the Salesian priests built a grotto to Mary, the mother of Jesus. She looks towards the mother of the ghats, from the first and highest of the hills that break into Sulcorna and then climb ahead.

It is a lovely place to sit, open to birdsong and moist breeze. By 2008, Mary, her hands stretched out in helplessness, looked straight across to three mining operations in the east, taking away ghat and forest and mud.

Near the point where the statue stands are three chains of hill and forest within which Goa's indigenous communities have their ancestral lands.

One major branch of this hill and forest comes towards us in Maina and Cawrem, and heads south and then westwards towards the sea. The other branch goes north with the Kushawati towards the village of Collomb, on the outskirts of Rivona.

Collomb was another village that was agitating against the mining. It was past this village that convoys of trucks piled high with ore drove to the barges in Sanvordem, a town barely a kilometre from the source of the Zuari. The trucks drove past twenty mines or so, including two on the banks of the Selaulim dam, which gives south Goa its drinking water. These stopped operating only because of the arrival of the Shah Commission.

Ahead of Sanvordem, as these ghats bend east to the other border with Karantaka, it actually gets worse.

Beyond the majestic Anmod Ghat, for instance, just past the border some 10 kilometres off the road leading further into Karnataka, one finds Goan indigenous communities who predate all the border delineations from 1947 onwards. They speak Konkani, eat food prepared almost the same way as it is done here in Maina and Cawrem, celebrate the same festivals and intermarry in Goa. While they are 'Goan' for want of a better word, they technically live in Karnataka and are therefore forced to study in Kannada if they want an education. Therefore, it is not surprising that most of the people who live here, even the ones in their late teens, have not studied beyond the fifth standard.

In the dispensations of the governments of Karnataka and Goa, they do not exist. They are the forgotten people of Goa.

The third and perhaps the most important branch of forest and hill is the one that leaves the meeting point with the other two as if it had never arrived, climbing even higher and disappearing southwards, behind the statue and grotto, into the remote villages from which some students trek a good hour to the Don Bosco school in Sulcorna.

These high hills and plateaus – which break down to sea close to Goa's southern border with Karnataka, bringing with them the rivers Galgibaga and Talpona, and include the Cotigao Wildlife Sanctuary – probably has the highest density of Goa's tribal population. It is another matter that their ancestral commons may well have been acquired by Goan upper castes in a land grab that goes back in time, perhaps even before the Portuguese were made to leave in 1961.

At any rate, it is too much to hope that the indigenous communities here will fare any better than their kin who fell prey to mining. With the ban on mining, they will face even more pressure from tourism and real estate ventures, the surrogates for mining.

They have already lost their land and livelihoods in the creation of the Anjunem and Selaulim dams, which provide urban populations in the north and south of Goa with water to waste. These very communities were also the ones who lost their lands to most of Goa's industrial estates, once flaunted as a boon for Goa but now beset with the rot that sets in after corruption has eaten its fill.

The Verna industrial hub, which one sees on the drive towards Margao from either the airport or Panjim, was once a forested plateau and part of the traditional commons of the Gavde communities and the surrounding villages. That land was taken away to set up the industrial estate as well as a famous fertilizer factory (surrounded by a sprawling slum that will give Dharavi in Mumbai a run for its money). Again, it was the commons that were taken away to set up Goa's university on the Bambolim plateau close to Panjim. In every single one of these deals, it is commonly known, if not legally proven, that there has been a politician who created a lot of wealth for the family fund. The rest of Goa, it would seem, applauds them for their luck and business acumen.

It is the indigenous communities that will lose their land and commons when the government fast-tracks a new airport for Goa on the Mopa plateau in north Goa. The plateau is home to at least fourteen perennial springs that feed the fields at the lower levels.

As they stand, all of these are temples to the bitter learning of Goa's indigenous populations, the agricultural and pastoral communities that are now being seen as an impediment to 'development'.

These could be Goa's 'unpeople', to use Noam Chomsky's formulation: people consciously de-recognized as being fellow human beings.[2]

The other story is that Goa's indigenous populations – both in their ancestral lands closer to the rivers and even the sea and those here in the forested areas of places like Maina and Cawrem

– have already been sanitized by a pincer movement: a heavy dose of evangelization from the Catholic Church on the one side, and fabricated theologies of right-wing Hindu groups and upper-caste interests on the other. These opposing forces came to the party with alien scriptures, chants and idols. They then worked together to convert or reconvert different segments of the village population.

The relative prosperity of some tribal populations, by way of doles, subsidies and other politically motivated entitlements from the eighties onwards, is no proof that Goa's governments and the general population recognized their special identity, culture, lifestyle or expertise over crops, fruits and non-exploitative modes of land usage.

Take the case of one of Goa's lesser-known rivers, the Sal, which passes through the western side of Margao in south Goa. This river was once the hub of Margao's commerce, the goods, mostly roofing tiles from Mangalore coming in by boat and docking at various parts of the river, including one point on the southern end of Margao when you cross the new bridge and drive to either Colva to your right, or Varca and further south towards Cavellosim to the left.

Twenty years ago, if you walked across the Sal at this point, you could see that it was still a free-flowing river. You spotted the boats, occasionally even a trawler bold enough to come in with the tide. There was an old curved bridge built with laterite and mortar, and it was just broad enough for a single vehicle to cross over. Today, there is no evidence of that tiny bridge. They probably just broke it down in their haste to bring development to Goa. Or, maybe, it was just overrun by the many weeds and grasses that now threaten to turn the Sal into a stagnant swamp.

Margao's sewage is now happily pumped into the Sal, while a new sewage treatment plant south of the bursting town perversely runs in fits and starts.

If you stand on this new bridge and the wide road that crosses the Sal at Margao, wishing that you were a bird, you would get an excellent picture of just how the Sal was destroyed – and, with it, the lives of Goa's tribal populations who farmed on either side of its banks. These were the Kunbi, and they also have a story to tell.

The Portuguese converted the Gavde community to the Catholic faith in the early part of the sixteenth century, although the community – much to the Church's displeasure – continued to follow their traditional customs, rituals and practices. It was, of course, the Portuguese who first began referring to the converted Gavde as 'Kunbi', a term the Gavde themselves consistently rejected because they knew it would cause a rift within the community. The Portuguese referred to the Hindu Gavde as 'Konkne Gavde'.

In the early twentieth century, the Gavde converts to Catholicism were re-converted from Christianity to Hinduism at the initiative of a Mumbai-based organization called Masurashrama, strongly supported by the rich Saraswat Brahmins.[3] Those who did reconvert were not accepted in the fold of their original caste, and became a new community called the Navhindu Gavde. This was a game of musical chairs both right-wing Hindu elements and the Catholic Church played together through the 1960s to cauterize the earth-centred but no-less-divine traditions and practices of the Gavde.

Until a generation or two ago, in south Goa, the names of those converted to Catholicism – Francis, Xavier or likewise – accompanied the surname Gavde (often erroneously spelt as

'Gawda'). This community comprised pious Catholics who went to mass every Sunday and seriously followed the rites surrounding baptism, marriage and death, besides participating in the annual church feast to whichever saint the church was named after. What the Catholic Church may never have understood is that the Gavde had their own affinities to the notion of the divine imposed on them.

Well into the 1970s and early '80s, the grounds around the cathedrals of Old Goa during the feast of St. Francis Xavier, Goa's Patron Saint, would be full of Catholic Gavde who came on foot from their villages, camping three days for what was to them a deeply sacred annual pilgrimage. They drank copious amounts of coconut feni, ate pork sausages stuffed in bread and played their gumots – traditional earthenware drums, the broader side covered with the skin of a monitor lizard, the other, far smaller in diameter, left open for the drummer to tamp with his palm. Then they atonally sang hymns of devotion to their patron saint in an all-night vigil. It is more than likely that the church of the day also saw this as a deeply pagan practice.

On the westward banks of the Sal river, most of the wetlands ran towards the sea, taking with them freshwater sources that literally bubbled out of the ground. It is these wetlands – now being steadily filled to construct new apartment blocks – that bring in the many migratory species of bird that use Goa as a halfway house.

On its eastward banks, its sources were the springs that once flowed down the plateau leading down to the village of Verna. On the Verna plateau above, one of the nine springs has already fallen prey to a water-bottling plant. There are eighteen illegal wells in this industrial estate, where – in the later eighties – some Goan politicians made a killing in land deals.[4] The other springs on the Verna plateau have almost all disappeared, choked by builders landscaping the land to suit their own interests. Left behind is now only a token strip of trees following the main spring leading into Verna. Many of these springs flowed into several lakes in the area that helped the village's farming activities, and kept its water bodies brimming. Much of the farming activities have ceased, with some villagers contemplating using the land for building purposes. Fallow land in the low-lying areas soon became a fetid swamp, and was polluted by sewage in many cases. The eastern slopes of the same plateau, where the villages of Raia and Loutolim are, have fallen to road widening and construction, and the springs and streams now have garbage thrown into them.

All the hills to the northeast of an ever-growing Margao were connected to each other and the Verna Plateau, before sloping north to meet the Zuari. Between all these hills, trapped for posterity, were those various water bodies.

The main hill overlooking Margao from the north-east, has now been taken over by a migrant vote bank population. As the non-Congress opposition consistently held, the former chief minister, Digambar Kamat, actively encouraged this. Though one of the springs on this hill still provides drinking water, a garbage dump has come up around it, creating filthy, stagnant water, toxic leaching, and twists and twirls of human faeces at the borders. The smaller springs around Margao appear to have died at the same pace that uncontrolled real estate projects grew.

Gogol, the part of Margao north of this hill overlooking it, once had a famous spring that came in from the higher hills and valleys east of the region. There was a stream that remained alive well into summer, merging with several others around Margao and joining the river Sal as it coursed towards Cavellosim. This was an area populated at that time by the Catholic Gavde, and they often farmed the area as tenants.

In the 1970s, when the monsoons would come to an end and the rice had begun to break through, the stream used to be deep enough for three young men to swim twenty yards downstream with the current, then take a shivering walk back to the small village bar on the banks run by an old Gavde woman called Marie. There, they could drink some more coconut feni (which was all they could afford), discuss philosophy and savour her dish of the day: freshly trapped field rat made fat by eating tender buds of rice. For every field rat brought in by a Gavde male, Marie would give him a couple of shots of the coconut feni that she herself brewed to about 60 per cent proof – strong enough to fuel a bike. She would then sell him a couple of plates of the succulent field rat – marinated in a paste of garlic, red chilly and vinegar, and stir-fried – for twice the amount he would have paid for the shots. Of course, he'd probably order two more shots before heading home.

I guess if you sit in Panjim or New Delhi, this is what you would dismiss as a village economy – a thing that should now be kept in a museum. After all, it had fallen to the power of development, infrastructure and garbage.

The little stream at Gogol that evokes such beautiful memories is also a horrifying example of a perennial water source that's now in its death throes. Is it any wonder, then, that as the eighties broke, most of the Catholic Gavde people in the area were buying mining trucks, which they then parked next to the new concrete houses they built and got a steady and growing income from hauling ore?

Going by the number of dumper trunks in the Gavde settlements north of Margao, It seems fair to speculate today that roughly one half of the community of Gogol may have gravitated to the mining business or into becoming road construction contractors. It helps to remember that their grandparents worked as manual workers in the mines. Right through the 1950s and well into the '60s, before the first mechanization of the mines happened, Gavde men dug the ore with shovels and the women carried it in metal tubs placed on their heads. The prosperity translated into first driving the trucks, then owning them. Meanwhile, the construction of roads and bridges, hauling of electricity poles and driving of trucks was done by Gavde labourers. They eventually gravitated to the construction business, and later became village leaders and real-estate builders.

It may have been real estate, which eventually cost the area this stream.

The concrete bridge that once crossed into this Gavde hamlet in Margao is still there, and the water below surprisingly crystal clear, even if it is partially dammed by garbage.

Upstream, where the spring originates, rest assured we will choke it with garbage. The stream will turn into a nullah and newer buildings will sprout up where it once stood.

The huge Nehru Stadium in Margao, which hosts one-day cricket internationals, and all the huge buildings on its sides have totally destroyed the wetlands – and worse, separated them from this very spring. So it is not surprising that the springs in Margao, which once fed the Sal as it passed by the Nehru Stadium, are themselves being killed by garbage.

Perhaps nothing could be sadder than what has happened to the tidal creek at Majorda Beach, not too far from Margao. This was fed by a spring south of the creek, which itself received water from smaller streams in the area.

In the 1970s, local fishermen refused to let a bridge be built across this tiny creek, arguing that people had to wash their feet in this water before they walked onto the beach. We never complained. We rolled up our trousers, carried our shoes and crossed it. Locals had a strange name for this spring, which became a beautiful creek and flowed into the sea even at times of low tide: Devcharacho Handh, the Devil's Hole. If you drank with them and asked them why, they'd tell you that it's because the water just came out of this hole in the ground. If you asked them if this meant that they wanted the devil to find a way to the sea and out of their lives, they would taciturnly answer 'maybe'. Then one of them would tell you that nobody dared drink its water.

Only God knows which panchayat member took how much money, but the big resort on the beach and a few other hotel and real estate projects in the area ensured that the Devil's Hole was eliminated – first sandbagged and then blockaded to death.

Soon, another resort will cover the mother spring with concrete, or it may simply turn into a garbage dump. Either way, preventing a creek from reaching the sea and turning it back to its own freshwater source while you choke that upstream is cruel. It is not unlike a man beginning to eat his own body parts: an image that comes to mind when we consider our inherent disregard for the sanctity of water that may come back to haunt us soon.

Something else we know is that the indigenous people in Goa, just like indigenous peoples everywhere, had their own site-specific understanding of what constitutes the divine.

On the banks of the Kushawati as it flows north, past all the mines that are illegally parked on its banks, one gets a truer picture of what this actually means. Close to the village of Collomb, one of the banks of the Kushawati swells into a piece of flat laterite big enough to accommodate a tennis court.

It helps to know that this is a site protected by the Archaeological Survey of India, even though an illegal open-cast mining pit used to operate at a distance of fifty metres or so. Though the pit has since disappeared, no attempt was ever made to repair the damage it had caused to the ancient monument. After all, this was mining – the 'backbone' of the Goan economy.

One walks on this huge bank of laterite, ever-conscious of the fact that many have come before us on this fragile planet, a knowledge that creeps through the skin from the ancient motifs and mandalas inscribed on rock.[5]

All over this bank, you find carvings where the thick laterite has been etched, scraped and furrowed into drawings that are as dark in texture and tone as the giant slab itself. However, in the early morning light, under a sheen of dew, they seem as if they were carved just a few days ago.

If you are alone, understanding the innocence and piety, zeal and longing of the ancient beings who hewed this rock can be an experience that's as humbling as it is unnerving. Did they do it in a single stretch while they were discovering the joys of feni? Or did they do it at regular intervals, week after week, carving diligently on solid rock so that their story could be told to the ones who came after?

After an hour or so, with the accompaniment of birdsong and the sound of water, it is not that difficult to understand the cyclical character of many of the carvings, and how most of them appear to celebrate birth and life as well as the abundance and generosity of nature. Look at the rock from a distance, and it would seem as if you were looking at a giant picture book carved out of laterite.

There is nothing soft about these carvings; one cannot simply say they are 'pantheistic' and then clothe them with some hoo-hah about life being holistic. They are raw and immediate, fuelled by a scream at a time when words and concepts may not have come as easily to the rescue, and the only aspects being revered must have been the earth and water that fed those ancient rock carvers. And, of course, the need for all those who followed to know the interdependence of people and animals and forests and water.

To understand the simplicity of worship without the appurtenances of theology and belief, one has only to listen to the story of Paikdev, known to every single Velip man, woman and child in Maina and Cawrem. It is a story oft repeated by their elders.

Once upon a time, a beautiful young woman from Maina was married into Cawrem. She was much loved in both the villages and was soon blessed with child, a bright-eyed boy who was adored just as much as his mother. While Maina and Cawrem received an abundance of rain, both were also dependent on a spring with water so sweet that it seemed touched with nectar. The spring was in Maina, a good forty-minute walk for the young woman who fetched the water while her husband tended to the fields, trees and livestock in Cawrem. One day, however, tragedy struck. She reached home with pots full of water only to find her baby covered with tiny black ants. They had left bright red spots on his tender skin.

People of both the villages offered prayers to their warrior deity, Paik, but to no avail. The little boy never recovered. His young mother, heart-broken, slowly drifted away from this world too. After a full year of grieving the loss of the two cherished lives, the girl's father, joined by elders from Maina, went to the spring that the young woman had gone to collect water from.

The father carried an empty mud pot with him. At the spring, the father's anguish and helplessness turned into great anger, and he smashed the mud pot at the mouth of the spring.

From that day to the present, villagers here say, Paikdev ensured that three-quarters of the water would flow into Cawrem and only one-quarter into Maina. Following this, the villagers of Maina and Cawrem began referring to the site of this miracle as 'Paikeachi Zor' or 'Paik's Spring' – a place sacred because it is where he manifested himself in water.[6]

When you tell this story to those who live very far from Maina and Cawrem, their eyes shine with compassion and their voices turn tender with hope, as if just knowing the story is enough to change the world. The story's indigenous roots lend it a touch of romance; Paik's people are described as 'good-natured' and 'close to the earth'.

But in the villages, you see alienation. As older men and women tell the tale, you can see their confusion and bafflement over what mining had done to their pantheon, and how their lives had changed irreversibly in less than six years.

The elders are the area's primary historians. They are also the saddest – helpless at being made redundant, disinherited in their own lifetimes. There are those who say that the Velip were systematically cheated of land that was once their traditional commons through papers and deeds drawn up by Goan politicians and their cronies with an eye on the till. The older ones, who refused to be taken in, were done in by their sons who sold the lands on their behalf. Overnight, the younger crop of this community turned into truck drivers hauling ore with their faces wrapped up in colourful bandanas to stave off the choking red dust. When they were not working, they hung around in little groups at the side of the road dressed in glares, tee-shirts, jeans and sneakers (some of them even showing off new motorcycles), but still eating dust.

Whoever the instigators might have been, there is no arguing that the Velip sold their rights to clean air, fresh water and forests to mining companies for Rs 350 a square metre (and a chance to buy a truck).

However, in 2010, the women of Cawrem suddenly realized what mining was doing to them. They came out on the roads in protest, strongly supported by village groups close to Margao, banding under a back-to-agriculture platform. They brought their faith in Paik with them.[7]

There was one old woman in a nine-yard sari though who seemed to find this particularly funny. Laughing derisively, she spat tobacco and betel juice to the ground when she heard another woman piously state that Paik would come through to help them.

'Paikdev?' she asked them in a high-pitched voice. 'How is he going to hear us when we have stuffed his ears with gold?'

In reply to someone saying that the government would have to stop the mining, she said – still laughing raucously as if demented and still spitting viciously into the dust – that those in Panjim would only understand how bad mining was when they opened their taps one morning and saw red dust flow out.

The few who didn't succumb to the temptation of the quick money that mining brought would tell you that farming and tending orchards was their culture, their way of life, something that they were born to and *gifted* with. They do not see farming by hand as the curse it is made to be by those who fear manual work because they have bought into automation and leisure.

Their demolition of this fear is simple: if you do not work the land and tend the trees, how will you eat?

There are people in their seventies who are still sprightly enough to take on a plough and two bulls, laughing as they tell you that every Sunday, as the sun rose, they would walk all the way from Maina or Cawrem to the weekly market at Quepem, selling the produce they grew here and returning, as the sun set, with provisions and articles they needed at home.

Those in their forties and fifties would do this even in the height of the mining season, not walking as their fathers once did but taking the bus and carrying to the market whatever produce they managed to grow in the face of the five ongoing mining operations in the area.

But today, the teenaged children of these men do not entertain the idea of letting their education take them back to farming. They just hang their heads and say, 'Yes, but ...' The 'but' is never elaborated on, no matter how much you try, because it precariously balances the weight of a brittle, tenuous 'aspiration' – the bombardment of advertisements whichever way they look, the possibility of being in a position to own a bike, a car, a new phone, a plasma TV or a house, to upgrade to what they see as better things.

At the base of the climb to Paikeachi Zor, you will often see firewood collected and tied with vine into scrupulously neat bundles. Every time the Velip take their cattle to the slopes to graze, they make two more bundles for someone younger in the family to later take home.

In the mid-eighties, both sides of this path were lined with thick forest, and trees would just grow wild, a proper lush jungle. The path was actually quite easy to find. You saw many fruit trees grown from seed, from tamarind to jambul, mango, jackfruit, kokum and even guava; you tracked more birds than you could count; and, on occasion, you came in touch with several insects that could bite with a vengeance. If you were lucky, you could catch a hare while it's still in half-leap, or manage to sidestep a snake slithering away. Often, it would just be a chameleon that had darted out of the way.

In the late eighties, however, Goa's forest department cleared the steeply rising hill of its tree cover and shrub. It cut terraces in the hillside and, in its place, created a huge cashew orchard that you could smell a mile off. Whether such was their intention or not, that move certainly made things easier for the mining barons. It's so much easier to say that you are clearing a few hundred cashew trees on land that belongs to the government, and not an ancient forest that must be protected.

This section of the climb to Paik's Spring was also the hardest, and many who came with us when we went to check on Joaquim's activities in 2009 ended up gagging on the overpowering fragrance of the cashew trees.

The cloying perfume comes primarily from the cashew flowers in early April. They then crinkle in the sun and give way at the end of the month to cashew apples that ripen in the hot sun and ferment even as they drop to ground – their bellies clinging to nuts that start out tender green and succulent and then develop a sharp, almost noxiously, acidic armour. This coats the nut and bears the brunt of the fall to the ground, preventing the juicy apple from disintegrating. In March, April and May, the fragrance of the cashew is overwhelming.

The cashew tree is just as precious to the indigenous people of these forests as the mahua tree is to the adivasi populations of central India. Both are instrumental in producing in a potent brew and the by-products of nut and flower. Like the adivasis discovered mahua wine, it is more than likely that Goa's indigenous populations gave the state its feni many a century ago.

Till today, in the deeper parts of these forests here, you will find traditional Velip liquor stills dotting the tiny Curca and its small tumbling waterfalls in April and May. While cashew apples are picked from the trees, the best are said to be the ones that fall naturally in the breeze. Arguments abound on the virtues of the colour of the apple – the yellow, some say, is conducive to excellent urak wine, while the red and orange are ideal for the more potent feni. One settles the issue by tasting the eventual products several times, and then blessing, as the locals do, the existence of the cashew tree.

The Velip leave the nuts at the base of the tree for others who have successfully tendered a contract to sell them and then head to their stills, where they stamp the apples with their feet while savouring the best of whatever remains of last year's feni. The collected juice is fermented in giant earthen pots and distilled twice, or even thrice – once to make urak wine, and subsequent distillations to make the cashew feni as potent as they want it.

The Velip and the Dangar, thanks to the possibility of a ban on mining in Goa being imposed in perpetuity, have at least got cashew trees as a link to their unique identity. Further along our journey, in the village of Ambaulim, the Gavde were not even left with their trees, the lands they tended or their water bodies.

We noted that the sounds accompanying us on the trek to Paik's Spring had changed. The old sounds of the forest were still there, but muted. You had to struggle to see or hear anything between the trees. All the monkeys and other small animals had already fled, taking refuge with the bison and the leopard in the forest adjacent to the farm or the thicker forests across the Curca where we knew the tiger to be.

As we climbed, we realized that the reason for this flight of nature was the low keening hum of machinery that seemed to reverberate in the background.

To those who know their ore from their mud, the first fifty metres or so of Joaquim's mine at Jollerancho Dongor was 'waste'. However, in agricultural terms, that translated to about two metres of ancient top soil comprising fertile dark-brown earth, and the rest largely laterite in various strata of maturity, colour and age. The riches that Joaquim sought lay anywhere up to fifty metres below all this 'waste', after the hill had been flattened.

When we climbed from the back to Jollerancho Dongor, we saw a convoy of around forty trucks working in a cycle, monitored at each stage by a battery of supervisors and engineers. They were excavating a flank that covered the northern and western slopes of Paik's hill. Like they made hills disappear elsewhere, in what was left of Jollerancho Dongor, they were making valleys at a lower level vanish, and with them, the natural courses of their water. The trucks took what was dug up from the side of the hill and dumped it outside Joaquim's lease area – into the very valley that comes out on the road leading to Paik's temple.

It was a simple operation, if you looked at it: first bulldoze the cleared trees into the lower valley and cover them with top soil and better soil, followed by lightly coloured laterite scree that turns darker as the excavators begin hitting lodes flecked with ore. Then they would start making their pits.

While all this happened before our very eyes, there was another sound, one far worse.

You hear it best after the engines have been warmed a good half hour, and primed to take away the earth: the high-pitched whine of anywhere between eight to twelve cylinders building to a deafening hum, then a growl and sometimes an angry roar. We could sense the resistance of the earth weakening and the blades pushing through, earth being swept ahead into a pile. Then, still crawling on our bellies, we heard the same powerful engine rev up, engage gear and settle into a hum of motor punctuated by shrieks close to a high C – like a bird crying out in terrible pain.

As the earthmover reversed, came to a halt, engaged gear and lowered its blades, we saw a bright, blinding orange light flashing in time with the loud shrieks. The wildlife was instinctively fleeing westwards past Paik's temple, or south towards the farm. The noise is deafening even at a distance.

There were four huge machines. Two were powerful bulldozers that pushed mounds of mud from the top of the hill where the trees and other elements of 'waste' stood. They bellowed with rage as they attacked the sides of the hill, belching massive bursts of thick noxious smoke into the air.

From behind the trees, the scenario was truly frightening. Even in the short time we remained there, everything from our clothes and hair to our skin was covered in fine red dust. The trees around us had turned a ghostly brown. With the sun dazzling our eyes, there was no thought of shade. And we saw the quantum of dust that those manning the machinery, driving the trucks and supervising the operations had to put up with every day.

If you crept to the very edge of the pit and peeked over, risking being seen by the battery of workers and security guards, you would note that the drop from the tree line on the hill was a good ten metres, if not more.

Assisting the bulldozers were two other mammoth predators, huge metal crab-like beings with a single deformed claw that would clumsily caress the mud before coming down again with force and lifting large portions of mud off the ground. Just three of these were enough to fill a large truck.

Steadily, the hill that was once Jollerancho Dongor diminished.

As we circled the mine, systematically photographing the destruction, we would gag with horror and fury. Behind the makeshift resting area, garnished with the usual tawdry accoutrements that are the lot of workers in this country, was a feculent garbage dump. We couldn't help but notice that the workers, truck drivers and security guards had made large portions of the forested land stink with an odour that seems to follow humans through all their conquests; unlike cleaner animals, our kind does not even have the decency to hide its own excrement.

It left us in a dark mood. In the mining seasons of 2008 and 2009, while we may have watched what the mines were doing, none of us really wanted to make the final part of the journey to Paik's Spring.

We decided the onset of the monsoons was the time to revisit the source of Paik's miracle and discover the forests around him even as all his flanks were under the attack of four mining operations.

Some 20 kilometres south-east of Maina and Cawrem by road, the dark cloud-framed ghats beyond Sulcorna are the mothers of the prehistoric hills, one of which I sat on.

It is a chastening sight. All the more so if you sit alone, a chill in the air and like the hills around you, feel under threat. They are bathed in a luminescence that looks and sometimes even feels like water. Let your imagination run a little more, and the hills begin looking like prehistoric creatures sleeping on their bellies. In this misted silence, you sense how the lives of forests and hills and wildlife and indigenous peoples are intertwined with the almost divine presence of water. In that Age of Greed, one would have thought it was the beginning of a surrealistic film if only it wasn't so real.

In any case, sitting on that hill in late June, where Goa's borders meet with Karnataka, you would have seen thick dark clouds over the high peaks surrounding the forests of Neturlim. Just before the rains break, the clouds turn even darker and thicker, just short of black, shutting down the light in seconds and sending lightning bolts across the sky. It seems as if the thunder is reverberating from the very bowels of the majestic Western Ghats.

It is here, at this very point where the clouds heavy with water meet the blackness of the last steep hills on the horizon, that the river Kushawati has its source.

To make the walk to Paik's Spring was to understand the difference between what is sacred and what is offensive. It involved running a gauntlet between thick forest land cleared by the government to plant cashew saplings and the slopes near Paik's Spring, where three different mining operations had acquired the necessary permissions to dump their waste.

Past this desecration, tucked in the slopes of the hills that form the cusp between Maina and Cawrem, is His spring. Paik's head is an old rock burnt dark with age, standing far taller than a grown man, his eyes blacker than the richest lode of iron. At the base of the rock is his succulent mouth, green and lush with myriad ferns and mosses and lichens. His hair is made up of the roots of a giant kusum tree, its branches and leaves like a plume reaching out to the sky; his tongue is a long swirling current of clear dancing water with streaks of fierce red as it flows over a bed of burnished laterite; his ancient beard flows with the fluttering white roots of plants and shrubs growing close, holding the mud back so His water is set free.

I have consistently trekked there from the mid-eighties, whenever I visited the farm, to drink of the sweetest water imaginable. It gushed out from the base of this giant moss-covered iron-laden rock that was indistinguishable from the steep hill that guarded it. Only in high summer, when the grasslands dried and withered, the shrub and undergrowth around the trees shrunk to twig and stick, did the path up the hill and down to the spring stand clearly defined. But then it had been paved over centuries by pilgrims making their way up at least once a year, and on other days by the feet of those who make their living from these hills as well as the hooves of the cattle they bring to pasture.

After we saw what the mining was doing, from 2006 onwards, none of us went anywhere near the summit of the massive hill that hid Paik's Spring from the three mining companies attacking its flanks.

We spent that time spying on what they were doing instead, and how they were doing it. There never was any doubt about the trickery that hides behind terms like 'sustainable mining'.

The heavy rains that visited Maina later told us Paik could speak back, whether we prompted him to or not.

The Space Theatre Ensemble that I worked with as an artistic director had just finished a long workshop with a school in Margao, and was now playing host to that same group of high school students and their teacher. They had driven to the farm in their school bus, and then joined us on a trek to Paik's Spring. We left with the sun shining through, and the monsoon clouds scattered to the edges of the higher ghats to the east. We would be back in time for lunch, we told them at the farm, maybe a little after noon.

One of the students, an articulate young girl in her last year of school, hailed from a prosperous Catholic family that owned one of the accursed mining leases granted by the Portuguese.

The lease owned by the girl's family, pulled out from some old cupboard or trunk, must have been worth a pittance when it was bought by some eccentric long-deceased relative. It was now worth millions if one also negotiated a percentage of the royalties with the mining magnate in desperate need of it.

Now, this young girl had seen the ensemble perform Creatures of the Earth, our dance performance depicting the horrors of mining through the life of a spring in a single day, and it disturbed her. She accused me of exaggeration. I told her that the performance was a metaphor to show the intrinsic destructiveness of this industry. Along the way, she walked with me and took pains to give me an elaborate argument on why Goa needed mining for its development and economic prosperity. Her presentation was so fluent it seemed as if she had rehearsed it in her head several times. She had already told me she had dreams of doing an MBA.

Much as you would like to, it's not advisable to throw ideology at younger people. You can't even throw it at their parents, who tutored them never to accept its existence. One broods darkly instead, hoping for a time people will see the world for what it is and what it could be.

'Did you see the mine when you were driving in?' I asked her. She said she hadn't.

This wasn't strange at all. We knew enough people who would go for weekend drives away from the hustle-bustle of Panjim or Margao to de-stress themselves by discovering Goa's natural beauty, but *never* see the mines. If we didn't stop the car and actually point a mine out to them, they would probably never have known of its existence.

Because I was so lost in thought, we got lost in the woods. I hadn't realized just how far we had come. Instead of taking the path to the west, over the steep bank of dark laterite and then into the valley down to Paik's Spring, I had led everyone further north to a point I had never reached before. Here, the hill bent its girth towards Cawrem and the summit, and the forest was like a wall, thicker and darker than I had ever seen.

On my right, barely 20 metres way, was a steep drop of at least 5 metres or so. However, you couldn't easily judge the distance because the ground below was overgrown with shrub and tree. A steamy, dank vapour blew from below, as if from deep water. Telling the children to stay back, we explored the perimeter cautiously and discovered a road close to the drop but away from the hill, big enough for a jeep or a small truck to pass.

I had been told about this by the local elders. We had chanced upon an old mine that was operated here in the late fifties by using manual labour. Even though the ore was of very high grade, it had been closed down due to transportation issues. At least two men in their seventies have told me that jeeps used to take this ore out in trailers, and there had been several accidents too.

However, a little distance away from this disused mine was the Magnum operation, the third along the road from Maina to Cawrem. Though it was separated from us by a clump of thick forest, the good folk at Magnum – with the kind of machinery and international expertise at their disposal – could easily spread their tentacles to this area in less than a year, provided their lease also covered the ground where we stood.

We had walked another fifty metres or so north, away from the mines, when we saw that the forest was giving way to a cashew plantation that climbed steadily up to the summit. We headed up because I just knew that the slope leading down to Paik's Spring would be on the other side. The climb was steep and exhausting enough to demand several halts to find our breaths, but with terraced holds firm enough to prevent any untoward incidents. Instead of skirting the last giant hill as we would normally do, we had climbed it.

At Paikeachi Zor, everyone fell silent, even the noisiest children who had been told that if they shout, they'd frighten off the birds. Is it because we are at the base of a valley surrounded and dwarfed by a steep, wooded hill that it feels like the base of life itself? Is it because the wind orchestrates the trees and brings forth warm breathy whistles and notes that sound close to a giant pan-flute? I glanced at the girl whose family owns the mining lease, but she didn't catch my eye. I remember hoping sincerely that she would catch a glimpse of the mines on the journey back.

On the way back to the farm, we returned the same way to make a new trail that was actually quicker by a good ten minutes, and far more mysterious. Close to the summit though, it started to rain, hard.

It was still just noon or so. In seconds, just as we hit the summit, clouds came together like a thick grey blanket and it felt like half an hour after the sun had gone down. A few thick drops stung us, as if they were carrying ice, and before even a shout of warning could be sounded, we were being pounded by a painfully heavy sheet of rain that went on for a good twenty minutes, accompanied by terrifying banshee-like wails. Without knowing it, everyone was being pushed downhill. We were all like dim shadows following dim shadows.

We had worked things out in a manner that each of the ensemble's actors had five children under their wing. We were all together when the rain abated, still in the same formations, and – thankfully – we had all moved together, hugging the hill in a horizontal curve till we reached a small clearing. People later said they were screaming out to the others. We were all doing that, and yet we could barely hear anything other than the deafening sounds of the storm.

I got lost again after the rains had slowed to a drizzle, and retreated multiple times in the face of the thick undergrowth and tree cover, and turned southwards to the farm after misjudging the slope. We had not only passed the disused Portuguese mine, but also moved more easterly than intended and were now much closer to the Magnum Mine. The trees above us were so thick that I couldn't get my bearings.

I was leading, a thick, cold mist blocking the view of what lay ahead, when suddenly – barely a few feet away – I saw a sharp drop and yelled to the rest to stop. The road from Maina to Cawrem that we have travelled on thus far was barely fifty metres away. We were at the edge of the Magnum pit. Ten more steps, and I could have hurled myself thirty metres or more below.

Just then, a gust of strong breeze blew the mist away in a lazy swirl, and some distance ahead, we could clearly see the cavernous mining pit. In the middle of what seemed like the set for a film on alien life lay two huge mounds covered with bright blue plastic sheets. Weighted with stone at the base perhaps, and tenting and sealing the ore, thick nylon rope coloured a pale green, like the shell of a pre-historic turtle. The group gasped collectively.

'What's *that?*' This was the young girl whose family owned the mining lease.

'It's ore they've stockpiled to send out after the rains,' I told her. After seeing the majesty and darkness of a forest's womb, the parasitic mining pit – with its laterite bleeding orange – looked like nothing short of an abomination.

It was close to three in the afternoon and everyone was hungry, thirsty and tired. Finding my bearings, I quickly put a plan in place. We could track westwards for ten minutes, veer south and then come out into Joaquim Alemao's Jollerancho Dongor mine and onto the main road – which was not even half a kilometre from the school. From there, I knew a short cut that would take us back to the farm in no time.

Joaquim's work came as even more of a shock for the young girl. Apparently, her family wanted to cash in on their mining lease, because it was still a mine in the making, an operation to clear away the rich topsoil so worthless to mining.

She brushed aside soaked leaves touching her face as we found the traditional path through grass and shrub growing as high as her knees. As we stopped to see and smell wild flowers that only come with the rain, she spotted birds taking shelter from the rain and screamed with excitement and frightened them away. And last of all, she joined us as we walked through a kind of a gateway between two slabs of laterite, and beyond this, Joaquim Alemao's mining operation that had ripped off the trees, then bitten into the side of the hill leading up to Paikeachi Zor from the southern flank of his giant hill.

We trudged down through bare, heartless scree that gave way under our feet, watching fat frogs drop into the many ponds, and picking our way across furrows left behind by the churning of truck tyres. Everyone suddenly saw themselves for what they were – a group of travellers within a lifeless crater.

The girl didn't look as confident as she was that morning. A bright sparkle of tears burst in her eyes.

'This is mining?' she asked me.

'*This* is mining.'

'*This?*'

'This.'

What would she say, I wonder, if she knew that barely a year-and-a-half later, the barren slope we climbed down had become a fifty-metre-high cliff.

3

The Mining Families

Goa's first business families were traders who hawked everything from cloth to curds as well as being well-known ships' chandlers and agents, with at least one among them making a killing after World War II by selling blockaded German penicillin stock across the then Portuguese border to the British and the Americans, among others. Then they all diversified into mining.

At the height of Salazar's fascist rule, in fact, Goa's mining families were not averse to wining and dining with the Portuguese dispensation, and at least one was bestowed an honorific title of the Portuguese equivalent of baronetcy.

Many say that Goa's first chief minister, Dayanand Bandodkar, was hand-picked to lead Goa by mining companies because they recognized both his acumen and his sympathy for their own greater cause. Even though he was not of their caste, he was himself the owner of a profitable mine. He was also their conduit to the underprivileged Goan.

What is far better known is that from the early 1960s, this wealthy mine owner emerged out of nowhere like the golden goose of Goan politics, in life as in the hereafter, ensuring that mining in Goa would be the exclusive domain of the few mining families who run Goa.

When Bandodkar's only son Siddhartha was killed after he accidentally shot himself through the spleen with a revolver – itself an incident coated with much intrigue and mystery at that time – his daughter, Shashikala Kakodkar, took over the mining business. And there she stayed till 1977, ruling Goa and protecting its mining families at the same time.[1]

It helps to keep in mind that the mining wealth in Goa, well before crony capitalism became the flavour of the day in the rest of the country, was controlled by just four thoroughbred families – Dempo, Salgaocar, Timblo and Chowgule. The first three, not unsurprisingly, are Saraswat Brahmins while the last comprises upper-caste early migrants from neighbouring Maharashtra.

Originally traders and shopkeepers, they now controlled 60 per cent of the mining leases. The remaining 30 per cent were controlled by Sesa Goa, which – before it was sold first to Mitsui and then to British behemoth Vedanta – was an Italian-German company that operated here well before Goa's liberation in 1961.

There were also smaller non-Brahmin but wealthy players like the Bandodkar and Bandekar families, and early migrants to Goa from Gujarat and Rajasthan who gobbled up the remaining 10 per cent of the leases. This was not even a fraction of the leases that Goans later found while rummaging through their old cupboards and safes.

Management consultant Rajendra Kakodkar, himself a vocal critic of mining, wrote in the press that every election in Goa since 1961 was fought with the help of mining money. It also played a great role in the coups, changes in leadership, and the many defections witnessed through its political history. Given that we all know now how much the mining families gave to politicians in the 2012 elections (the information was available to the public),[2] he wrote that it was highly probable that they supported Bandodkar in quelling two inner party rebellions, one in 1967 and the other in 1972, both of which saw him come back stronger than ever before. The extent of how much the mining families pull Goa's strings can be adjudged by the fact that there were eleven chief ministers in Goa between 1987 and 1999.[3]

Kakodkar also noted that, in comparison to Goa, 70 per cent of the mining leases in Karnataka were owned by public sector units NMDC or MML, and the remaining 30 per cent by at least 100 families.[4] In Goa, the declared profits of mining – amounting to around Rs 12,000 crore – was shared by a handful of people. If you take the fact that there are 2 lakh families in Goa, Kakodkar added, this could have meant a 6 lakh-rupee windfall for each family.[5]

It is not surprising that former chief minister Digambar Kamat was connected by ties of marriage, fealty and caste to the traditional mining lobby. His daughter was married to Govindraj Sinai Dempo, the scion of a premier mining family in Goa, recently incriminated by the tax authorities for stashing money outside the country.[6] This followed a peculiar practice followed by mining and other Saraswat Brahmin business clans, who, wishing to keep this under strict supervision, married children within a few families – following, no doubt, strict astrological codes and mathematical permutations culled from appropriate Vedic formulae.

The community's publicity, largely funded by the mining families and written up by well-known members of the community, trumpets its peaceful and loving ways, its love for culture, arts and the good life, and even its 'unique' cuisine, which has been influenced by several indigenous practices, including basic spices and coconut. As in all cases where wealth and status decide what's best, their food is much richer in ingredients and, therefore, of better flavour, texture and even subtlety.

What may actually stand out is the success of this small but flourishing community in keeping its purity and wealth intact – a practice that goes back centuries, through various ruling dispensations in Goa, and which even absorbed the shock of being converted to a foreign religion.

One credits the Portuguese and French for introducing the shrewd practice of 'assimilating' the native colonized population into their culture, education and even class. But the Saraswat Brahmins of Goa understood this as a means of keeping valuable resources in their hands. It was a kind of reverse-colonization, a practice that worked for them for many centuries.

The mythology surrounding this community says that before settling in the Konkan region, the sage Parashurama presided over yet another yajnya to which he invited sixty-six Brahmin families from Trihotra in present-day Tirhoot. He then chose from among them ten hand-picked gotras, Brahmins with records and history documenting and determining the purity of their ancestry. These families, at his invitation, spread themselves over the Konkan and came to be known by the names of the ninety-six villages they were given as the 'promised land'.

There is no doubt that Bandodkar brought into being the Bahujan Samaj, a classical social reform-style movement to empower the underprivileged across the length and breadth of Goa. His singular feat was the passing of a bill in the early 1960s that gave tenant farmers (mundkars) rights to the fields they tended, and landlord's status over the land on which their huts and houses stood.[7]

Ironically, when he passed these populist, quasi-socialist acts, few beneficiaries had the education, acumen or funds to develop them. The early 1970s may have seen the first instances of land grab taking place, with relatively poorer indigenous people selling out to investors. That story continues to stretch into the present.

In gratitude for the gains they got, thousands of the former mundkars, Catholic as well as Hindu, became Bandodkar's captive vote bank. It helps to keep in mind that he would have lost miserably in several Goan villages had the lower-class and lower-caste Catholics backed the Catholic-led opposition party of that time, the United Goans Party of Jack Siqueira. While a few may have backed that party out of loyalty to a shared faith, most knew it to be led and advised by upper-caste land-owning Catholic and Hindu Goans of whom they would have remained tenants.

However, back then, none of Goa's voters were to know that they were participating in the first move to put Goa's unique system of the many communidades, the village-governed commons, on the back burner.[8]

Brahmin sycophants posing as historians will tell you that Bandodkar's 'most historic and significant contribution ... was the undertaking of land reforms and resolving the complex issue of land ownership'. The real focus should be on how he systematically devolved, if not neutered, the indigenous system of governance. It was a system of village governance that the shrewd Portuguese chose to accept because it was already in place, and would therefore allow the payment of taxes to the colonial power to be negotiated over a table – instead of being extracted by threat of the sword.

The Portuguese, quintessential bureaucrats, wrote this into a sophisticated code with laws and by-laws, and maintained a carefully annotated documentation of amendments made over time and the reasons for having done so. They referred to it as 'communidade'. One often wonders how much more Mahatma Gandhi's ideas of village government would have been enhanced if he had just been given a translation of the communidade notification that the Goa government brought out in a Gazetteer.[9]

There is a strong feeling in many villages in Goa that only the revival of this system of village governance will save this tiny state from ruin at the hands of the industrial-development lobby. In destroying the communidade and conveniently devolving the power down to village panchayats which had fallen into the hands of political rogues climbing the ladder of corruption right from the late 1970s – this poor little state was given no chance.

It was Bandodkar who first consolidated matters by ensuring that his hand-picked candidates came to power at the panchayat level too. He chose to ignore the corruption slowly multiplying along the coast, where – thanks to tourism – two generations of Goans came to see the panchayat as a cash cow. The journey from there to a ministerial berth as the eighties ended was not a very long one.

From the time the former mundkars got the land in their names, they were fair game. For the people in pursuit of the real estate and tourism businesses, their land was the next frontier. It became a vicious circle, a wheel that expanded even as it turned. After their parents died in the eighties, at least one generation of former tenants, who now owned prime land, became rich overnight.

Supporters of the status quo in Goa will tell you that 'the mission of comprehensive land reforms initiated by Bandodkar was abandoned by the subsequent governments'.[10] Or that 'after 1979, Goa saw drastic land use changes detrimental to the local ecology and environment', and that 'abandoning land reforms meant creation of a "free-for-all" situation that spawned a new class of cut-throat land speculators who began to influence Goa's post statehood politics'.

This only sounds good on TV. The looting had already happened, and many pockets filled. The communidade system was dismantled and shredded twice: once to create a vote bank, and the next to open the door to privatizing the village commons.

Bandodkar's business acumen and political astuteness also translated into Goa's polity being communalized, and probably for the first time, two communities that had co-existed in peace began to bare their teeth at each other. On the flip side, it allowed the better-educated, more affluent Brahmin elite to corner the prime parts of business in Goa.

His strength lay in dividing the Hindus and the Catholics on two fronts, seeking to not only deny Konkani official status as a language and give this distinction to Marathi, but also hold an opinion poll at the start of the 1960s to find out whether Goa was not better off merged with neighbouring Maharashtra.

Bandodkar lost that opinion poll when the mining families realized that their privileged status would be done away if Indian regulatory mechanisms came into play, and backed the anti-merger forces instead.

In bringing his Bahujan Samaj together, Bandodkar subverted a network built over two decades by earlier freedom fighters in

Goa from the areas around the mining town of Bicholim. These were volunteers of the Rashtra Seva Dal, a Maharashtra-based organization that blended its socialist-Gandhian beliefs with regular story-telling workshops and literacy drives to popularize Marathi, its language of use.

It doesn't take a political or economic analyst to tell you that, in the annals of Goa's business history, while the fields and coconut trees and small plots were given out to Goans of a lower caste and status and then bought back again, the chambers of industry and commerce were stacked in favour of the elites – the bulk of whom happened to be Saraswat Brahmins.

From that point, bringing in all the factories and the new railway line that cut right through the heart of Goa – and the over 2,500 hotels, resorts, bars, restaurants and boutiques that now dot the length of its coast – was not that big a deal.

Yet, if talk in the bar among the older folk veers back to the first two decades of governance under Bandodkar, there is still an undertone of reverence.

The fascist Portuguese government of the fifties, paupers as they were, left Goa with next to nothing by way of even basic infrastructure. It was Bandodkar who personally supervised the putting in place of an amazing network of paved roads linking smaller villages to the markets of main district towns and rapidly electrifying even the remotest of villages.

In twenty years, Goa had transformed itself. The early eighties and some way into that decade may have been Goa's golden period, with excellent statistics in healthcare, education and agriculture. The foundation for this was laid by Bandodkar.

And yet, he may also have been the first person to foist down Goa's throat the poisons of growth and development that have come back to haunt us since, predicated as they were on the premise of creating jobs. Nobody stopped to think that this may not have been the best model or paradigm for Goa to follow. While Jawaharlal Nehru promised Goa Special Status when he came visiting, not many others – apart from the first batch of senior bureaucrats – took it up with any serious thought or resolve. They were more focused on coin.

In the main, for civil servants who wanted the good life without the intrigues and lobbying that go with the job, Central government postings in Goa were enviable. Such bureaucrats consistently saw to the interests of the mining families. Digambar Kamat was faithfully served both as Goa's minister for mines and later its chief minister by an IAS officer called Rajiv Yaduvanshi. He remained the secretary of mines for eight straight years, and was ably assisted by two pliant directors of the state's mining department – one of whom served for six years and the other now remains suspended pending an inquiry.[11] The feeling on the street is that the Goa government-instituted probe will create a few fall guys while the real crooks are allowed to go scot-free.

Across India, thanks to the Supreme Court order dated 4 December 2006, there can be no mining within ten kilometres of a wildlife sanctuary.[12] But this was Goa. Here, Yaduvanshi, quite unbelievably, noted that since Goa was such a small state, it did not really need a 'large' buffer zone around its wildlife sanctuaries.[13]

In 2009, Gaurav Shirodkar, a young Goan working for an organization that closely observed environmental irregularities in the Western Ghats, heard that the Chowgule family had given the go-ahead for a 'raising contractor' to take out stockpiled ore from a mining operation closed down by a court order.

Gaurav alerted several organizations in south Goa, including those working with mining-affected villagers as well as groups that monitor and protect water resources from the powerful real estate lobby, and they immediately sprang into action.

After a meeting, they sent a delegation to the chief secretary in the secretariat just outside Panjim – fully armed with statistics, a few Google maps on a pen-drive, and a thorough knowledge of the law.

Goa's secretariat and assembly building, across the bridge from Panjim to Mapusa, was perched like an ugly bird overlooking the Mandovi. It stood like a lighthouse for the hundreds of barges that carried ore from the destroyed ghats at the sources of the river. Not too far from where it stands was once a ferry at Betim that took you across to Panjim. Those days, the bridge was even closer to the secretariat, which was housed in a smaller building that could not accommodate the burgeoning number of men and women who wanted to become politicians and make money overnight. About the time the new secretariat was coming up, a part of the first bridge that made the politicians richer fell down, and the ferries came back. Sooner than you think, there was this big shiny secretariat on the hill and, below it, like greedy hands reaching out for more, there were now two bridges in the place of one. As of updating this chronicle, they have started building a third bridge. They will build another two if they can, because that is where the money is.

Striding into the secretariat from a white limousine with a red light on top, followed by a retinue of fawning officials and bootlicking serfs, is very different from walking into the vast grounds, past the security guards, and into the palatial entrance.

From the bus-stop at the foot of the hill on the Panjim–Mapusa road, one sees that this ostentatious edifice with lawns of rich grass, saccharine flowers and manicured trees was born out of the tattered remains of what were once groves of cashew, jackfruit, mango and coconut. For all one knows, these may have been the traditional commons. Now the hill has been cut and shaved twice, once to broaden the roads, once to landscape – and all you see are the quick-growing, easy-to-fool bright green of the Australian acacia, casuarinas, beheaded and dwarfed forest alstonia, and the occasional splatter of gulmohar and jacaranda, all neatly hemmed in by water-guzzling duranta.

Past the tasks of filling in details and getting out slips, and having bags and files and pockets patted and searched, the secretariat is a many-sided beast. It could be the foyer of a somewhat upmarket but government-run hotel or the entrance to an upmarket hospital. Everywhere you turn, there is the unseemly sight of uniformed men and women armed with brooms and mops and buckets constantly sweeping and mopping the floors and staircases to free them of footprints, leaving behind just the fragrance of fried fish-imbued jasmine disinfectant. It is the nature of government employment: services outsourced. So huge is this building and so intimidating its style that one might think that it would have an endless stream of visitors going in and out. But this is not the case. Apart from those who work there, there is not a soul to be seen. The quieter places in the building may even remind one of a university, of silent corridors and closed doors behind which students or professors sit and read, or maybe listen to Bach.

While the temperature outside may be in the high thirties, the hotel-like ambience of the waiting room purrs at a steady 21.5 degrees. A crisp Shimla at the height of its summer, perhaps.

It is in the waiting room and office of the PA where you are reminded that this is a government office. You see freshly shaven senior officials and police officers in smartly pressed uniforms, most carrying files or notebooks, walking in, chatting with each other, one eye peeping in to see who may be sitting in the waiting room, and then, seeing only a delegation of ordinary citizens not worth a second glance, breezing past.

When you see trays of coffee, tea and biscuits going in, you know that the wait will be anything up to an hour. But this delegation, which intends to report an illegal mining operation in the Neturlim sanctuary, is obstinate. While some plot further recourses to the law, others note the paucity of reading material in the waiting room. Some among them, upon encountering the head of police for south Goa, inform him of the illegal mining operation, reminding him that a letter to that effect is on his desk. 'I will look into it as soon as I read it,' he tells them affably, baton firmly under his arm. But he will do nothing.

As the chief secretary has such a packed schedule for the next few days, his assistant has no appointment to give to the delegation. She agrees to take in their letter encapsulating the illegal operation and comes back with it initialled to the secretary, forests. But the delegation is informed that the said individual, who also happens to be the secretary, mines, and yes, water, is also busy. They are asked to come back in the afternoon, although it would suit the secretary, forests if they made an appointment for the next morning.

I was part of that delegation. We were all angry. We took the letter back from his PA, pushed the door open, and crowded around his desk. Rajiv Yaduvanshi, perhaps more frightened than he had ever been in his life, bleated harmlessly that he was busy.

Regardless of which avatar the secretariat uses to greet you, one thing remains forever true: politicians, bureaucrats, assistants and clerks are both privileged and empowered to work for the people, should they so want. The secretariat could easily be a great headquarters for a privileged activist group. The whirring of air-conditioning systems, the ringtones of phones and the almost silent patter emanating from keyboards linked to the net. Seeing all the technology around us, we realize that Goa's government, if it so wished, had everything it needed to make the state a model for the rest of the world. You soon know why this will not happen.

The secretary, forests goes on the back foot when faced with a delegation of nine men and women, ranging from age twenty-three to fifty-nine, each competent and guided by no less than their concern, interest and outrage. The complaint is noted, and a prompt and stern phone call is made to the director of mines, who, in turn, informs the secretary, forests that he can only meet the delegation at three in the afternoon.

In Goa, among people who made up delegations such as these, who asked for nothing but that the law be applied to all equally, such phone calls – from government to government, government to police, government to anyone – were known as being 'kicked into the long grass'. It was an expression coined by a young advocate in Goa to denote how the authorities collude to keep what is exactly as it is, and doing, or rather, not doing, what the law says.

While the letter was being duly sealed, three younger members of the delegation – in what can only be called a swift guerrilla movement – took over his computer and went straight to the Google Earth website and keyed in some coordinates they knew by heart. Soon, they were showing Yaduvanshi a mining operation located barely 200 metres from the eastern shoreline of the Selaulim dam, built expressly to store drinking water for south Goa.

Clucking sympathetically, the secretary, water, promised to pursue the matter.

In early May 2009, the mine next to the dam still continued to operate, truck after truck leaving with ore and skirting the dam's southern shores. They did this till the Shah Commission first visited.

In the early 1970s, Goa was actually picture-postcard perfect, one season passing into the other rhythmically and the summer temperatures far more bearable. In comparison, Kenya was not considered a safe place by Goans born or settled there.

Those were the days when many Goans who were either born in East Africa (like my grandmother, my mother or me) or who had settled in East Africa from the late 19th Century (like my father's side of the family), headed off to the UK on British passports through 'vouchers', a kind of luck-driven lottery. Better-off Goans took their money out and applied for Canadian citizenship. Quite a few who detested the extreme cold went to the US or Australia, some even to New Zealand. A few, perhaps out of loyalty, looked for investments in India particularly Goa – because that was where their roots lay.

When I was in college, I drove a Goan investor from Kenya, a friend of my father, up to the plateau that overlooked the long stretch of beach from Candolim to Baga. There was no iconic hotel then, no helipad, golf course or exclusive cottages. It was yet to become a place that hosted leaders from all the Commonwealth countries for an exclusive retreat.[14]

He was depressed. He desperately wanted his business partners in Kenya to invest in Goa, and had made this trip to give them proof. Instead, after visits to two government departments and a couple of banks, he totally rejected Goa as a possible destination for him and his three friends. Too many bloody 'licence' problems, he told me, poor infrastructure, corrupt government officials, lazy people, bad roads with cars that should have been abandoned long ago.

He looked at me witheringly. 'You Goans are too laidback. That's not the way to progress.'

The view from the top of the Aguada plateau was spectacular, the sun not even at 9 o'clock yet, and the air clean and salty to both eyes and tongue. The beach was like a fat well-fed snake with its tail tucked under the plateau on which we stood, its body stretching all the way north from Candolim to Baga, where it rested its head just below the plateau that blocked Anjuna from view. The old Jesuit Retreat House at Baga was perched on the cliff overlooking the creek, like a tiny white bird. The shiny white steeples of all the churches before it, adjacent to mango trees that were just as tall, stood out against a backdrop of ripening rice stalks and the occasional tiled roof. In seeing the Goa of that time, I felt like a bird born to the pleasures of topography.

The view brought him alive.

'This is virgin territory,' he said to me.

He had been telling me what he and his partners had seen on the Spanish coast, which was just opening out to investments in tourism. 'The guys there know what they have,' he said. 'Not like Goa. They're at the airport the minute you land, a car at your disposal, suites in a hotel, appointments set up to meet guys who know what they're doing, meeting with bank managers who want your money and are not throwing bloody rules at you ... I mean, look at this beach. It's empty; it should be full of tourists bringing in money to Goa. On that hill there ... I mean, imagine the view for Christ's sake ... there'd be luxurious apartments ... there and there and there ... and think of all the jobs Goans would get ... They wouldn't have to leave Goa to earn a living!'

He had painted a perfect picture of the future, right down to the final stroke.

In the Age of Greed, even a distinguished representative like Pratapsingh Rane – US-educated man, veteran politician and former chief minister with a long royal lineage – was not left without egg in the face. It was he, after all, who opened the door to let the loot begin while conveniently looking the other way. There was also a concomitant rise in his assets. While his assets were worth close to Rs 9 crore during the 2007 elections, they had nearly doubled by 2012.[15]

It was he who appointed Digambar Kamat, who defected from the BJP to save the Congress government, as his trusty minister for mines. Kamat later went on to take the reins of the government from him.

Pratapsingh's son, Vishwajit, was Goa's minister of health in the former Congress government. Though inducted into politics by his father, he was not blessed with the same charisma and charm – a factor that resulted in him becoming an important behind-the-scenes player. While there were many allegations of his direct involvement in mining, as 2011 ended, we came to know that intelligence agencies were tracking his bank accounts in Dubai, London, Portugal, Switzerland, Germany, Mauritius and Russia.[16] As the website goachronicle.com told us, they suspected that his funds came from real estate, drugs, deals with casinos, money laundering, providing escort services to the rich and famous, and a few so-called self-owned businesses.

On 3 March 2010, the same day that a few thousand grossly overloaded trucks hauled out ore to Sanvordem and left Quepem and Sanguem talukas in ruins, Vishwajit held a press briefing. Goa's minister of health was obviously rankled by a letter from the Ministry of Environment and Forests, New Delhi, putting a moratorium on all new mining clearances.[17] The decision had been taken after Jairam Ramesh, union minister of state, environment and forests, inaugurated a conference aimed at saving the Western Ghats from mining operations as well as ecologically damaging industries.

This was what Vishwajit said: 'Legal mining is something the chief minister wants to allow in the state, and in my constituency, there are certain villages where we want mining to happen. If the people in those areas want mining to happen, then it should be allowed ...'

As if the message was not clear enough, he stressed: 'Mining activities with legal permissions, valid licences and clearance documents from the authorities should be allowed. I think the union minister has unilaterally put everything on hold: the chief minister's letter had categorically stated that the mining policy was in progress, and it's a question of another fifteen days, so let the legal process move on.'

Like Joaquim, Vishwajit also told everyone that people had a constitutional right to do business, and if anyone wanted to mine or extract sand (a big business in his neck of the woods), they had the 'right' to do so. To quote him: 'No one can cancel or keep it on hold ... mining will continue in Goa because it contributes to the state's economy to a large extent, but at the same time, with the mining policy, illegal mining will come under control.'

Driving through the mining country, an arc right through the Western Ghats as they come into Goa, we find evidence enough to know the travails that dust can bring to everyday life, drastically changing it from the sublime to the ridiculous. Study after study has painfully documented this sorry fact. When the Goan health minister was asked how concerned he was about accidents, congested roads and dust, he replied: 'That is why I was asking the chief minister to sit with the mining community in mining areas and discuss the matter with them.'

When one perused the papers in Goa in the Age of Greed and actually read what its elected representatives had to say, he did not look for coherence, articulation or even provocation. The magical word was actually 'elasticity' – the ability to adjust or even sugar-coat something as grossly reprehensible as mining to make it look like the panacea to all ills, and act as if the piles of money made out of it were just another side-effect.

On the other side of the curtain in this farce stood Manohar Parrikar, once Kamat's chief minister and later the leader of the opposition in the house. Kamat held the portfolio for mining in the BJP government as well as the Congress government (which he defected to). Before he was inducted into the BJP government at the Centre as the defence minister, it was Parrikar who became custodian of both those offices in the state government.

From late 2008 onwards, Parrikar started declaring vociferously to anyone willing to listen that the mining operations in Sattari and Sanguem talukas, and Quepem, the taluka where both Maina and Cawrem are situated, were illegal.[18]

When Jharkhand's chief minister Madhu Koda was caught in a mining scam and the story broke in Goa, Manohar Parrikar met the media with a sheaf of papers in his hand, his tenor undergoing falsetto shifts of excitement as he claimed to possess proof that the mining in Goa was 'illegal'. He even said that he could link Koda and the money looted in Jharkhand with the same scams occurring in Goa and Bellary.[19] And there, the matter was laid to rest, while they all forgot a certain Justice Santosh Hegde.

Perversely, Parrikar now takes credit for exposing the 'irregularities' behind the patently illegal mining. He claims to have done it in his capacity of chairing the Public Accounts Committee, which, incidentally, was never allowed to table its report. If it's not tabled, it is not an annual PAC Report.[20] Ergo, it can be ignored.

Such were the Marquez-like scenarios that played out in Goa. It seemed obvious that all the actions taken by the newly elected Manohar Parrikar government would have just two possible outcomes: one, that they would be caught out, but the authorities – on close scrutiny – would discover only a fraction of the loot; second, that the Centre, only too willing to kick-start growth, would intervene and bring things back to normal. That way, the ransacking of the forests would be done at a slower pace. Instead of finishing five hills in four years, they would do it over eight.

As the Age of Greed built up, the people's movement against mining – constituting many who were on the same side but not necessarily on the same page – caused the mining barons a whole lot of discomfort.

There was little the government could hide. Digambar Kamat bleated to the media in 2009 that no new mining operations would be allowed in the Western Ghats. Less than a year down the line, Jairam Ramesh stood at Kotagiri in the Nilgiri Range and declared a total moratorium on mining in Goa. The audience applauded, thinking that they had won.

Alas, all of this was akin to building a brand new stable a good six years after the horses had been killed. Digambar Kamat had forgotten to tell the media that none of the five mines between Maina and Cawrem had waited for their clearances before they began upending the earth.

This may have been made easier for Kamat thanks to two men appointed to head the Ministry of Environment and Forests (MoEF): T.R. Baalu, who led it from October 1999 to December 2003 during the BJP-led National Democratic Alliance government, and the man who succeeded him, Andimuthu Raja (of the telephony scam fame), in charge from May 2004 to May 2007. During their terms, the MoEF gave itself the self-certification option – exempting project expansion and modernisation proposals from seeking environment clearances – through an amendment to the Environment Impact Assessment Notification, 2006. The power these men wielded was such that the ministry chose to maintain no database showing compliance to norms with regard to projects cleared by it.[21]

Activist groups used to joke that Andimuthu Raja's appointment was akin to the MoEF being issued a death certificate, and it wasn't even funny. In 2009, a report by the feisty environmental group Kalpraviksh – 'Calling the Bluff: Revealing the state of Monitoring and Compliance of Environmental Clearance Conditions' – showed that ever since the new Environment Impact Assessment notification came into force in September 2006, every industrial project for which approval was sought had been cleared (until September 2008). As many as 952 industrial projects were cleared and not a single one rejected. Besides this, 134 thermal power plants, a nuclear plant, 1,073 construction sites and 577 non-coal mining requests had been given the go-ahead.[22]

Actively assisting A. Raja in doling out environmental clearances by the dozen was R.K. Chandolia, then director of planning and coordination in the ministry, and Niira Radia, the now infamous 'publicist' whose phone calls were tapped and later leaked, and is now known to have 'facilitated' deals.[23]

Raja gave 'environmental clearances' to 169 mines in Goa – clearing 120 mines in 2007 alone – giving us the annual figure of more than 50 million tonnes of iron ore being exported.[24] Between 2007 and 2008, after Raja was given another ministry and his portfolio taken over by the prime minister, as many as seventeen 'clearances' were given to mines within the Netravali Wildlife Sanctuary in Sanguem Taluka – despite a 2000 Supreme Court order denying mining companies permission to operate inside wildlife sanctuaries.

When the authorities were approached about matters pertaining to mining, we found that they had been tutored to be polite. Security guards searched us for guns we only wished we had, and gave us entry slips that were stamped at two different points. We were led into silent, air-conditioned corridors and rooms where everybody from the minister to the bureaucrat dutifully took down our complaints and told us with great sincerity that they would look into the matter.

They are still doing that – looking into the matter. This was not apathy, as some may like to think. This was proactive collusion, the outsourcing of greed.

Why would you not then have the royal entry of Vedanta and Posco into Odisha and governments across ideological spectrums, willing, ready and able to bend the rules? Or various parasitic hydro-electric power projects and nuclear power plants to give the cities even more power; fast-tracked industries needing land but not the people dwelling there; the absurdities of a Formula 1 racetrack, or malls after malls, with retail outlets tested to see what can be sold to India's gullible upwardly mobile middle class and nouveau riche so that they can spend all the money they earn and ask for even more electricity for the cities; to more prominent instances of someone like Jharkhand's chief minister Madhu Koda who was caught with his fingers in the till with mining loot; and the best known of all, the Mining Kingdom of Bellary ruled by the Reddy brothers, BJP ministers in government.

The Shah Commission rained on everybody's parade when it declared in its report that 'iron ore worth Rs 35,000 crores was plundered by the mining companies, committing theft of Government property'.[25]

As in other parts of the country, perhaps, the law in Goa was used to spit in our faces and get away with it. Bear in mind that between 2004 and 2010, every truck, barge and railway carriage carrying ore within Goa, into Goa and out of Goa, was loaded to the brim. Trucks, in fact, in contravention of prevailing law, even added depth with additional boards welded to the sides and back. A study by the Central Pollution Control Board in 2007 pointed out that on just a single six-kilometre stretch of road near a large mine in northern Goa, overloaded and speeding ore trucks generated as much as 2,770 tonnes of ore spillage per year, largely in the form of dust.[26]

While everyone in government was quick to admit that such overloading was illegal, the time taken to travel between Margao and Panjim to file charges and the subsequent bureaucratic delays ensured that the offence remained unchecked for the longest time. And if an honest government official did try to throw a spanner in the works, he would be transferred before any damage is done, buying the mining lobby a few more months. They did this for more than six years.

It was also during this period that the expert appraisal committees set up by the Ministry of Environment and Forests capitulated to industry yet again. The expert committees are supposed to give environmental clearances to sectors like mining, thermal power, river valley projects and industries. They have a critical role to play under the Environment Impact Assessment (EIA) notification of 2006. These committees, meant to be transparent and honest, were only required to give reasons for their decisions when rejecting a project. M.L. Majumdar, chairperson of the expert appraisal committee that oversaw mining, was also the director of four mining companies, namely, Uranium Corporation of India Limited, RBG Minerals Industries Limited, Hindustan Dorr-Oliver Limited and Adhunik Metaliks Limited.[27]

He was anything but impartial. Ritwick Dutta, the noted Supreme Court lawyer who argues cases for the environment, told us that Majumdar held the dismal record of clearing about 150 mining projects related to Goa in an hour and a half flat, spending ten minutes or even less on each of the 200-page proposals that sought the so-called 'environmental clearances'.

When Jairam Ramesh came in later to whitewash what his predecessor A. Raja had done, he sacked Majumdar for failing to disclose that he was on the board of a few mining companies. However, they did not revoke the clearances that he handed out.

The fact is that, for the mines between Maina and Cawrem to operate and function, both the state's collector and the Goa State Pollution Control Board had been acting as willing couriers. They forwarded what public opinion in Goa overwhelmingly believed to be illegal and fake documents to the MoEF, where environmental clearances were granted a good year – if not more

– after someone like Joaquim Alemao had already eaten his way into Jollerancho Dongor.

Meanwhile, both the government and Goa's mining families claimed every chance they got that what was actually destroying the hills and forests in Goa was illegal mining – with which they held no truck. They claimed that their operations were 'legal', and referred to their method of pillaging the land as 'sustainable mining'. Each mining family maintained at least one model mine to show visitors, but criminally ignored thousands of other hectares they had been destroying systematically from the late fifties.

However, what exactly constitutes illegal mining has never been specified for obvious reasons. The school of thought that holds that the ban on mining be imposed in perpetuity, the loot recovered down to every last paisa, and those who committed the offence jailed and fined, say that when push comes to shove and the documents are strictly scrutinized, not a single mining operation in Goa would be found legal. Our activist friend at Bicholim, Ramesh Gauns, said this to several newspapers, every opportunity he got. If one goes by the law strictly applied, that is.

But the sheer brazenness with which the mining was carried on in 2008, following not even the most paltry guideline set by the Ministry of Environment and Forests, made us wonder whether we were the ones who were – in fact – misguided into thinking that the mines were illegal.

Does 'illegal' refer to the contractors and politicians who act at the behest of a mining family, freely disbursing large amounts of money for what Joaquim memorably said was his 'constitutional right' to mine? We often wondered why it was not the constitutional right of villagers near these forest lands to continue with their way of life.

As wags at the bar used to say: we know there are forty thieves elected to the legislative assembly, but who is Ali Baba?

Between 2006 and 2008, getting what was euphemistically referred to as 'environment clearances' in order to mine – basically, the official sanction in New Delhi to do away with forested hills – was the easiest thing in the world. It only required a document officially known as a 'Rapid Environment Impact Assessment' form, abbreviated by mining companies and ministry officials to EIA to give the illusion that matters were not as rapid as they actually were.

Such 100-page reports were conjured out of a hat and customized by a firm in Hyderabad called Bhagavathi Ana Labs, which opened a branch in Goa in 2008. From reading several such reports, it did seem that with one tap of the mouse, a menu opened out with set templates, and they were on the road. It boiled down to having an office of young men good with software, and others with below-par skills in at least three languages, but doing what most high school students could have done – cutting paragraphs and sections from previous reports and pasting them into a new document.

These so-called EIAs are now being scrutinized by the Goa branch of the Centre for Environment Education, Ahmedabad.[38] What will they find out today that we did not know between 2006 and 2008? When we scrutinized the EIAs for Maina, Cawrem and Collomb while tracking those so-called 'public hearings', we knew they were flaunting the rules and laughing at us at the same time.

Fake EIAs are just one part of the story.

In three of the mining operations here, including the Fomento mine behind the school, there appear to be no records to show that genuine public hearings were actually held and not just populated with truck drivers and owners. In those days, no one in the area had any idea about either EIAs or public hearings; the three mines just came out of nowhere, people said.

In 2008, Fomento was not interested in justifying its right to mine anymore. Around the time the monsoons ended, it went on a 'corporate social responsibility' drive, printing a glossy publication showcasing the positive aspects of mining with large photographs of children smiling into the camera. Instead of photographs of overloaded trucks, bulldozers biting into mud and children as well as adults choking in dust six days of the week, you saw lush green fields and the Goan stereotype of simple, happy people – pictures probably sourced from the stock of the in-house magazine that services the same family's famous Cidade de Goa hotel.

In Maina, Fomento opened two clinics in areas they had colonized. At the peak of the mining season, these were always covered in dust. Doctors visited only every alternate day, or once a week. However, now that the mining has come to a halt, the clinics are closed. But they are not covered in dust.

As the rains came to an end in 2007, we also saw that Joaquim Alemao had started believing that it was only a matter of time before his Raisa Mining, much in the fashion of what Fomento did behind the school, could begin a pincer movement. Alemao would extend Jollerancho Dongor south, moving the village community there to some other illegally acquired forest land, and going east of Paik's temple, down to Curca, where the farm was.

In the gym that he went to on some evenings, more to keep an eye that his flock didn't stray than work to trim his ripening body, he would snigger publicly about Cheryl on the farm, knowing that his words would reach her ears. Everybody has a price, he would tell his close cronies, it is just a matter of time before she realizes who I am, and breaks.

At stake for Joaquim, was getting the 'environmental clearance' to mine Jollerancho Dongor that ironically, his Raisa Mining had already started destroying before such clearances had actually been issued. When we brought this up, they threw at us the magic word – 'deemed'.

It now appears that the Congress government deemed anything to do with mining legal. They clicked their fingers, and as if by magic, the plundering and looting turned into mining families working for Goa's development.

The original leaseholders to Jollerancho Dongor were the Gujarati firm Shantilal Kushaldas and Brothers Pvt. Ltd, early settlers in Goa.[29] They were elbowed out of the business by the Goan mining families, and the lease for Jollerancho Dongor was, at some point, miraculously passed on to Anil Salgaocar by the time the Shah Commission arrived.

Joaquim Alemao would never attend a public hearing in Maina, where people only bowed their heads in deference and hoped that he would take out his wallet. To Maina, he sent his minions.

First to enter the 'community hall' near Paik's temple were the managers of most of the mines in the area. While leaseholders and lease owners may have been separate entities, the staff at the various mines – who often shared the same contractors – worked as a consortium protecting their own interests. Most were brought from places outside Goa.

At the public hearings that we attended, the managers ensured that workers and related employees – comprising anybody from truck drivers to random elements – were present. Later, they would be treated to drinks at the local bar. The managers would bring in a few hundred letters supporting mining, to which their clerks dutifully added random signatures and fake addresses. A jeep bringing in snacks and drinks followed close behind, and the children and women were quickly served under the solicitous eye of the mining staff.

Nothing ever began until the collector arrived, invariably late and usually escorted by two unarmed, nervous policemen.

By the time the collector arrived, the staff of Bhagavathi Ana Labs and officials from the Goa State Pollution Control Board would have set up their equipment to present the 'facts' and videotape the proceedings. There would even be a printer ready and waiting. When the collector finally arrived, the farce would get underway.

The master of ceremonies was invariably a lecturer from a local college who was tasked, at every public hearing, with the responsibility of translating the EIAs into Konkani. He was a consummate actor who knew the script of every single EIA he had to translate because they were all the same, and the predictable sequence of the power point presentation projected from the computer. He never used his notes, just the screen to get the figures right. His performance was always flawless. When you asked him whether he didn't feel bad translating false facts to the Goan public, he would reply that he was just doing a job.

However, what no one expected at Paik's temple that morning of the hearing to clear Jollerancho Dongor mining was a 'community hall' packed with close to 200 people. Even the collector, who arrived an hour late and still insisted that he had to rush to another public hearing, was taken by surprise.

There was a reason for the gathering. The Catholic Church in Goa and particularly its shepherd, the Archbishop of the Diocese of Goa, kept sitting on the fence even when everybody else was protesting against the illegalities of the mining industry. In fact, one of the 'brothers' from the Salesian order was even silenced, and then transferred out of Goa for crying out against mining. Later, a priest from the same order was also transferred for taking part in the agitation in 2008.

But there was at least one community of nuns who were not as sanguine as the Archbishop of the Diocese of Goa. The Presentation Sisters, who run two well-known schools in south Goa, had also been exposed to the hazards of mining thanks to the work they do in Zambia, Odisha, Jharkhand and Chhattisgarh. They knew exactly what ruining the land and displacing its traditional inhabitants meant.[30]

They saw the devastation caused by mining in Goa first-hand. Among the order, at least two nuns had held evolved training sessions for other nuns on the theme of 'ecospirituality', a need for the religious Catholic to understand the feminine in the divine and the inherent spirituality of the earth. They had their community house in a village just outside Quepem, once inhabited by the Gavde community but now in the throes of either disinheritance or change – whichever comes first.

At the meeting at Paik's temple, the two nuns brought in a seventy-member contingent of women, from teenagers in skirts to older ladies in saris. They had all contributed and hired a bus, and were loud, hearty, spontaneous and infectious. What followed next was pure magic. The Velip women from Maina and Cawrem – who had either come in an open van or walked in their traditional nine-yard saris and flower-bedecked hair to the venue – were astounded to see the Catholic women arrive.

Slowly, they stood up, parting to let the visitors in. The whole hall was abuzz with excitement and laughter.

Father Matthias, a Salesian priest from Sulcorna, was moved enough to say: 'You know, when I see something like this, all these women sitting like this, not bothering whether they are Catholic or Hindu, but just fighting for a common cause, I feel there is hope for the world.'[31]

However, when the meeting got underway with the master of ceremonies smoothly accelerating, changing gear and getting into the flow of his Konkani translation, we were left with reality flickering on a screen, half-washed by a bright glare that only highlighted the quality of the larger farce, giving it a touch of the surreal.

In between, you saw gems flash on the screen, like the wonderfully misconstrued, 'The local people have benefited from the infrastructure provided.'

At other times, you found out that Joaquim Alemao's accountant had set aside the princely sum of Rs 50,000 to replace the thousands of trees that would be hacked down; Rs 120,000 for tankers to sprinkle water on the roads and bring down the dust; and in case all that fails, Raisa Mining would 'develop a green belt along the boundary wall of the mine to reduce the visual impact'. Not as incongruous as you would think: all along the mining corridor, operations either grow Australian acacia and casuarinas to blanket the entrance from the horrors beyond, or raise a high fence over which one cannot see. It's like closing your eyes to wish the destruction away.

At any of these so-called hearings, when the mining company finishes its presentation, the real feelings of the people come out. Everyone who opposes mining does so, taking the microphone and speaking into the camera, in many instances railing against the collector for overlooking illegalities and demanding to know why the Goa State Pollution Control Board remains silent.

It was frustrating – knowing that even the law wouldn't help. Ask the Pollution Control Board officials, and they would say that they are just doing their job. Corner the collector, and he would hem and haw and try to convince us that there are grey shades in everything, including the law.

At this particular meeting, as the public finished raising their objections and the collector was about to draw the curtains on the farce, Podiar – a man who waited for his well-respected freedom fighter father to die before selling the family land out to mining interests (Alemao and Fomento) – stood up and said, 'I wish to speak.'

When Podiar walked somewhat cockily to the microphone, he was greeted with silence. He tapped the microphone and cleared his throat. From the back rows came some comments that drew a few derisive hoots and some chuckling from the women in the front.

The collector slapped his palm on the table and called for silence. Both he and the mining representatives at the meeting were already rattled.

Podiar introduced himself, saying that everyone there knew him as he and his family were from this very village.

'What do you want to say?' one of the men asked.

'Why are you wasting our time? Say what you want, and then go,' said another, glaring angrily.

Podiar did not know that villagers in this area had already attended another such public hearing where opposition to the mine far outweighed support, but the motion was still passed in New Delhi. All they had left was seething anger.

Somewhat rattled, the old freedom fighter's son bleated: 'There are a lot of people who say that mining will be bad for our villages ... but I just want to tell you of the many ways it will be good for all of us, good for our village—'

It was the moment many had been waiting for. Pandemonium broke out. A few spat on the ground, and many – with arms whirling as if they held stones to hurl – screamed words of terrible abuse.

Shouts of 'Eat dust, eat dust, eat dust' filled the community hall in a raucous syncopated refrain.

A few of the younger, more hot-headed men had to be restrained from physically assaulting the freedom-fighter's son, while two or three well-built goons quickly formed a protective shield around him. The mining officials made soft cooing sounds intended to palliate matters, while their underlings hastily brought in tea, samosas and soft drinks for the villagers. The collector, totally ignored during this time, was not overly concerned. He simply wanted the pollution board to print the minutes, so he could sign and dispatch them to Delhi.

Then an elderly woman in a nine-yard sari, her pallu tucked around her bent waist and a shiny orange wreath of abollim in her oiled hair, walked up to the freedom fighter's son and threw a roundhouse slap at him.

Such cheering broke out!

Podiar couldn't ward off the slap. He clutched the left cheek and his eyes were smarting.

There was chaos again. While the goons tried to calm the old lady down, the public exhorted her to hit him again. She did not. With tears in her eyes though, her voice rising and quivering as she shook off the hands restraining her, she cursed: 'I don't want to know how much money you have eaten, but that money will never make you happy. I know that for what you have done, selling your father's land to these mining people, you will never be happy, and neither will your children.'

The applause rang loudest among the women and children as well as those impoverished and landless, while the few who had sold out looked sheepish. It seemed like a new religion in the making.

Not that their seething anger did any of us good. In the ensuing weeks, in village after village in Quepem and bordering Sanguem Taluka, clearances to mine were given at the drop of a silver coin. All of them sought to regularize the environmental havoc created over the past two decades.

That night itself, even as some villagers patted themselves on their backs, truck owners seated in nearby bars boasted that the so-called 'environment clearances' had already been procured in New Delhi.

In any case, we sent the EIAs for Jollerancho Dongor and the other mines in this area to the Centre for Science and Environment (CSE), New Delhi. Their response was prompt, thorough and damning: there were five mines already surrounding Jollerancho Dongor, and the cumulative effect would be disastrous.

CSE also stressed the need to conduct a cumulative environmental assessment of Maina and Cawrem. It duly noted people's objections to a false map given in the EIA, and the more serious objection that, though the hearing was held in August 2008, the excavation had begun as far back as early 2007. While Bhagavathi Ana Labs had stated there were no perennial water courses, rivers, streams or water bodies within the lease, the CSE noted that the villagers claimed just the opposite. While Bhagavathi Ana Labs stated that only 46.8 per cent of the total area in the buffer zone required by law was forested, villagers said this was as high as 95 per cent.

The Mining EIA mentions the presence of kraits, lizards and fresh water snakes in the core zone, but forgets to make a note of the mighty king cobra, wild boar, bison, hare, deer and mongoose, which also have their home here. And as in every EIA close to forest areas, mining companies refuse to mention leopards and tigers.

CSE's investigators noted the anomalies we had come to accept: on page no. 2.5 of the document, it was stated that the life of the mine was twenty-eight years with planned production of 0.10 million per annum. However, on page no. 4.15, this was changed to twenty years, while at the same time, deliberately increasing the original distance they had given in the same document between the mines and human dwellings surrounding it.

And worst of all, it would consistently understate the ore to waste ratio, or just not mention it at all. (This is a serious omission, because on average, mining means excavation of around 3 tonnes of mining waste – overburden and good soil – to produce one tonne of low-grade iron ore.)

The CSE critique put it like this:

'If all the iron ore projects submitted for clearance since June 2007 are cleared, 55 million tonnes of waste will be generated on an average every year – assuming an average generation of 2.75 tonnes of waste to extract 1 tonne of iron ore. This is a huge quantity and would also require a large amount of land for its disposal. In a state that is already witnessing a number of protests on account of mining waste destroying agricultural fields, these new projects could become a major bone of contention – especially taking into account the hilly terrain of the proposed mines and high rainfall.'

CSE also stated that Joaquim Alemao's mining operation at Jollerancho Dongor made big claims on its corporate social responsibility policy, which were subjective in nature and incapable of being cross-checked. He needed to provide 'quantitative figures on how he was going to invest on the uplifting villagers in the area through education, health services and other programmes', it noted.

But thanks to the Shah Commission, Jollerancho Dongor was never to reach operational levels, where the entrance to the mine would have required the road to be broad enough for one convoy of trucks going in empty, and another coming out overloaded.

Something like that could not deter a man like Alemao. A few months after the Supreme Court ban on mining, he smoothly shifted gear, selling some of the land he had bought in Maina, not that far from either Jollerancho Dongor or Paik's temple, to someone who promptly converted it into small 'dream farmhouse plots'. They managed to acquire environmental clearances for this deal too.

The week after the public hearing at Maina, another so-called public hearing was held at the Collomb temple. News of the one held at Maina the previous week had filtered down, and a busload of villagers opposed to mining arrived that morning. There were people from Benaulim, Sanvordem and Panjim, all intent on letting the MoEF in New Delhi know that mining activities were unwelcome in the Western Ghats, one of the world's most important biological hotspots.

Proving that politicians will grasp at any straw, this particular meeting was disrupted by the presence of then leader of opposition Manohar Parrikar and a large entourage of male followers.

Villagers from Benaulim had come all the way here in two buses to show solidarity with the people of Collomb. They had already seen how the government and its many functionaries had sold the ground from under their feet to tourism-related ventures and real estate sharks in the name of infrastructure building.

Women in both groups had already intermingled with each other. The frocks and jeans, tops and headbands worn by the Catholic women mixed and matched with the nine-yard saris, strings of mogra and bakul flowers, and salwars and kurtas of the Hindus.

In any case, two Goan men were all they needed to put paid to an occasion of genuine public discourse. Two taxi-drivers from Benaulim shouted abuse at the BJP leader of the opposition, demanding that he and his male entourage leave the public meeting. Parrikar welcomed the attention. Bringing his skills as a facile orator to bear, he demanded that the public hearing be cancelled because it was illegal!

There was a show of force, and even as Catholic and Hindu women nervously stood aside, their husbands spat and hissed at each other.

This hostility was a result of the systematic polarization between Catholic and Hindu from the mid-1960s. Parrikar, a devoted RSS acolyte, represents for many Catholics, an extremist form of Hinduism. Some would say this divide is only increasing.

Soon, the police walked in, escorting the district officials and those from the State Pollution Control Board back to their cars. An event where people could have reasoned with each other deteriorated into a sham that was sad and predictable.

The leader of the opposition stood up, acting as if he was speaking to hundreds of cameras, even though there was just one in the room. His stage-managed bravado apart, all his rants that the mining lease would not be allowed came to naught. The so-called 'environment clearances' had already been procured; in fact, the mining operations began even before the public hearings were held.

The old scene that we saw at the hearing for Joaquim's mine was enacted all over again ten days later, at another community hall in Rivona with the same characters – an additional collector with an official from the Goa State Pollution Control Board; two secretaries to record the minutes; a young man to videotape the proceedings; two technicians from the Hyderabad-based company to project slides with tables and statistics; and the same Konkani lecturer, all set to translate the claims to Konkani and make some money on the side.

At this particular hearing, they presented a person whose father had a colonial lease that had long since lapsed, but which he now sought to hand over to a mining company. A successful farmer of some standing, he had recently sold his farm for a few crores of rupees. A person at the meeting actually asked him why he needed even more wealth, and did he really need to sell the valuable forest land that his father had procured from the Portuguese.

'Don't tell me about fighting mining,' he replied defensively. 'I have been fighting them for over ten years.'

Then why give up now, he was asked.

'It is iron,' he replied. 'The whole world needs iron. Can you tell me if there's anything that you use every single day that does not have iron?' He pointed at the watch of the person asking the question, his spectacles and his belt buckle. See, see, see, he said, nobody can do without iron. Then he sat down, folded his arms across his chest, and sank back into himself.

4

Cheryl's Last Stand

Joaquim Alemao looked all set to be our neighbour.

While he went about getting 'environmental clearances' to mine behind the hill leading down to the farm in the cover of the night, Alemao's Raisa Mining sent drilling teams to prospect and test for ore all over the land he had bought from Gaonkar.

After my sister Cheryl[1] left Varca to settle on the farm with her husband and newly born daughter, she knew that the land on which her house was built contained the richest lode of all. Alemao knew this too. So, more than anything else, it was this farm and the bedrock of ore beneath that he craved.

He made quite a few personal visits to Maina and Pirla behind us. In fact, his mining kingdom stretched all the way to Collomb, where our friend and anti-mining activist Rama Velip had been tracking his moves. He had also moved into the Catholic mining belt of Sanguem town and its environs, sniffing out mining leases in the adjacent hills and water bodies. He harboured dreams of making his son, Yuri, head this section of his mining empire.

When Alemao visited, he came in a Pajero with darker-than-legal windows and a red light flashing on the car roof. A police escort followed in a jeep, only too willing to let the siren rip and instil fear.

He had largesse to bestow and the people took it, probably thinking that they will deal with what comes later. This largesse, assurance and promise he offered to all and sundry, especially the Velip squatting for some thirty-odd years on the land that Gaonkar sold and Alemao bought. It is another matter that it may not have been Gaonkar's to sell at all, but village commons land that he colonized and made legal through the passage of time. Joaquim had two neighbours, and he hoped to buy them out to establish his dream of creating a mining pit starting from Jollerancho Dongor and extending to the edge of the Curca that curved in a bend, kissing the farm at the point where it met Paik's Spring waters flowing south of his temple.

Richard Dias, a successful real estate builder from Margao, had bought land here in the late nineties. He and Ninette, his wife, had turned the land into a farm-cum-weekend home that they maintained most religiously. Whether out of fear for his family's safety, or pragmatism, Richard was not averse to selling out to Alemao. In those days, the myth in everybody's head was 'You can't stop mining' – the subtext being, 'So you might as well cash in while you can.'

However, to get to Richard's land, Alemao would have to first go through Cheryl's farm. Now, there he had a problem. I have been told more than once how the mining baron in a moment of desperation and hatred – described her (spitting before he said the word) as a wagin, a 'tigress'.

Since the nineties, she had given the Alemao familia several reasons to despise her.

Cheryl bought her farm, fields and cashew and coconut orchards from an old Catholic landlord who had bought it with clear legal title in the early 1960s, thinking that his sons would continue farming. The land had come into her possession in the mid-1980s, when she ran a successful, high-end furniture and restoration workshop, which in those days was consistently among Goa's highest foreign exchange earnings for small-scale units.

Her furniture workshop was in the village of Varca, a once-sleepy fishing village that has now changed into frighteningly bizarre suburbia. In the late 1980s and early '90s, it was better known for the infamous Churchill Brothers.

While the Churchill Brothers are better known as a football team today (its patron and benefactor being Churchill Alemao, former chief minister of Goa and Joaquim's brother), the term – in those days – literally denoted a family of brothers whose writ ran large in and around Varca through various rackets, including smuggling and extortion.[2] The battering ram they used was Ciabro, a younger brother who dwarfed the Enfield he rode.

It was Ciabro who had approached Cheryl, asking for money to 'protect' her furniture business since he had heard of threats being made against her. She had pointed to the two German shepherds she had at that time, Virginia and Woolf, who rode with her in her post office-red Tempo Trax, as if to say: 'That's all the protection I need.'

If there is one thing that raises the hackles of macho Goan males, it is the sight of a woman driving a large vehicle. It was not difficult for Ciabro to talk one of the family drivers into frightening Cheryl. The driver, over-eager to please, did worse. Past the Varca church, where the drop to the field below is close to two feet, he drove her right off the road. Even as she flew off the road, skidded and braked, spinning round to face the road, Cheryl spotted Ciabro's jeep disappearing at full speed. Putting her vehicle in gear, she climbed back onto the road before heading straight to the Alemao mansion, banging the knocker of the door like it was Ciabro's head.

A grinning Ciabro opened the door with only a towel wrapped around his waist. His mother was standing behind him.

'Is this how you open your front door to visitors,' Cheryl asked Ciabro witheringly. 'Have you no shame? Please put on some clothes before you come and talk to me.'

While he slunk away, Cheryl took the opportunity to tell the mother exactly what her son was up to. When he returned in tee-shirt and jeans, she told him that if he ever tried such a thing again, she would lodge a police complaint against him and his driver.

Chastened, the Alemaos behaved themselves for a while. And then, one day, Cheryl booked an export order for 150 hand-carved fireplace mantles for a well-known Canadian dealer who had sold out the twenty-five test samples taken earlier. She was asked to deliver in less than three months for a bonus payment.

The Alemaos decided that this was a time when Cheryl would be vulnerable, working to meet a deadline, and therefore amenable to their 'protection' offer.

First, they got the linesmen in the electricity department servicing the area to disconnect her power supply. Complaints made to superiors resulted in prompt action, but there was no assurance that the supply would remain stable. Her phone connections were plagued with the same problems.

Thinking ahead, she had a generator installed. Sure enough, during the week leading to the deadline, both the phone connections gave away. Cheryl began using the public phone booth across the road.

The night before the container was to be shipped, the Benaulim police arrived in a jeep and hauled off Cheryl's foreman and her chief polisher (who still had at least ten mantles left to finish) on a flimsy pretext. The plan was to keep them there, delay the container, and get Cheryl to face losses all the way up. They wanted to teach her a lesson.

I was working on a theatre project in Goa at that time. One visit to the police headquarters at 8 the next morning to discuss the specifics of the incident with a bored khaki-clad gentleman working on a newspaper crossword puzzle resulted in two phone calls.

After the first call, a paunchy Goan gentleman hurried in and saluted the police officer awkwardly. He said little other than 'Yes Sir' several times as the boss told him to settle the dispute before it flared up.

A second call was made from the lower body's shabbier office to an even lower body at the Benaulim police station in a tone that seemed to be a cross between childish scolding and a whining plea. Whatever they did, it seemed to have some effect: a police jeep took both the workers back to the workshop before hastily beating a retreat.

But Ciabro was not done yet. When the huge truck bringing in the container approached Varca from Margao, the driver and his two cleaners were met by Ciabro's hoods, brandishing iron rods and chains, who said they could drive the truck into Varca, but would have their legs broken if they tried to take it out.

When she heard about the incident, Cheryl made two calls from the phone booth across the road (they had cut her wires again a day ago). One call, loud enough for Ciabro's goons to hear, was to Canada – a voice message clearly stating that the consignment was on track. The other was to the manager of the container company in Vasco, assuring him that his crew, truck and her cargo would be unharmed. As she paid the lady at the shop, Cheryl said, 'Let's see who tries to stop me.'

At five-thirty, with enough time to spare for the ship's departure from the docks, Cheryl started off in her Trax, with the towering truck in tow. At the main road, she saw Ciabro's goons on bike and foot, lining either side of the road. The last trick in their book was to feign an accident under the truck, and file a false police report.

Ciabro would have known by then that I had put the Alemaos' earlier tricks in writing, down to the last detail, at the police headquarters. He would have been more than wary. The goons on the road were just part of a face-saving exercise, and Cheryl duly acknowledged that. She smiled at Ciabro, enquired about his mother with exaggerated politeness, and then politely requested his help in clearing the road of his supporters and letting her cargo through.

Till the truck had reached the limits of their 'territory', Ciabro's bikers behaved like dogs chasing a car that they had no hope in hell of actually biting. They accelerated up and down, coming close and swerving, while Cheryl and the truck set a steady unwavering pace of 30 kilometres an hour till they reached the Zuari. Then the truck headed west to the docks, and Cheryl turned back and returned to Varca.

It was only by the end of the 1990s that two of the Alemao brothers, Churchill and later Joaquim, turned political leaders and kingmakers. By 2012, they had brought in their children too.[3]

When Cheryl bought the land in the mid-1980s, everyone laughed and said that she was crazy. In those days, when she first saw the land, she had dreams of diversifying into a wildlife resort that she could run in cooperation with the villagers in the area.

This may have been an idea planted by our father, Peter, who, till he died in the late 1980s, kept insisting that India needed to rethink the idea of cooperatives.

So when Cheryl married Tony, a college friend, and the two had Aki – born on 1 January 2000 – they closed the workshop.

Without an architect or engineer, they built their new house as carpenters would. Cheryl designed the space using straight lines, right angles and exact measurements, while Tony fulfilled the duties of a foreman-cum-worker.

When they were testing the soil, they were told to forget farming and turn to mining. They were shown the spot where the lode was the richest – ten feet is all they needed to go. They built the farmhouse at that very spot, its proportions all wrong but mighty enough to withstand several onslaughts of a bulldozer.

In 2006, when the farm and its orchards – populated with cashew, mango, coconut and chikoo trees – were up and running, Tony was tragically electrocuted on Richard's farm, trying to help them reconnect a transformer cable that had come loose.

Joaquim Alemao smelled blood.

He waited for the period of mourning to get over before pouncing. He assumed that with the husband gone, the wife and child would be at their most vulnerable. He had read Cheryl wrong.

Alemao approached her through an emissary, offering Rs 25 crore to buy her out. Cheryl asked the emissary whether the party on the other side thought she could be bought so cheap. The next day, the emissary offered to double the amount, even take it a bit higher, given the 5,000 crore Alemao was likely to make from the ore under her house.

When people urged Cheryl to move on to a new life, she echoed our mother Dora, asking how anyone could accept the kind of money that takes away forests, land and water, and still manage to look at themselves in the mirror the next morning.

So, like his brother Ciabro, Joaquim tried resorting to muscle power.

In 2007, he ordered Gaonkar to bring in a gang of workers and hack down the trees on the hill leading up to the farm. At six in the morning, as she headed out to drop Aki to school in Margao, Cheryl saw twenty to thirty trees lying on their sides. She turned her Gypsy around and gunned it back to the farm.

By that time, I had moved to the farm, well and truly a nomad shifting between Pune and Goa and balancing teaching work with activism. We all sensed that things could get hard for their all-woman household: Cheryl and Aki; our mother Dora; Rita, the family retainer who had brought up Tony as a child; and Shashikala, who helped out with the chores.

The day they cut the trees, Aki got a day off from school, which pleased her to no end. By 7 a.m., Cheryl and I were at the officer of her lawyer, Mario Pinto-Almeida.

He dictated, I keyed in. We made print-outs, got them photocopied and signed by Cheryl, and neatly packed them into envelopes before sending them off. When the secretariat in Panjim awoke after the lunch break, I was handing out sealed envelopes like Father Christmas, faithfully recording receipts for the same. It was a detailed letter to the chief minister, listing instances of his minister's skulduggery; and it was copied to the chief secretary, ministers for environment and water, and secretaries, forests and water. I also went into Panjim and handed a copy to Shashi Kumar, the conservator of forests. It is laughable that, in the Age of Greed, there was someone who answered to that description.

Cheryl, meanwhile, handed out copies to the forest department at Quepem, her taluka headquarters and to the forest check-post before Cawrem.

That night, Gaonkar hid himself at home and did not even make his regular evening jaunt to the village watering hole. The next morning, we drove all the way to Panjim and personally met Shashi Kumar again. He smiled as he always did whenever anyone complained to him about mining, and shrugged.

'I have seen the letter,' he told Cheryl, 'but my hands are tied. All my people in the south have been bought out by mining companies.'

We demanded that he follow it up till they photograph the felled trees, file a case and fine Gaonkar. We took to walking around Joaquim's new property with Cheryl's two large Rottweilers, and a young playful Great Dane with a bark that would have sent the shivers into anyone. That put paid very fast to the men Alemao had brought in to do the preliminary drilling and prospecting. But Cheryl was also forced to put a wall around her own property, digging her heels in and consciously deciding to take the mining companies head-on.

Alemao was not done yet, though. He made his next appearance in Pirla, where he sought another public hearing for clearances over a mining lease that had actually lapsed.[4] He assumed that since he was the minister for urban development in the government, chief minister Digambar Kamat would do his bidding as he had done with several others.

Before they get to the public hearing stage, the village panchayat and people must pass a declaration stating that they all favour mining in the area. So, in mid-2008, having 'officially' won in Maina, even though the people had unequivocally declared that they did not want mining, Alemao launched the process of getting clearances to mine in Pirla. It was a truism in Goa's Age of Greed that regardless of what the local population, particularly the women, said against mining, the clearances would happen.

He arrived at the panchayat office at Pirla in his Pajero, with a bright red cherry stuck on the top, escorted as usual by a police jeep. At this meeting to declare the village's support for mining, Cheryl was the lone opponent. She listened to the local government officials telling villagers that mining would be good for them, while Alemao stood smirking at the side. When it was time for the villagers to speak, Cheryl told the gathering that their local government officials had been bought out by the minister.

'Look at the minister,' she told them. 'Look at his shoes ... they are Italian and cost 6,000 rupees ... look at his watch ... do you know how much it costs? One lakh rupees! Do any of you have shoes? What about a watch? How many of you own a watch? How is it that only he has the money?'

Turning to Alemao, she asked politely: 'How have you come to this meeting with a police escort? Is this an official escort? Are you entitled to it?'

The police inspector accompanying the minister shuffled his feet uneasily; the constables hunched over and tried to blend in with the villagers.

'All of us in the panchayat support mining,' one of the local officials bleated.

The minister, not expecting her presence at the meeting, just tried to stare her down.

'I oppose the mine,' she replied. 'And I want my objection to be put on record.'

She handed in her objection in writing, methodically noting the havoc that mining would wreak on traditional agricultural practices and natural water sources.

Muttering threats under his breath, Alemao walked to his car, followed closely by the police escort. Engines gunning, red lights flashing and a siren blaring, they left.

'You are the only person here who doesn't want the mining,' one of the officials told her, smiling. 'You can't stop it.'

'Think about what all of you are doing,' she told the rest of the gathering, most of them men. 'You will get peanuts while the minister makes crores of rupees. Can you even imagine how much money this is? You will lose your fields, and they will be covered with mud and stone so hard that your ploughs will bend.'

She pointed into the distance, beyond the panchayat office, where the hills loomed large. 'You will lose those and all the water beneath. The weather will change, it will be much hotter in March, and May will be totally dry. What if the rains don't come? Will you be able to live with just what the mining company gives you? How long will that money last?'

The panchayat officials stood there, smiling even as she started her Gypsy and drove off, her tears of anger mixing with the uneasy knowledge that it was dust the villagers would opt for.

5

Money Drove It All

From Jollerancho Dongor, the old freedom fighter's house is due east, at the lower reaches of the hill. To reach the house by road, you cross the school and the Fomento pit, then the mud turn-off going left to Paik's temple. And just before you reached the bend, again on your left, you would see the entrance to Joaquim Alemao's mining office at the foot of Jollerancho Dongor.

Before you hit the bend and the house, you see how there's only about half of Jollerancho Dongor left. The southern side of the hill that once fed water to the river Curca behind the farm stands as a sheer laterite cliff. From 2008 onwards, the only water to be had on the southern slopes of Jollerancho Dongor was between September and early November, when cattle in the area would find the occasional pool of water left over from the rains – a green, viscous mess congealed with mining slurry and their own dung – from which the frogs had long fled.

Alemao spared the northern portions of the remaining forested hill, but that didn't mean much. In 2008, MFC Industrials Pvt. Ltd – a Canada-based company working with its Indian subsidiary, Magnum Minerals Pvt. Ltd – had already secured all the necessary permissions to totally destroy the eastern flank of the same hill as it climbed further to its highest peak in Cawrem. Behind this mine – not even 75 metres west of the summit and going downhill – was Paik's Spring.

As the mining money came in, the dwellings around the old freedom fighter's house changed. Once, when you visited him, you would sit on a cemented bench built into the veranda in typical Goan style, while he reclined in his easy chair. His eyesight was getting poorer, but his memory for old stories was just fine. You had a panoramic view of his property across the road, lush with cashew trees climbing to the very summit. Year after year, he leased these out to people who make cashew feni or collect the nuts to sell.

Alemao and his mining cohorts were attempting to buy the fields and properties that the old freedom fighter owned. From there, they could open a new flank to the farm and the river Curca, one that would take them all the way up to the land Alemao had already acquired from Gaonkar.

The old freedom fighter's son had already sold the hill with the cashew orchards his father had planted to Fomento. They had fenced it all the way to the road, leaving only a small portion of the old man's property across the old house. Behind that hill, Fomento had excavated a huge portion and created a carefully graded mud highway down to the main road. This was to bring in empty trucks from one side, load them and take them out through the other. And there would still be space left for a third lane, in case circumstances demanded it.

Even after the old man died and his son sold more of the land, getting his hands on more money than he knew what to do with, the house was not torn down. It was perhaps dealt a blow far worse. Almost overnight, it was changed in form, shape and texture; extensions were made on all sides, and bars put across all the new window frames of the new rooms. The old veranda was sealed off with a wall as well as aluminium frames and tinted sliding windows. The old whitewash, which had seemed so natural in the 1980s, gave way to expensive paint in colours that were mismatched and garish, yet quite at home with the life around them.

Then the son started bringing in truck after truck, until he had twelve of them neatly parked in the small service yard he had cleared of trees.

Around mid-September, Alemao and his men got the heavy machinery serviced and ready. The labour contractors had already brought in migrant workers. They waited for Ganesh Chaturthi to pass, and with it, the last of the rains. Then they uncovered one small portion of the giant stacks of ore stockpiled during the previous mining season, which were being sheltered from the rains under about half a hectare of tarpaulin. They gunned the earth movers and called in the mining trucks.

Eventually, the new house and everything around it was covered in a fine sheen of dust that dulled the bright walls as well as the shiny coats of the family's new cars. Even as the new century broke, you could see children in the area playing outside their houses and family members enjoying the breeze on a cool evening. However, six years later, the doors and windows of the houses were seldom found open. The dish antennae atop each of the dust-covered houses and the occasional flicker of TVs behind the tinted panes were the only indication that there was any intelligent life in these parts.

As if fleeing curses rained on them by those forced to remain in the area and eat dust, many a family who sold land to mining bought land elsewhere or simply moved to Margao, where they bought a flat. But the old freedom fighter's son did not move. His luck, in fact, changed for the better. By 2008, he had plans to bring in another six trucks. He could be heard boasting to his newfound admirers that he had even bigger plans of venturing into real estate, which was Goa's other cow for slaughter. Sadly, the curses mouthed by old Velip men and women as they passed Podiar's house – spitting on the ground as they did it – seemed to hold no magic powers. For when the mining ban set in, he changed tack by selling off half his trucks and venturing into agriculture, putting up sheds for cattle and growing grass for them in the fields adjacent to his house.

But back in those days, when you passed his house, you got a very strong sense of just how mining was changing our world. The trees and bushes some metres off the road were painted dirty brown and the potholed road seemed like a grimace of horror. All along the road, taking the climb westwards was Fomento's high barbed wire fence encircling the entire hill. Just ahead, as the climb got steeper, was the new mud highway. At the foot of this road during mining season, they employed a few older, unemployed Velip men, paying them a couple of thousand rupees a month to cover their heads in cloth, and wave green or red flags to give right of way to the mining trucks.

You pass Alemao's mine and Fomento, and before your engine can even brace itself to make the climb, the third mine, run by Magnum Minerals Pvt. Ltd unfolds in front of your eyes.

This was once a hill that sloped all the way down to the road at a gradient of forty-five degrees. At the very top, still some way from the summit, you still see a whole line of trees tilting outwards, just waiting to fall, at the edge of a man-made cliff much higher than a fourteen-story building. Below it, the pit is so deep that you can hardly see its bottom from the road.

The Magnum mine was shrouded in secrecy from the day it was born. None of us heard about the so-called public hearing held to give it the requisite environmental clearances. One day, as we drove by, we saw men putting up fences and barbed wire around the thickly forested hill slope. They worked fast. At that time, we took it to be a forestry project by the government.

Before we knew it, bulldozers started clearing away the trees that once crept all the way down to the road. Of course, whenever they have a mine in forested areas, the proposals that seek environmental clearances describe such thick forest as 'scrub'. They do not mention the existence of hills or perennial springs in the site they wish to target. They note the existence of monkeys, hares, deer and wild cats, but blissfully ignore bison, leopard, wild boar, otter, python and even that most majestic of animals – the tiger.

Till 2009, none of us even knew who owned this mine. By law, every mine must have the necessary signage stating ownership, environment clearances and lease area, among other details. As with all the other mines between Maina and Cawrem, the signage here only came up a couple of months before the Shah Commission's first visit, and that too, in the form of hurriedly hand-painted boards.

The digitally printed reinforced-plastic signage – like the brightly painted fences and posts, and slick godowns and sheds – came much later. After the Shah Commission's two visits, the Central Empowered Committee arrived in Goa and damned the mining companies yet again. As the Goa Foundation's website reminds us, it was their petition (No.435/2012) that led to the Supreme Court passing its famous order of 5 October 2012 disallowing the re-start of any mining activities in Goa and injuncting anyone in the state trading or transporting mineral ores. The order also directed the Central Empowered Committee to examine the various findings of the Justice Shah Commission and make recommendations.

Australian acacia was planted fitfully along the mine's edges – miserable clumps of foreign forestry that even the crows avoided. And even as they wilfully destroyed traditional water sources, the miners brought in tankers of water to spray on the roads and put down the dust, so the drivers of the overloaded mining trucks could benefit from a better environment.

There were all sorts of rumours floating around this third mine on the road. The truck drivers in the bar said it belonged to a person from Karnataka. No one had seen him. Others mentioned a company in Panjim that was said to rent or lease out earthmoving machinery manufactured in China, but which was actually contracted to extract the ore at this mine. And yet others said this was a partnership between a politician or two and a big player from Bellary – which, at that time, was also reaching its nadir in terms of greed.

A few residents of Cawrem held that the mine actually had two owners, one from outside the country and one from Karnataka. Someone else, closer to Margao, said that the owner from Karnataka occasionally visited Goa, and when he did, he worked out at a gym just outside Margao. He was said to have two bodyguards, one of whom supervised his heart-strengthening exercises.

All we ever saw was, once, a monstrous black SUV drove into the mine on a Sunday morning, followed by a more ordinary jeep with managers and other functionaries. Before the dust could settle, the guards in the mine had come to attention in the hot sun. The jeep behind disgorged men, and the best dressed among them literally ran to the SUV and stood eagerly at the driver's door, fanning the dusty haze.

When the dust went back to ground, another man – well dressed, in a long-sleeved shirt and tie – got out of the back of the SUV.

Given the setting, it could have been a B-grade Bollywood film, with the desert landscape of burnished laterite, scree and waste dumps towering to the skies.

The boss appeared to be inside the air-conditioned car. Then, word was apparently sent out from the driver's half-lowered window because another senior mines manager approached the SUV and started nodding like a marionette. The whole episode lasted barely ten minutes. The window went back up, the manager returned to the group behind, shook the hand of the well-dressed person and escorted him back to the door, opening it, bowing and then closing it again.

The SUV drove away, its huge tyres kicking up dust over the guards still standing at attention and saluting.

It must have been a very good meeting – perhaps with promises of additional bonuses if the ore was brought out faster – because no sooner had the SUV hit the main road than there was much backslapping and shaking of hands all around, the laughter and mirth echoing in the caverns of the mine and reaching us all the way to the top, where we crouched.

We found out eventually that the mine belonged to Magnum Minerals Private Limited, a business establishment registered at New Delhi in February 2005, giving the c/o address of S.N. Dhawan and Company in Connaught Place (it was probably the firm that registered the company). Some years later, the company was to state that its directors/officers in New Delhi were one

Dragan Arsenijevic and another Slobodan Andjic. Very little could be found out about them.[1]

Then there was a small flutter. Suddenly, out of nowhere, a certain C.A. Aziz Khan from Bangalore popped up, claiming to be the real owner of Magnum Minerals Pvt. Ltd. On an online consumer complaints forum in Bangalore, we saw a terse sentence pointing out that the real owner of Magnum Minerals was one Prashant Sahu. There were several posts condemning C.A. Aziz Khan for hoodwinking people in Bellary, where he was said to be a mining contractor, and in Chikmagalur, where he was supposed to have interests in coffee.[2]

We discounted neither party, believing it quite likely that this was a business deal gone sour. Matters were later set right when all the parties came to the conclusion that there was more than enough of the loot to go around.

Prashant Sahu, of course, was much more than just the simple and real owner of this mine. We found out that, thanks to him, Maina and Cawrem were involved in a truly multinational operation – something that would make any proponent of a globalized economy proud. When the Goa Chamber of Commerce and Industry, for instance, invited Prashant Sahu onto their expert panel to streamline operations and improve the infrastructure for mining in the state, they knew that he was the executive director of MFC Industrial Ltd – a Canada-based global supply chain whose business centred on its commodities as well as mineral interests.[3]

At the very outset, therefore, Prashant Sahu was not to be compared with the likes of Digambar Kamat, a powerful politician. Or with Joaquim Alemao, who wanted to become a mining baron because he had come to believe that the mining industry controlled the affairs of Goa. Sahu is not even to be confused with the scions of Goa's mining families, who got everything on a platter.

No, Sahu was big time. The global company he oversaw was like a shopping mall – a kind of corporate equivalent of Walmart with shelves for minerals, metals, chemicals, plastics and wood, built on a solid platform of more than sixty years of experience in supplying various commodities.

They would buy these resources at competitive rates from Asia, Africa, Europe, Australia, the United States and the Middle East, and put them on the shelf for buyers from places across the globe. Anybody in need of resources and commodities just had to approach them with a fat bundle of money.

By the time Sahu joined them, MFC had ventured into areas like merchant banking and financial services, specialized banking, third-party financing, investing and, of course, real-estate trading.

Listed on the New York Stock Exchange, its shares traded at \$10 at the beginning of 2005 and climbed to a high of \$44 in 2007. During the slump of 2009, these figures sank below the 2005 level but recovered. Being largely liquid, they have the reserves and wherewithal to pay out money when needed and continue to do business and grow.[4]

MFC began its journey as Terra Nova Royalty Corp., a company set up in Canada in the early 1950s, but traced its origins and sourcing skills to an older parent company in Austria. It derived its income in those days through a sub-lease at the Wabash iron ore mine in Labrador, an operation that commenced in 1956 and is due to expire in 2055 (or sooner, depending on how much is dug out from Wabash, and how fast). That initial income seeded their knowledge and expertise as a commodities middleman.

Since then, it has had other faces, or masks, depending on your point of view. In a long but steady process of divesting, their name changed from 'MFC Bancorp Ltd' to 'KHD Humboldt Wedag International Ltd' in 2005; then to 'Terra Nova Royalty Corporation' in 2010; and finally to 'MFC Industrial Ltd' in 2011 to reflect their new focus as a global commodities business.

MFC Industrial Ltd could be said to be a good, safe, reliable, risk-free investment that established its global presence and put its money in carefully selected baskets all over the world. They will make you money in the long term while you fiddle elsewhere. Admittedly, it won't be at a rate as rapid as the mining barons in Goa, but at a saner pace with the knowledge that shares could be traded later to fetch a good price. You could probably take a time-share for a week in Bali every year, but not have enough to buy an exclusive villa in Goa.

It is also sad but true that the villages of Maina and Cawrem, and even Goa itself, will leave not even a speck of dirt on MFC's highly polished shoes. MFC Ltd was doing legitimate business in Goa, and involving us Maina–Cawrem folk in a truly global operation. It would not help matters in any way if we moaned in indignation that they took away our hill – or weep because they almost wilfully destroyed the left arm of the aquifer that fed Paik's Spring.

Long after the carnage at this mine as well as the Shah Commission's initial visits and just before the Supreme Court-appointed Central Empowered Committee came to Goa, MFC miraculously transformed the mine, putting up a huge, semi-translucent, milky-green fence that blocked the view of the mine all along the road. They also installed proper sheds for the workers and equipment, and did whatever they could to hide the collateral damage. In the proposals to get their environmental clearances, they actually list the use of such fencing to 'reduce the visual damage to the environment'.[5]

Their international business, in fact, did a lot more than okay.

At the end of 2011, for instance, Prashant Sahu took home $319,244 from MFC Ltd, which included his salary of $89,224 and an additional $230,020 as part of the annual incentives he was entitled to. While Sahu's chairman and CEO, Michael Smith, was in the millionaire's club, the other Indian on the board, director and executive chairman Ravin Prakash ('with over 35 years of corporate banking and financial management experience', who also 'specialized in recovery and restructuring of doubtful assets'), was not that far off.[6] He took home $961,888 by way of salary, options-based awards and annual incentives.

Another Indian, Indrajit Chatterjee, was hired in 2005 as a director with Mass Financial Corp., presumably a smaller arm of the company. He was later elevated to the board of directors of Terra Nova Royalty Corporation, a much beefier arm.

Chatterjee, 66, is a retired businessman, once 'responsible for marketing with the Transportation Systems Division of General Electric for India ... experienced in dealing with Indian governmental issues'. He fulfilled his duties admirably and, at the end of 2011, took home a 'retirement' bonus of $248,685. This was computed as $96,500 by way of salary, and $152,185 by way of incentives and awards. More than enough, you could say, to buy an exclusive villa in a gated colony in one of the more scenic areas of Goa.[7]

The villages of Maina and Cawrem were never intended to leave egg on the MFC's handsome global face. They were clear, business-like and thoroughly professional.

This is what they wrote in their annual report 2011: 'We have entered into agreements through a subsidiary with third party leaseholders of iron ore mines in Goa, India, pursuant to which the leaseholders agreed to sell iron ore to our subsidiary at a fixed price per tonne, based on the extraction costs plus a royalty payment to the owner dependent upon the iron content of the iron ore. Pursuant to the agreements, our subsidiary has also been contracted to extract iron ore on behalf of the leaseholder at a fixed fee per tonne. The agreements are presently in force and continue until September 4, 2014, and our subsidiary has been granted the right to renew the agreements for three-year terms until September 4, 2020.'

Given that their annual report mentions mines (in the plural) in Goa, it is not unlikely that all the ore taken out from these five mines between Maina and Cawrem was actually lifted by MFC Ltd.

In the final analysis, MFC will claim to be a transparent global company. Had they remained till their contract expired in 2014, the pace and efficiency with which they worked from 2005 till early 2012 would have ensured that Paik's Spring was completely destroyed. They would have commanded and coordinated assaults on five flanks that protected and nurtured the mother aquifer, taking away the hills for the ore that lay deep below the aquifer.

They were also pragmatic. In that same annual report of 2011, they dutifully acknowledged that their business was conducted 'in countries with a history of corruption', and that this could only compound their risks. In fact, they added that further international expansion would only involve greater exposure to such practices. They left a window open to wash their hands.

In November 2012 the company's press release noted that a court in India had 'issued an interim order on October 5,

2012 prohibiting mining activities in the State of Goa, India'. The company noted that the order was passed 'based on a petition filed by a non-governmental organization, Goa Foundation, in light of a report which was tabled in Parliament on September 7, 2012, alleging that billions of dollars were expropriated by illegal mining companies in the region'.

The press release further noted that MFC's Indian subsidiary 'previously entered into agreements with third party leaseholders of iron ore mines in Goa, India pursuant to which our subsidiary is the sole contractor, and the leaseholders agreed to sell iron ore to our subsidiary at a fixed price per ton based on the extraction costs. Our subsidiary has provided materials on our activities and environmental policies to the government and we are optimistic that such activities are in full compliance.'

MFC's heart was in the right place. 'The Government of Goa,' the press release duly noted, 'is under strong pressure to expedite reopening all of mines as 75% of Goa's economy depends on mining revenue. The mining industry is the largest employer in the state, employing: 52,000 general truckers, 26,000 mining trucks, 7,000 bargemen and another 75,000 people directly employed in the mining industry.

'While there can be no assurance as to the outcome of the proceedings,' the company said, 'we view the suspension to be temporary and are reasonably optimistic that iron deliveries will be resumed before the mining season ends.'

They were so optimistic, they concluded the press statement noting that they were 'continuing the process of obtaining all the necessary permits respecting the purchase and sale of iron ore from a new mine owner that has a property located in Goa, India. We have entered into an agreement with the mine owner.'

In November 2012, MFC gave us the good news that their new mine in Goa was in very 'close proximity to their existing iron ore sources in Goa'.

The posh office of MFC's Indian subsidiary Magnum Mineral Pvt. Ltd in Goa is housed in a property developed by the flamboyant mining magnate-cum-politician Dinar Tarcar, whose own mine, as we shall see, is cheek by jowl with the Magnum mine, and was also charged with being illegal.[8]

They did arrest Prashant Sahu in early 2014, but not for the fact that Magnum Minerals Pvt. Ltd ran an illegal mining operation.[9] He was arrested and remanded to two days' police custody for calling the Income Tax Department in Panjim in September 2013 and pretending to be the revenue secretary, Government of India. In this silly bit of playacting, Sahu had demanded that the department probe the assets of the Margao-based Kadnekar family.

Here too it was a question of mining. It was the Kadnekar family that owned the mining lease, which was not renewed in 1988 when it should have been, but Digambar Kamat had condoned the delay when he was chief minister.

Magnum Minerals Pvt. Ltd, designated as the Kadnekar family's 'raising contractor', exported more than 1 million tonnes of ore, earning something in the region of Rs 150 crore. When the Kadnekar family asked for their royalties, they were told by Sahu to collect the money from MFC Industrial Ltd in Canada, the company to which Magnum Minerals Pvt. Ltd had been sold. And here too, it was not just Sahu who had his hand in the till.[10]

After the call was traced and found to come from Prashant Sahu and not the revenue secretary, the income tax department filed a complaint with the Panaji police in October 2013 and asked it to investigate the case. The case was later transferred to the SIT.

So, what happened in the end? Sahu got away with a slap on the wrist.

We were never to find out whether it was Dinar who had agreed to sell his purportedly illegal mining operation to another such operation between Maina and Cawrem.

On 1 April 2013, MFC's global corporate communications told us that 'in September 2012, the Indian government halted all mining activity in the State of Goa following the tabling in Parliament of the Shah Commission report on illegal mining. Subsequently, in October 2012, the Supreme Court, acting on a filed petition, stayed all mining operations, including transport of mined minerals (iron ore and manganese), in the State until further orders.'

MFC had had enough perhaps. 'We believe the orders will take many years to resolve for the existing mines and that there is a very strong possibility that no new mining will ever occur,' they wrote. 'As a result, it was our decision to move on and recognize a loss on our investment. We have sold our position for nominal consideration, consisting of an interest in any future cash flow if mining actually resumes. With this former subsidiary being sold in 2013, MFC recognized an impairment charge of $42.6 million on these interests and a $19.4 million write-down on inventories. The total impairment and write-down was $48.2 million, net of an income tax recovery of $13.8 million. MFC has no further cash flow obligations associated with these operations.'

Truth be told, Sahu's mine is what educated us. We hated it the most because every single day till the ban, we saw exactly what they were doing to the side of the hill that towered above the road. The operation ran parallel to the road. The security was so tight, you just couldn't get past the guards who lined the entire section. They even had guards up on the hill, stationed on both sides of the canyon being created below.

We got to see what exactly they were doing by climbing the hill towards Paik's Spring, going behind Joaquim's mine at Jollerancho Dongor, and then veering to this mine. The guards standing watch on the hill in their thick black uniforms and grey berets were the easiest to handle. All you had to do was hide in a thick clump of bush and disturb it, then make a few deep, growling noises. Being members of a theatre group, these sounds came easily to us. Sometimes, we would make it sound like two animals were fighting.

If they bent down to pick a stone, a second set of growls – this time of some wild animal ready to attack – would get them running all the way down the hill and back to their tin-shed barracks. At the shed, they would call the other men out and point towards the hill. They would watch for fifteen minutes hoping to see a leopard. We waited to see if anybody would come out with a gun someday.

So, between 2007 and till the day the Shah Commission happened to save Goa, this mine appeared to have more than doubled its speed. It made the operation at the Fomento Resources behind the school pale in comparison. We didn't need figures, the number of trucks driving in and out of Maina was proof enough. By early 2011, there were close to four times the number of trucks loading up and going out.

Piles of mining waste, adorned by a few recently planted trees, now form a ring around the mine. The hill and its forests have been replaced with a deep mining pit.

When a mine gets this far, you don't even need bulldozers to move the trees to get to the rock beds and ore. All you require is a carefully charted line of explosive charges and a plunger. So deep do they go, one barely hears a muffled thud if he is a kilometre or two away in Maina or Cawrem. The trees, the fertile topsoil, the earth, the water and the rocks, all tumble down into the pit already mined for ore. You do that over and over as you take away the hill in ever-increasing circles. The mining industry refers to this as 'scientific mining'.

Even all these years later, what hits me most is the total disrespect for water. No one knows just how water behaves, and seeing how everybody from hydrologists to humble villagers are completely dependent on it, experts have spent their whole lives trying to figure it out. On the face of this same hill, a phenomenon occurred that ought to have been filmed for posterity to show those in the mining industry as well as the bigwigs in our government just how sick and anti-life the concept of 'scientific mining' is. As the mining contractors took away the hill, widening the wound and extending operations by creating a machine-made terrace to get at the ore, they sprang an aquifer free – guiding it away from the pit and into the agricultural land in the valley below.

Setting this particular long-dormant aquifer free was like watching a frightened leopard being chased into an open ground by poachers. First, it became a waterfall wide enough to wash over four mining trucks abreast, a veritable sight for tourists, with an explosive gush that lasted well over four days. However, with time, the water petered down to a trickle that – after three days in the hot sun – left only stains on the mud. We were so disturbed that we did not even think of photographing it. I never wrote about this before, either. I kept it for this travelogue.

It would be impossible to calculate how many litres of water were wasted, and how long this aquifer – if retained in its original state – could have provided the population of Quepem town with drinking water. As it is, the water flowed into fields below, and through these, into brooks and streams and back, if one wishes to be scientific, into the Curca, then on to the sea as the Kushawati.

The villagers below, dependent as they happened to be on farming (and water) for their livelihood, were given a pittance by way of 'welfare' by the mining contractors.

We took hundreds of visitors past this mine over four years, all of whom reacted to the 'visual impact' that Magnum Minerals Pvt. Ltd (India) didn't quite manage to hide.

One of them kept saying 'Oh My God! God! Oh God!', as if she was, in actual fact, entreating God to do something. There were more people than you could count on your fingers and toes who had tears in their eyes. A young man just couldn't stop saying the f-word, his outrage rapidly turning into disbelief. As for one particular young woman, she just maintained a brooding silence through the trip from one mine to the other, all five of them. It was only when we reached the end of our journey in Quepem town that she mumbled under her breath: 'This is sick.'

6

Politicians, Activists, Journalists

Shortly after the rains ended in 2008, before the mining season could start, I left for Pune to take up a short teaching assignment that ran till the academic break in Christmas that year. I admit that I ran away shamelessly. I would return, of course, but at that moment I desperately needed a break from having to see and hear about the mining every single weekday at close quarters.

By August 2008, the mines managers were openly boasting in Maina and Cawrem that they were going to start ramping up operations by many notches. Then the looting really took off. Soon, whenever they passed us, the managers in their company jeeps would slow to a crawl, roll their windows down, and push their heads out – smirking like cats sighting cream.

I began making notes for this chronicle as far back as 2006, wondering what mining would do to entire landscapes that I had cherished for years. I had long lost faith that the feeble opposition to mining in Goa would bear any kind of fruit.

I saw this chronicle as a factual blow-by-blow account of what actually happened on the ground – left behind like photographs in monochrome and sepia. Only when there was nothing left here, except the pockmarked ravages of open-cast mining, would everybody know how this part of Goa had been upended in a frenzy fuelled by greed.

I wanted to speak for the earth's injured voice, but needed to run away from my own notes and the pictures in my mind. By early August 2008, they were beginning to eat circles in my head; I could even see them in my sleep. Those days, I felt like swinging at anyone who even suggested that the greed could be halted with our tactics and strategies. I may even have had a breakdown of sorts. Everyone noticed it too, which is what probably made me take off.

Regardless of what madness possessed me, I always knew I would keep this chronicle for the very last. Not like a dessert or iced liqueur-laced sorbet, but like a cup of bitter coffee on an empty stomach.

It was Justice Santosh Hegde, the fiery and conscientious peoples' judge from Karnataka, who prevented this uncalled-for surprise by systematically deconstructing the extent of the fascist criminality at play in the once-flourishing mining empire of Bellary in Karnataka. We need to keep in mind that his first report on illegal mining in Karnataka was submitted to the government as far back as 18 December 2008.[1] It opened a can of worms that would subsequently shame governments at the Centre as well as several states across party lines.

Justice Hegde handpicked his team of five officers based on their reliability, understanding of issues, and above all, courage.

Before he submitted his final 466-page report on 27 July 2011, indicting the then Karnataka chief minister, B.S. Yeddyurappa for illegal mining, to Governor H.R. Bhardwaj and Chief Secretary S.V. Ranganath, his team of five officers had scrutinised 400,000 documents and assessed 4 lakh bank accounts.[2]

It was his first report in 2008, however, that had started the tremors. Justice Hegde's investigating team not only retrieved substantial evidence of skulduggery but also gave the government reason enough to think that that they had barely scratched the surface of Bellary's mining scam.

It was unfortunate for the infamous Reddy brothers, who ruled Bellary in very much the same fashion as Goa's mining families did here, that the man Justice Hegde chose as his chief investigating officer was U.V. Singh, Karnataka's chief conservator of forests. He happened to be a man of integrity.

When U.V. Singh visited Bellary in 2009, he came across Somashekhara Reddy, MLA of the region and brother of the shrewder Janardhan. Somashekhara arrogantly asked Singh whether he had the permission of the minister in charge of Bellary to enter the district.[3]

'As a citizen of India,' Singh told him, 'I do not require anybody's permission to visit Bellary.'

In September 2011, speaking at a workshop at the International Centre in Goa after his retirement, Justice Hegde was quite clear that his team would have nailed everyone involved in the Bellary illegal mining scam. 'Mere five officers scrutinized four lakh documents and assessed 4 lakh bank accounts. If we had got two more months, we would have literally nailed everyone involved in the Bellary illegal mining scam,' he told the press as well.[4]

While he acknowledged that there were more people as good as the small band of officers who served him so well, equally, he said, the numbers on the other side were growing. In any case, he added, 'he was retired not tired'!

Justice Hegde had reason not to be cynical.

His more-than-capable protégé, U.V. Singh, was promptly inducted into the investigating team of the Justice M.B. Shah Commission set up in November 2010, reluctantly instituted by a once-complicit Central government.[5] Their hand had been forced. It was by then impossible to ignore the reports of large-scale illegal mining and the abject failure of several states and even the Centre to curb this disease from spreading.

It must, therefore, be said quite emphatically that it is the Justice M.B. Shah Commission's investigations that finally saved Goa's forests and water, and not – as may now easily seem to be the case – its home-grown, well-meaning, but eventually frustrated, judicial activism spearheaded by Dr Claude Alvares of the Goa Foundation.

In fact, as events on the ground unfolded from 2007 onwards, those who opposed mining were an amalgam of many creatures.

The most influential in the Age of Greed were Goans (or those who had come to settle in Goa as the promised land) who allowed themselves to be wooed by the argument that industrialization was a necessity in Goa. They may have been incapable of seeing the virtues of plotting a distinct path for the state that would take it back to its remarkable social indicators of the late 1970s and early '80s. They knew, perhaps, that their own personal success depended on the assertions of growth and development. They concocted situations where both sides could win. Let's do this by consensus, they said, let's decide how much environment must go if we are to 'develop'.

It would not be unfair to say that the anti-mining lobby in Goa suffered from its fractured sense of 'politics'. Those who ought to have known better chose the easy, comfortable route of launching an NGO or two and putting down a paper trail. They spurned the plea that the battle had to be fought away from the courts and on ground zero for it to make any headway at all.

What could we say when 'anti-mining activists' actually suggested in good faith that NGOs help the mining companies re-green some of their old mines?

But if they were to drive about 60 kilometres from Panjim, they would see how the rogues here weren't even leaving any dumps on which they could plant trees like they were supposed to. They were digging their old, once-discarded pits, even those adjacent to the Selaulim dam – which provides drinking water to south Goa – in ever-widening concentric circles, leaving behind a bare carcass of earth. The 'Grand Canyons of Goa' as some put it.

By 2008, there was enough evidence that all was not well with Goa's forests. But people consciously chose to look the other way, and why wouldn't they, when Goa was on the move. By 2012, Goans topped the country's per capita income index by taking home Rs 192,652 on an average per year. Bihar, languishing at the bottom, stood at a mere Rs 24,681 a year.[6]

It also helps to keep in mind that the strategies and tactics adopted by the anti-mining lobby in Goa were unilaterally arrived at, under the guise of a broad consensus. The loosely formed anti-mining group was never on the same page from the very first day. Beyond the sound and the fury, there appeared to be only one line of attack: petitions, petitions and more petitions filed against mines littered across the place.

If one was lucky, one could even attend a token protest meeting or send strings of group mails to a closed internet community. Meanwhile, precious time rolled by.

The legal precedent with mining-related cases as far back as the 1970s, as everyone knew well (or ought to have known), was what happened when the Dempo and Sesa Goa mines were beginning to expand their operations around Bicholim in north Goa.

Ramesh Gauns, the well-known anti-mining activist grew up and lives in this area. Speaking of the old days, he told us that it was common knowledge that aggrieved parties, whose rice fields and orchards were inundated with mining waste after the rains, would receive little help from the magistrates of the day. In a very patronising tone, they would just be told, 'Arre baba, how can you fight these big companies with just one or two families in the village. Take their money and be happy. What else can you do after all?'

That kind of fatalism, historically, was the terrain on which the law would run its course on anything to do with mining in Goa. Even more antithetical to the belief that a struggle for the environment must emerge from the affected areas, and not be top-down, was made painfully obvious to us much later, and much before the ban on mining kicked in.

Dr Claude Alvares, the well-known director of the Goa Foundation, was the de facto leader of the anti-mining movement because of his long-standing expertise and experience, his passion, and – most importantly – his willingness to pursue matters (even though he was always badly strapped for funds and always severely understaffed). He remained at its helm until the day the Justice M.B. Shah Commission relieved him of his onerous responsibilities and forced the law to take a stand.[7]

In all fairness, the Goa Foundation had worked well within its self-imposed restrictions. A research report by it identified fifty-seven mining companies operating without consent under the Air and Water Acts. The Foundation then went on to file a writ petition against the Goa government asking the chief wildlife warden to issue wildlife clearances holding back the sanction.

Even more revealing, the Goa Foundation's petition challenging the government's order to the chief wildlife warden was held up because one of the judges refused to hear the matter because of his relationship with one of the mining companies.

It was also the Goa Foundation that tallied all the production of the mining companies and matched it with the data tabled in the assembly by then minister for mines Digambar Kamat. Not surprisingly, the Foundation discovered that forty-eight 'legal' mines had conveniently taken out 11 million tonnes extra. (It is another matter that on ground zero, we knew from 2006 itself that there was no distinction between 'legal' and 'illegal' when it came to the mining operations between Maina and Cawrem.) As the Foundation pointed out, this was in violation of the Environment Protection Act and the terms of consent under the Air and Water Act. These violations had, of course, gone to the Goa State Pollution Control Board – toothless in the Age of Greed.

It was only as late as 2012, more than four years into all the looting, that the Goa Foundation did to the mining industry what that industry did to the earth.

They went through approximately seventy-four reports of the monitoring committee, which visited several mines from 2008 and 2009, and sent these tabulated lists of violations to the chairman of the Public Accounts Committee, Manohar Parrikar (who was the leader of the opposition at that time) and to the

Western Ghats Expert Panel. A little later, they withdrew all the cases filed by them in Goa's courts, and moved the fight to the Supreme Court in Delhi.

In retrospect, it was those eighteen petitions filed by the Goa Foundation and a few more reports put forward by other legal collectives and concerned citizens, all well researched and meticulous, that provided the preliminary data for the Shah Commission. This, in turn, led to the Goa Foundation coming out with its own recent and totally damning report on illegal mining.

However, the courts themselves may not have been as seized of the matter as they have been of late.

For instance, the High Court of Bombay, Panjim Bench took eight years to pass an order in favour of the Goa Foundation's first petition – filed in 1992 – which took the Goan expatriate Chowgule family, pioneers in the Goan mining industry, to court for setting up a beneficiary plant in a protected forest about 15 kilometres northeast in Maina.[8] This is the same mine that they then leased to a raising contractor, who happened to be another politician, in the Age of Greed. That was when we caught them and lodged a complaint with Rajiv Yaduvanshi.

So, should one assume that the Chowgule family functioned 'legally' in that period of eight years? How is it, then, that they left in their wake a tract of land that today, regrettably, makes a deathly moonscape appear tame? For this too, there is photographic evidence.

Still, there are complexities that one cannot wish away.

One of the cases filed by the Goa Foundation pertained to a certain area between Maina and Cawrem but did not have its genesis on the ground. The petition was filed on behalf of the villagers of Maina and Cawrem but did not actually begin with them, or even allow them the space to actively support proceedings.

This was activism once removed. It consisted of carefully plotting the mining leases and companies owning them, then poring through documents and 'laying down a paper trail'. There is no denying the importance of the work they were doing, of the groundwork they laid for future events – but it was work done in isolation. For all practical purposes, the Goa Foundation's petition had been filed without consulting the villagers of Cawrem. The papers of the petition were not easily available to those affected either.

It was Claude Alvares who, well before the mining season of 2008 broke, arranged a meeting between the chief minister, Digambar Kamat, and the who's who of the anti-mining lobby. Everybody had put aside ideological differences to be present.

As Cheryl did not want to see the former chief minister's poker face, as inscrutable as a boiled potato on most days, she sent me instead. It was at this meeting, in full view of the twenty-five-strong anti-mining lobby, that the chief minister promised a blanket ban on mining until his cabinet's Draft Mineral Policy was properly discussed. He said this the day before his Draft Mining Policy was made public, and it was something that eventually turned out to be embarrassingly pro-mining.

He made this promise in response to my angry statement to him that every single one of the mining operations in between Maina and Cawrem was illegal, and he was duty-bound to stop them and institute an investigation.

I was hushed, the matter played down, even the threat of confrontation denied. As with all meetings where activists or afflicted citizens meet the chief minister, far too much respect was accorded to the man. That he was accused of corruption many years later was small consolation to me. Sadly, many in the anti-mining group took his Draft Mineral Policy seriously, actually engaging with it instead of pressing for a blanket ban.

They all chose to ignore that Kamat's words were just that.

Cheryl went to every single meeting of the anti-mining movement in Goa from late 2006 at my behest, so she could help widen the opposition to mining. She was the only woman there. Worse, she sensed that the rest of them seemed to see her as a woman who had a farm she could lose to mining, and was, therefore, at the meetings for personal reasons. She didn't have nice things to say about the meetings, but went anyway.

At the very last meeting she attended, however, I think she realized she had had enough of the alternatives on offer: confident pronouncements that letters of complaint were being written, cases were being filed and steps were being taken. She told the members present that mining was being taken up at a faster pace than ever before. She had seen the trucks getting ready, had seen them lining up on the road outside the mines. Claude graciously admitted that he had done whatever he could in the courts, and that Cheryl could expect no recourse there. He said that she may 'have to take the fight to the streets'.

It may have been the wrong thing to tell her because, despite our best efforts, desperation had crept into all of us at the farm.

It was like what happened when my eighty-year-old mother, Dora, faced the magistrate at Quepem's district court in early October 2008. From the great height of the bench, she frowned as she looked above her glasses and asked Dora quite sternly –

some would even say rudely – whether she even knew that the barrier to the mine she chained herself across was legal.

She stressed the word 'legal'.

The judge was definitely not prepared for Dora, who – resplendent as only she could be, with her tight mop of ash-grey curls and honest, unblinking eyes – retorted in a rising and angry alto: 'What is legal about taking away forests and water?'

In 2013, just before Dora passed away, that same magistrate had the decency to look sheepish when she threw the case out of the courts. She too may have taken solace in the fact that the larger investigation was now with a higher authority.

That morning in 2008, though, she sent Dora and three other women to the Fort Aguada jail for one night for chaining themselves across Dinar Tarcar's mine. Sharing the large women's cell with Dora that night were Cheryl, Rita and Shashikala.[9]

I got several irate calls questioning my political wisdom. One of those calls was from my older sister Camilla, a Canadian citizen since the early 1970s who – like so many non-resident Goans – was clueless about the realities back at home. I heard the usual mouthful of words that have haunted me for the last forty years or more: of how one needed to grow beyond 'radical ideas' and become more responsible, and see how the world is no longer trapped in the 1960s with the hippies and leftists. She was in the process of asking me how I could even think of forcing poor old mum into blocking a 'goddamn shitty mine' and courting arrest at the age of eighty when I said 'hello' a few times and switched off the phone.

A good two hours before Camilla's call, I had received calls from various friends in Goa who were on their way to the Quepem police station. They were appalled that I had talked my mother into blocking a mine chained to her wheelchair. 'Isn't this taking your passion for theatre too far?' one of them asked sweetly.

Among the nicer calls was one from the near-septuagenarian Mario Pinto-Almeida, Cheryl's lawyer and an old friend going back to the heady sixties. His dissident and rabble-rousing ways far predate mine. But now, given his age and wisdom, he brings with him a touch of fatherliness.

He laughed, long and low like a baritone sax, till he choked on the smoke. I said nothing. He cleared his throat.

'It would be nice if your family learned to be a little calm, but I suppose that is asking for too much,' he said. 'Okay, let's understand one thing. It may have been a good idea; it may get everyone to start doing something about this mining ... but then, it would have been nicer if you and your sister had at least told me about this earlier, so I could plan for it.'

I laughed nervously. He had already told me he was driving to the Quepem police station, and I guessed that he may be more than just a little peeved about having his well-oiled routine thrown out of gear.

'Listen, I like your politics,' he told me. 'I appreciate your politics; I understand your ideology or whatever it is you want to call it ... I support it too, you know that.'

'Hey, thanks for saying that—'

'But, arre baba, listen ... have some little bloody sense at least. If you and Cheryl want to do something crazy, then you and Cheryl go do something crazy, I don't care about that, that's your bloody headache ... but why do you have to pull your poor mother into it?'

'I had nothing to do with this, man. I'm in Pune, teaching.'

Mario cut the call.

It makes so much sense, therefore, to narrate the conversation I had with Cheryl when she was sitting in the back of a police

Gypsy at Tarcar's mine. It's a bit like a play, but definitely worth recounting.

Hi...

Hi...

You busy?

Sort of, yeah...

Okay, look, I don't have too much time ... in a bit of a hurry here. You got some time?

Sure, tell me...

Okay, we've just been arrested by the cops.

Who's been arrested by the cops?

All of us...

All of whom?

We blocked Tarcar's mine—

You blocked Tarcar's mine?

Yes, chained ourselves across the bloody gate—

Nice! You and who else?

The old bird, Rita, Shashikala and me ... Aki's gone to her granddad in Baga—

Oh s*** ... you got the old bird into this too?

It was her bloody idea—

Her idea??

She's said it's the only way to stop the b*******!

When Cheryl called me from the back of the Gypsy, the persons in uniform were taking a snack break – and you can't blame them, considering that the siege had gone on for nearly four hours.

We got ten minutes on the phone for her to recount what exactly happened.

Thanks to the suddenness and secrecy of the action, and the fact there was little mobile coverage in the area between Maina and Cawrem, everyone was caught with their pants down. Neither the staff at Dinar Tarcar's mine nor the Quepem constabulary and their superiors were remotely prepared for anything like this. (We were subsequently informed by someone lower down the pecking order that several calls were exchanged between certain politicians, mining officials and senior police officers over the day).

By eight-thirty, when the barrier to the mine was still down, the four women had chained themselves across it, and were standing there with grim smiles on their faces. Cheryl and Dora genuinely angry and well past the point of no return, and Rita and Shashikala frightened out of their wits but trying hard not to show it.

In ten minutes, the trucks had started piling up on the road from Quepem, coming into the area where Maina and Cawrem stand separated. By ten o'clock, the women were joined by about a hundred others from Collomb and Rivona, led by our friend Rama Velip and his colleagues, Xavier and Matthew.

Matthew, strange though it may seem, drove a mining truck because that's the only way he could support his aged mother. There were too many like Matthew who hated mining but had to be a part of it because that was the hand they had been dealt in the circumstances.

Among the people who came to show solidarity with the women was Father Matthias, a priest from the Salesian community at Sulcorna, some 12 kilometres south of the farm. Father Matthias had a special relationship with Dora, given that he had spent time with East Africa's Salesian communities, and spoke fluent Kiswahili to Dora whenever he visited her. It took them both back in time to happier days and memories. It was Dora, of course, who sweet-talked him into joining the blockade.

Father Matthias may have got it in the neck from his higher-ups later, because shortly afterwards he was spirited away to a safe house never to be seen again. But that magical day, there was no way he was not going to join Dora and show everyone what Goans from East Africa were all about.

Kurush Canteenwala – my friend, one-time teaching colleague at college and a documentary filmmaker – was also with them at the barricade. Dora had informed him about their plans, following which he caught a bus from Mumbai. At our insistence, he had already visited Maina, Collomb and north Goa several times, staying with us as he shot a short but blistering documentary on mining, Goa, Goa, Gone.[10] While that was already gathering critical acclaim, he added footage of the mine being blocked – as taken with a tiny video camera – in the second cut.

The women were also joined by Sebastian Rodrigues, or Seby, as he was better known. He had his own organization, Mandgoa, representing tribal rights and causes. He worked largely in the Collomb and Rivona areas, where he too was the de facto leader of the anti-mining movement. He had received modest funding from agencies in Scandinavia to study the issue of mining, and he toured there now and then to attend seminars and speak about the ill effects of mining in Goa. Seby also ran an anti-mining blog that was very much in the news, thanks to his dogged perseverance in keeping tabs on the mining companies.[11]

That blog of his, methodical and precise, was to get him into big trouble in the years to come. So Seby comes back into this narrative a little later, when he was forced to abandon his righteous leanings under sustained pressure from both the mining lobby and the government.

Not too far off from where the women were standing was Quasim, Dora's driver from Quepem, who had to drive her car back to the farm later. Just behind Cheryl was Robert, the well-built Goan she had brought in as a bodyguard after she began receiving calls threatening to teach both her and Aki a lesson. Robert had worked in a gym catering to the US Special Forces in Iraq, and had learnt quite a few tricks. Though he cost Cheryl a bomb, she needed all the help she could get in her fight.

Around this core were villagers from Collomb and Rivona, some hundred or more men and women who came only because Dora went to call them personally. This was important, given that when the people of Collomb had agitated against the Timblo-owned mine there, the villagers here in Cawrem, beholden as they were to the local Timblo mine, did not join them. It is an indication of the pettiness within the anti-mining campaign that no one in south Goa had tried to pull these factions together like this before.

While we later teased Dora, saying she could stand for the elections and win, the Quepem police and their notion of law and order on the morning of the protest seemed to disillusion her a lot. They came to Tarcar's mine in force, more than capable of asking the four women chained there to leave peacefully, or if seen fit, taking them to the police station in Quepem to let the law run its course.

But they came there under strict instruction. Like voyeurs, deliberately and consciously, they chose to stay at the side. 'I will teach you a lesson, you will never forget,' an officer in khaki told Cheryl before thumping his shiny baton in the palm of his hand and walking away.

Like newspapers in Goa later reported, quite a few police and government officials in Goa had a truck or two in the names of their relatives. Even a minor delay in this lucrative trade could be calculated as a loss in thousands. The police may have had no choice but to look the other way.[12]

As the heat built and the mining trucks came to a grinding halt, blocking the entire stretch of road from Quepem and throwing everything out of gear, the managers at Tarcar's mine and the transport contractors from Quepem played the oldest trick in the book.

While Quepem's constabulary stood watching over the blockade, they drove the truck drivers to the three bars in the vicinity and talked them up, plying them with booze and fried chicken.

Just before noon, with enough time for them to still eat a good lunch later, the truck owners and contractors drove to the barricade in mining jeeps and an open truck. Cawrem villagers, who had a stake in Tarcar's illegal operation, cheered them on. Then, even as the police watched, they separated the four women from their Collomb and Rivona supporters. They were not to know that this would be a coordinated attack involving the mine managers, transport contractors and truck drivers that was aimed at killing such protests once and for all.

Barely a few feet from Cheryl and the other women, in full view of the police, the truck drivers thrashed Dora's driver Quasim as well as Robert, the bodyguard.

'There were just too many of them,' Cheryl told me later, describing Robert in the skirmish. 'But you could imagine what Robert could have done if he wanted ... none of them could actually hit him, he was that fast at avoiding the sticks and blows.'

The other men were not so lucky. Father Matthias was slapped, hard, twice. He was asked whether, as a priest, he did not know better than do something as stupid as this. When Dora screamed abuses at the man who did this, he turned to her and told her to shut up if she didn't want a slap herself. Kurush was slapped, punched, pushed to the ground and kicked. Seby got the worst of it, as if he had been consciously targeted by them.

They also damaged Dora's car, which was parked nearby.

When the attack on the men started, Cheryl freed herself from the chain and started pushing the goons back, daring them to hit her and yelling at the police to stop this. They didn't touch Cheryl, and reluctantly moved away to let the police take over. However, they abused her in the vilest language, with their leader telling her exactly what they would like to do to her. While the posse moved towards the women to haul them off, the inspector stood aside, still tapping his baton on his palm and staring at Cheryl with a smile. 'See, I told you...'

Interestingly, none of the men from Collomb or Rivona were attacked because the truck drivers and even the police knew they would be biting off more than they can chew. Unlike those from Maina and Cawrem, the villagers of Collomb and Rivona, led by Rama Velip and his associates, had remained steadfast in their opposition to mining right from the late nineties. Like us in Maina, they knew about every single mining operation in their villages that was operating illegally because they had circled the perimeters.

Before the women could be taken to meet the magistrate in Quepem, a detailed report on the incident had been put up on various websites. It went up faster than either the mining companies or the government could have anticipated.

From 2007, we had contacted every single news channel in English that provided some coverage of the environment, either by phone or email, including Damian Grammaticas who represented the BBC in New Delhi. He said to me: 'Oh, what a terrible pity, I was just down in Goa with the family, on a vacation ... lovely place I must say ... How I wish I had known about all this illegal mining business earlier.'

Our own channels were even more blasé: 'Oh, illegal mining in Goa, but we just did a story a few months back.' I got this from three media organizations that I approached. Cheryl had actually joked about this, saying that nothing short of her head being smashed would strike them as newsworthy.

So we milked this unwanted publicity for all that it was worth, using it to highlight the mining operations in Goa. Cheryl told everyone who could listen how she had sought and received an audience with the chief minister at his residence in Margao, and reminded him yet again about his promise of a blanket ban on the mining in Maina and Cawrem.

The chief minister had told Cheryl that his hands were tied.

Someone wisely said that 'democracy must be something more than two wolves and a sheep voting on what to have for dinner'. What was happening in the mines between Maina and Cawrem was exactly this, and Dora had only intended that the truth be brought out.

She was the conscience that said you couldn't take money in lieu of the mud, trees and water.

The hill that stood guard in front of Dinar Tarcar's mine only showed you the entrance, and the broad road that cut into it before snaking upwards and out of sight. It was only a facade, like the set of a play. You could see the barrier that the women and others blockaded, and the security cabin-cum-room for the weighbridge that was probably never used. Then you saw the road going into the mine, climbing a hill beyond which you couldn't see. While Tarcar had installed CCTV coverage of strategic points along the road to the mine and around his offices, there was little either he or the guards could do when we followed old cattle paths, climbed to the summit and saw what his operation had actually done.

The 1994 Environment Impact Assessment notification of clearances was only for five years. In Goa, this translated into fifty-four mines whose environment clearances had expired, and should, therefore, have applied for renewed clearances in order to continue their operation.

The lease for Tarcar's mine was held by one Zoiram Neogi and an application for it was filed in 1996. However, Dinar Tarcar – who appeared as the attorney for all the legal heirs of Zoiram – argued that the delay must be condoned in 2007 when the Chinese market was hot. Former chief minister Digambar Kamat 'condoned' the application, handing over not just this operation in Maina, but also two other mining leases in the villages of Rivona and Sulcorna to Tarcar's company, Minescape Earth Movers Pvt. Ltd. His mine in Rivona was heavily guarded at all times. On paper it was owned by one Haider Kassim Khan, but operated by Tarcar through a power of attorney.

The delay was condoned on two grounds. First, a family crisis due to the death of Zoiram. And second, the government of Goa was taking a 'liberal' approach to condoning delays. Kamat also did this with Magnum Minerals' operation, with Alemao's Jollerancho Dongor and with the Xec Hasan mine in Cawrem.

The signage outside Dinar Tarcar's mine announcing his company and other details came up twice: once just before the first visit of the Shah Commission, in the form of a hastily hand-painted signboard where paint had dripped; and the other before the second visit, when Tarcar invested in a large plastic, laser-printed board to give credence to his theft of resources.

Given the secrecy and stealth with which he was allowed to function, Tarcar's operation was also the most heinous. It made all the earlier mines seem like they were done with some sense of a 'science' – no matter how horrific – at work.

Tarcar's operation was a slash and grab-as-much-as-you-can routine. While other mines had surveyors and engineers who plotted on large paper which area fell under the blades of the bulldozers first, here it seemed like a free-for-all. The area was attacked from every conceivable side.

To keep the population happy, he doled out favours to the men while bringing the women of Cawrem into his headquarters at the mine. He gave the younger girls gainful unemployment that involved sitting in front of a computer and lazily keying in falsified data for later use, and put their mothers to growing vegetables at the base of the valley, where his mine had gouged out one side of a hill. This, they watered from a dying spring.

This was Tarcar's idea of corporate social responsibility.

In fact, the man was so cool that he didn't even need to hold a public hearing. Entry to that meeting to get his necessary approvals was an in-camera affair, restricted to truck drivers and the mining-addicted. Tarcar, like everyone else, just used his wealth to buy the necessary clearances.

In the mining season of 2009–2010, way after he had killed the spring and stripped Tembechem Dongor bare[13] (but surely sensing the heat of an impending investigation), Tarcar instituted a non-profit venture. He placed signboards warning the drivers of his transport contractor, Subhash Phaldesai (later BJP MLA) that they needed to drive more sedately.

About twenty signboards were placed all along the 12-kilometre stretch from the mines at Cawrem, past the forest check post and all the way down the plateau to Ambaulim, a prosperous village of truck owners where the hills plateau out. Each signboard carried small placards – one proclaiming that the venture had the endorsement of whichever panchayat the board falls in (which is not surprising, given that at least half of the panchayat members owned trucks working at his mine) and another saying that the public service was courtesy the Dinar and Manisha Tarcar Foundation.

As may happen all too easily in this country, the case made its way to the district court, just slow and steady enough to harass Dora and the rest who had blocked Tarcar's mine for more than four years.

But the four women perversely attended every single court hearing – Cheryl taking time off from work; the household thrown out of gear at least two days before each appearance as alternative arrangements were made to drop and pick up Aki from school; and everything adjusted just so that they could respect the law.

At the two hearings before they finally threw the case out, we saw Dora's stubbornness and resolve at work yet again. The first time she made a few phone calls and asked for favours, and was therefore carried like a queen, still sitting on her wheelchair, up the old wooden staircase of the court. I carried her walker, which Dora insisted on using to stand when the same magistrate walked in to preside.

The second time another hearing was held, Dora had just come out of the hospital. Cheryl and I told her that we could easily get her a medical certificate exempting her from attending court.

'They dare not reject that,' I told her because she looked a little worried. I should have known better.

'Medical certificate?' she snorted. 'You want me to ask for a medical certificate when I'm fit and fine? The b******* want to harass us, let them harass us ... We'll see who wins.'

She sat in the car and waited three hours in the shade reading the papers, while the court deputed the proper authorities to verify that she was in fact alive but unable to climb the staircase leading to the honourable judge's court. This was like a Dario Fo play: the designated officer refused to walk to the car park, a short distance away. 'She must come close to the steps of the court,' I was told.

Dora had told me to be polite, and not lose my cool. I backed the car in through the narrow gate, and with a few contorted manoeuvres, managed to bring Dora's side of the door parallel to the steps. The appointed officer waited for me to get out of the car and open the door at her side before verifying Dora's inability to climb up the steps. He then made an officious tick on a piece of paper and signed it.

'Okay,' we were told peremptorily, 'You can go now.'

In 2007, when Dinar Tarcar ran against his friend Manohar Parrikar of the BJP in the assembly elections for the prestigious seat of Panjim, he effectively split the vote and lost on a Congress ticket. His declared assets then amounted to a little over Rs 5 crore, most of it made from his timely forays into the real estate business as the new century broke.

Everybody kept saying at seminars across the country that men like Dinar Tarcar were creating jobs, driving the economy and setting the benchmark for growth and prosperity.

It helped none of us, least of all Dora, that at the end of February 2012, the National Election Watch – an arm of the non-profit Association for Democratic Reforms – released the findings of a study on thirty-five candidates contesting the elections the year before in Goa. They hit the nail on the head with their argument that the finances of Goa's politicians had gone through the roof in the Age of Greed. They found that the average assets of Goa's MLAs had grown by a whopping 200 per cent in 2012.[14]

While Congress candidates were worth around Rs 8.44 crore on an average and the BJP stood at Rs 4.21 crore, the seven-member Maharashtrawadi Gomantak Party – which Dinar Tarcar changed sides to join – was worth a whopping Rs 33.5 crore.

How's that for a growth story?

The mining of ore, not unexpectedly, played a crucial part. The perennially independent candidate, Nirmala Sawant, whose family had a sizeable and flourishing stake in owning, building and repairing barges, was worth Rs 36.30 crore. Joaquim Alemao was worth a cool Rs 31.26 crore (his net worth was just Rs 9 crore in 2007). The mining territories of Curchorem, Sanguem, Sanvordem and Bicholim exemplified the power of mining.

Shyam Satardekar, the Congress nominee from Curchorem, saw his assets grow from close to Rs 5 crore in 2007 to just over Rs 30 crore in 2012. He ran against the BJP's Nilesh Cabral, who had trucks, barges and assets worth over Rs 13 crore.

The BJP candidate from Sanguem, Subhash Phaldesai, was the mining transport contractor for the mines between Maina and Cawrem. He owned eighteen trucks and was the voluble president of the Mining Truck Owners' Association. He was worth just over Rs 7 crore in 2011. To accommodate him, the BJP denied a ticket to their two-time MLA, Vasudev Gaonkar. Phaldesai ran against Yuri Alemao, son of Joaquim Alemao, who was the NCP candidate and worth Rs 4 crore. Given his tender years, this was not bad at all.

Sanvordem, another adjoining mining constituency, was represented by Goa's prominent mine owner Anil Salgaocar who won as an independent MLA in 2007 when his assets came up to Rs 70 crore, a sum that went up to more than Rs 90 crore in 2009 and possibly more in 2011. He made way for his son, Arjun, to also contest the same seat as an independent candidate. Arjun was worth Rs 19 crore by way of assets. Anil Salgaocar believed in spreading the butter. His other son, who contested the 2011 as the Trinamool Congress candidate from Mandrem in north Goa, was worth Rs 15 crore.

The BJP, after much confabulation, fielded Ganesh Gaonkar in Sanvordem. He was a mining transporter with assets worth Rs 7 crore. The Congress picked Govind Sawant, a big transport contractor, worth over Rs 7 crore, as its candidate.[15]

Interestingly, as the heat intensified on mining violations in the post-Shah Commission period, it was only Anil Salgaocar, mine owner and once-independent candidate from Sanvordem, who admitted to any illegality. He told the state mining department that he had exported about 1.2 million tonnes of iron ore in one year without paying royalty. However, no one knows whether the department actually fined him to the tune of approximately Rs 30 crore, or he was just another bright red herring thrown our way.[16]

In 2012, Dinar Tarcar contested the elections from the constituency of Santa Cruz, close to Panjim, running against former Congress minister for town and country planning Babush Monserrate.[17] Tarcar was in good company. Babush and his wife Jennifer were worth a cool Rs 20-odd crore each. Babush, interestingly, had also been accused by the income tax department of taking a bribe of Rs 4 crore to sanction the conversion of large tracts of farmland for residential and business use. In that case, he may have actually been worth far more.

In any case, all the money that Babush and his wife had between them was a very small drop in the ocean in comparison to Dinar Tarcar, who, in 2012, declared his assets as Rs 211.76 crore. Now, that's what you call a really good growth story.

To Sreenivasan Jain on NDTV, Tarcar giggled, hemmed, hawed and said nothing. He stopped them from filming him. To the press in Goa, he was far more forthcoming. A dashing smile on his face, he put his wealth down to good financial management and a galloping share market, and promptly dismissed accusations that he had made his money through illegal mining interests and land grabs. He admitted to being 'a little uncomfortable' about being touted as Goa's wealthiest political candidate. 'How much is too much?' he asked reporters. 'I think we have enough.'

He also self-righteously told reporters that he pays taxes on the money he makes.

Now, had the agitation against mining continued on the streets after Dora's arrest, Tarcar may not have had to pay those taxes because he would never have made that kind of money.

In March 2012, the Goa Foundation was emboldened enough to write a strong letter of protest to the then chief minister Manohar Parrikar, informing him that Dinar Tarcar was continuing to run his mine on the basis of a fraudulent order issued by Digambar Kamat. They added that the mine's operation was indicted by the Public Accounts Committee, probed by the Justice Shah Commission, and found by the Indian Bureau of Mines to have doubled the production allowed in the approved mining plan. It had also issued a notice to Tarcar in 2010 for expanding the size of the mining pit beyond approved limits, and as if that was not enough, he did not even have the required approvals under the Forest Conservation Act, 1980.

In case the chief minister did not take him seriously enough, Dr Claude Alvares, on behalf of the Goa Foundation, demanded that the Tarcar mine be shut down forthwith, failing which the people of Cawrem would take the necessary steps in this regard.

Apart from Goa's *Herald*, the English press in Goa was studiously silent on the illegal mining that occurred between 2006 and 2011.

None of this was surprising. Goa's oldest English newspaper, *The Navhind Times*, was owned by the Dempo mining family. The other, *The Gomantak Times*, was once owned by the Chowgule mining family until they sold it to the Maharashtrian Sakal media group, which publishes a Marathi newspaper of the same name and is headed by NCP leader Sharad Pawar's brother.

The monthly magazine, *Goa Today*, was once iconic for the independence and straightforwardness of its founding editor and publisher, Lambert Mascarenhas. However, it was taken over by the Salgaocar family, who reduced it to a quasi-glossy periodical without an identity of its own.

However, as 2011 drew to a close and elections to a new assembly were in the offing, even the *Herald's* owner allowed the paper to be subverted by employing a former staffer of Fomento Resources, Sujoy Gupta, as its editor-in-chief.

So much has been written of this man in the Goan press, with various blogs and websites rapping him on the knuckles, one doesn't have to hold back for reasons of propriety. It got so bad for Sujoy Gupta in Goa during the Age of Greed that at a posh function in a Panjim hotel, owned ironically by the Salgaocar family, designer Wendell Rodricks and a few others asked him and his companion to leave immediately. It made the front page of the papers the next morning.[18]

Gupta came to Goa as a journalist to take up an assignment as the editor of the *Gomantak Times*.

Proprietors in Goa have always had an important business or political stake in forming opinion, or indeed suppressing it. So it is accepted practice that editors are hired from outside Goa and paid handsomely to ensure their compliance. There are barely three or four instances from the 1960s to the present where Goans have been appointed as editors of English newspapers. And none, barring two, lasted the course to retire from service at the paper.

One wonders about the mysteries of coincidence: on the World Environment Day of 2008, Sujoy Gupta was formally appointed as the vice-president (Media & Publicity) of Prudent Media, set up by Audhoot Timblo's Fomento Group.

Gupta's boss was Arvind Bhatikar, a retired IAS official who was the managing director of Prudent Media. Also in the team was Sandesh Prabhudesai, a once-fiery student leader in the 1970s who had resigned his job at the Dattaraj Salgaocar-owned Konkani newspaper, *Sunaparanta*, to come in as the chief editor.

The anti-mining lobby had a lot on Sujoy Gupta.

They recall a short, bespectacled, paunchy man pretending to be a protestor outside the Timblo mine at Collomb in 2008. At this protest, Gupta walked all the way with a delegation from Panjim, who had come to show solidarity with Rama Velip and his fellow villagers. Gupta suavely walked them to an office. Here, he miraculously brought out a sheaf of papers that convinced them that the Timblo mine was legal. Faced with evidence on paper, they naively returned to their comfortable lives in Panjim believing the myth that all Goans wanted to believe, that the mining was 'legal'.[19]

However, it was also around this time that we came to know that Gupta had filed, on behalf of the Timblos, a defamation case of Rs 500 crore against Seby, citing his blog.[20]

I may have been one of the first persons to call Seby after this news broke. 'Ignore the summons if it comes,' I told him. 'They'll be forced to send someone from Kolkata to arrest you, and we'll meet them with you and resist this.'

Though still in Pune, I volunteered to make it to Goa and contact as many people as I could. 'Let's go to town on this,' I told him. 'Let's make this really public.'

Seby refused. I got a lecture instead. 'We should have some respect for the law,' he told me.

Still, in solidarity, I put out an online petition protesting the idiocy of the suit. A few well wishers, barring me, started a campaign to raise funds for Seby to fight the case in Kolkata, and as the new year of 2009 started, a protest meeting was held at the hallowed TB Cunha Hall, a place that had been a site of radicalism right through the 1970s. However, in 2009, they found it unable to accommodate any more than twenty people, and some of them squeezed into the small balcony to give the illusory impression of a large crowd.

Chaired by Pravin Sabnis, a soft skills trainer who doubled as a social activist when the mood took him, the protest meeting adopted three strong resolutions. The first called for an immediate withdrawal of the defamation case filed against Seby by Fomento; the second warned of taking the issue to all villages till the accusation was withdrawn; and the third called upon eminent persons, artists and other people to undertake study tours to mining sites and check out the extent of the destruction.

Seby said the suit violated his freedom of speech, and lamented that the 'intellectual class in Goa was mum on the whole issue of destructive mining'. Much venom was spewed on Sujoy Gupta.

Floriano Lobo of Moira village, leader of the fringe Goa Suraj Party, was also in attendance since Seby was an important member of his party. In fact, the gathering decided to hold a meeting close to Gupta's house in the village of Moira in that coming week to show solidarity with Seby. Floriano was nothing but stern with Fomento's patriarch.

Audhoot Timblo is a very dear friend of the Goa Suraj Party, he told the gathering. 'He must immediately correct his foolhardiness of filing the suit in the Kolkata High Court. He should file it in the Bombay High Court if he feels Seby's writings were defamatory.'

Those kind words from Floriano, imploring a weird sense of justice from a dear friend of his party, appeared to determine the fate of the Rs 500-crore defamation suit against Seby till the day it miraculously disappeared, and nothing more was heard of it again.

By the time the women had courted arrest, Manohar Parrikar, as the leader of the opposition, raised the bogey of 'Naxalites' in Goa, pointing the finger at poor Seby, who stood with the women in the blockade. Come to think of it, they ought to have looked more closely at Dora.

Before 2009 was a quarter of the way through, we saw the tempo of the mining work increasing. Dora, as feisty as ever, was convinced that civil disobedience was the only route to take. Again she said, somewhat presciently, that they would never stop mining unless they were forced to. At the farm by then, I was again amazed by the hard line she was taking.

Dora and Cheryl vetoed the idea of me joining the blockade at Tarcar's mine the second time. 'They'll target you and break your head,' Cheryl told me emphatically. 'This isn't Uttar Pradesh yet, so they won't attack a woman.' We both browbeat Dora into withdrawing her plan of courting arrest again. Instead, every single day, she would be driven in her Swift to visit the chief minister in Panjim and harangue him. Cheryl put together what we referred to as a 'jail bag' containing her toilet essentials and three cigarettes that Dora had stitched into the lining.

This time it was decided that Cheryl would take Aki with her and block the mine, just the two of them. Aki would have to go to the juvenile remand home, where she would be picked up by her grandfather. Aki and her vision-impaired grandfather would visit Goa's totally blind minister of environment and forests every day and make him see again. Cheryl would pointedly refuse bail, and force an investigation into Goa's mining scams.

This time round, I took Mario's advice, planning it systematically and keeping him in the loop, and even finding a spot where one of us could hide and film the new blockade. We made a list of media persons who would be informed. All the people who had been there for the first blockade were told about our plans via a detailed email. The only person absent from this emailing list was Father Matthias, who had been sent to his Gulag.

Seby, given his credentials and the fact that he had stood with them the first time round, was on that list.

But Seby, for reasons best known to him, sent an email response strongly advising Cheryl against courting arrest and marked it to a much larger group of people – opening plans of the arrest to all and sundry and subverting the planned agitation.

Close to two years before the elections of 2011, the mining lobby was gearing itself to ensure a government that would be compliant with its own interests. Audhoot Timblo, the suave head of Fomento, was a close friend of chief minister Digambar Kamat. The whole of Goa witnessed how close this relationship really was. Kamat had conveniently dug out an old state ordinance from the cupboard to bypass a Supreme Court order won by the Goa Foundation against several illegally built structures around Cidade de Goa hotel, Timblo's showpiece of taste and excellence.[21] Nobody batted an eyelid. For two weekends in a row, a small group of affluent Goans took to picnicking on the beach in protest. However, when that fizzled out, they also accepted the fact that that the chefs at the Cidade de Goa were probably quite good for the brand name that was Goa.

So sure was Timblo that he wrote a long article titled 'Mineral Farming brings Health and Employment' in the *Herald*'s edit page.[22] It conveniently ignored the well known fact that manufacturing contributed 25 per cent to Goa's GDP using less than 2 per cent of its land mass, while mining used 8 per cent of Goa's richest land mass and contributed only 4 per cent to the state's exchequer.[23]

The article stated: 'It is well established that these (mining activities) and other streams converge to give us labour-saving devices, creature comforts, longevity and other benefits that we crave in modern times.' It went on to add, somewhat disingenuously, that 'education, health and the equitable distribution of wealth is synonymous with mineral development for over 100,000 families in Goa.'

Venita Coelho, a writer and feisty columnist who lives in Goa, was quick to take him on. She retorted that though Goa constituted only about 1 per cent of India's land mass, it exported 35 per cent of the country's ore. She gave him facts that other Goans needed to hear too: for each tonne of ore that Timblo 'farmed', three tonnes were discarded as waste. His 'farming' misplaced more than 9 million tonnes of barren soil, which leached into water bodies during the rains, silting them, and playing havoc with ecosystems and marine life. Venita also informed him that Goa's famed Mandovi River carries around 2 million tonnes of sediment every year.[24]

However, Audhoot Timblo was not to be chastened by Venita's ire. He was already plotting how to keep holding on to all the strings. There is a lot of likelihood in the story that a deal was cut out between the Saraswat Brahmin mining families and Timblo himself. As the heat built against Digambar, the combine didn't leave him to the wolves. They set about figuring how to save face, building walls of legal protection around them while planning for the future.

They smoothly shifted camp to the BJP's side, and with finesse that would have shamed a good card player. Audhoot Timblo, once again turned to Sujoy Gupta, who worked to neutralize the quite-justified concerns that Goa's Catholic polity had with the BJP's rightwing, pro-Hindutva stance.

The *Herald* actually stands apart, given that it was born again from an old and highly respected Portuguese paper printed by the present owner Raul Fernandes's father, and possibly his father before him. That periodical, in fact, continued a tradition of liberal writing by Goans, many of whom were pro-Indian in colonial times. Raul's father however, was not exactly a liberal.

In the 1980s, on an assignment from Delhi, the *Herald*'s then editor, Rajan Narayan, let me use his typewriter and telex operator to file my story.

While I was doing this, Rajan called a meeting of the staff because the owner, Raul's father, wanted to address them. They gathered around a large table in the centre of the office. When Raul's father walked in, he berated the young journalists there in Konkani. 'I am the owner of this paper,' he told them. 'Do you know what this means? All of you are sitting when I walk in? Is this showing respect? Stand up!' They all stood. Rajan is perhaps the only non-Goan editor to take on the political despotism and bear the scars for doing this – he was attacked twice – but he too remained silent.

Whatever his boardroom manners, Raul's father was a pillar of the Church, and a known philanthropist. He also ran a hugely successful stationery enterprise and an excellent printing press. Under Raul's leadership, their ventures now include real estate and hospitality at places as far afield as Thailand.

Whether their newfound revenue changed the course of the paper from its once independent, largely pro-Goan moorings is anyone's guess. But some months before the elections of 2011, Sujoy Gupta walked through the door of the *Herald* as its new editor. Two journalists promptly resigned.

Gupta first side-lined, then displaced, Ashwin Tombat, the last vestige of decency prevailing in the Age of Greed, a firebrand leftist in his college days. While Ashwin had mellowed into pragmatism since then, his essential moorings were intact. It was he, in fact, who opened the pages of the paper to criticism of mining when the looting began in 2005.

Given its ownership, the *Herald* was still a paper trusted by most of Goa's Catholic population. Curiously, the Church in Goa privately decried the corruption and nepotism of some of the elected representatives belonging to their flock, but publicly skirted the issue, choosing – like it did with mining – not to see it. If they chastised such people in the confessional, duly handing out strenuous penances, we were not to know. Given the riots in Gujarat and the anti-Christian attacks in Odisha, one would have expected them to be circumspect about this campaign to bring the BJP into power.

Typically, a few compliant Catholic candidates were inducted into the BJP and portrayed as an 'alternative' to the corrupt Congress politicians.

Sujoy Gupta, ironically, also started a virulent attack on 'illegal mining', trapping all the known rogues belonging to the Congress, and (it is said, at the behest of Audhoot Timblo) carrying out a series of exposés on Dinar Tarcar. Gupta and his team actually gave us even more information to damn him.

Gupta was always careful to make a distinction between 'legal' and 'illegal' mining, the former posited as the route to much good.

Not surprisingly, the BJP routed the corrupt Congress. Some Catholic intellectuals and columnists wrote of 'change' and a 'new dawn' for Goa. Gupta celebrated the occasion by emblazoning the *Herald's* front page with a massive and somewhat colourful headline: 'Goa Sacks Congress' – 'Goa' in black, 'Sacks' in flaming orange and 'Congress' in bright green.[25]

Audhoot Timblo, ever the king-maker, was not done yet. While Gupta worked at *Herald*, he continued to be a freelance consultant with Prudent Media. There were far bigger plans afoot. Within months of handing the Catholic population of Goa to the BJP on a platter, Gupta jumped ship and became the editor-in-chief of *The Goan*, a glossy weekly published by Prudent Media. He took several journalists with him.

The *Herald* stuttered for a few weeks before bringing in Ishan Joshi, an assistant editor from the *Statesman*, Kolkata, as its new editor in September 2012. They had already brought in Devika Siqueira, a senior journalist, a month or two before that. They had to coax her away from her decades-long stint as the *Deccan Herald's* very competent correspondent in Goa, and getting her to test-run a few magazine pages with a view to launching a Sunday newspaper. There could not have been a better person to bring real independence to the press in Goa. The new pages, brought out on a regular basis over the long weekend, gave ample evidence of just how different the news was from that featured in *The Goan* every Saturday.

Then Ishan Joshi left the *Herald* in December 2013. In early 2014, after a brief holiday, Joshi too joined Timblo's Saturday newspaper, *The Goan*. Like a game of musical chairs, a few months later, Sujoy Gupta returned to the *Herald*, first sitting out a notice period because Fomento threatened to sue if he did not. Under Joshi's tutelage, *The Goan* was recently launched as a daily newspaper.

Even as Sujoy Gupta continues to helm the *Herald*, it is rumoured that the Timblos have filed three cases against him. Devika, in total disgust, put in her papers and got down to finally working on her book. But one must never forget that this is Goa, and weather-cocks can change with the most gentle of breezes.

At the Semana da Cultura Indo-Portuguesa held in Lisbon post the ban on mining, a jamboree to promote cultural and business ties between Goa and Portugal, Audhoot Timblo was heard telling Portuguese investors they would be better off not coming to Goa because it had too many problems – including an overactive judiciary, and an intellectual class that stood in the way of most development projects.

'We have an overworked and underpaid judiciary coming in the form of judicial activism,' he told a gathering of people that included European businessmen as well as India's ambassador to Portugal Brij Tyagi, Deputy Chief Minister Francis D'Souza and NRI Commissioner Wilfred Mesquita. He told everyone that a quarter million people suffer from malnutrition and deprivation in Goa, and thanks to the mining industry being shut down in Goa, '30 per cent of Goans are unemployed'.

'That's the reality,' he told them, 'I don't know what's next. Until 1992, India had red tape. These days it has green tape, and even the deputy chief minister's speech stressed on "green, green, green".' Then, 'speaking from the heart', he said: 'Everyone will say welcome, welcome. Hospitality is upfront. But don't be misled. Goa is a very nice place, but it's also a very terrible place. We have a lot of problems of the haves and have-nots, and the have-nots are agitating. With massive unemployment in the intellectual class, you have an agitation.'

Everyone scrambled to cover their tracks. The deputy chief minister couldn't do much to stem the damage. He said that while he concurs with some of the points raised by Timblo, specifically that India suffers from the curse of bureaucratic red tape, there was 'no need to publicly say so' and create an embarrassment.

D'Souza also told the press that anyone wanting to set up industry in Goa would have to follow the environment laws. 'I told them our NGOs are very environment conscious and favour the green industry. We have to respect that, just as the decisions of the courts have to be honoured.'

Prudent Media, the media arm of Audhoot Timblo's Fomento Resources, was far from done proving that mining was the lifeblood of this tiny state.

In late March 2015, Arvind Bhatikar, former IAS official and managing director of Timblo's Prudent Media, met the press in Goa before the release of his book *The Rudderless Democracy*, eleven chapters and 400 pages arguing that neither our governments nor the Supreme Court had taken into account the economic importance of mining for Goa before banning operations.

'The Goa government took a stand in the Supreme Court that action will be taken against the mining companies for the alleged illegalities committed by them. The Goa government in the Supreme Court has rejected almost all the findings made in the Shah Commission report.'

Bhatikar also told the press that the stated loss of Rs 35,000 crore to the exchequer due to illegal mining operations was a myth, and the state administration would be unable to establish it. 'It will be like trying to find a black cat in a dark room blindfolded,' he said. He termed his book 'a critique of the reports of the M.B. Shah Commission, the Central Empowered Committee, the judgement of the Supreme Court and governance at the Central and state levels, on the alleged illegal mining in Goa'.

'I found that the comments made by the Shah Commission in its report were not appropriate in many places,' he told *The Times of India*. 'The commission's repeated observations that there has been a tremendous degradation of the environment due to the alleged illegal mining seem to be exaggerated.'

He kept his best for the last, repeating what we had said too: 'If the mining industry had been properly administered from 2005 to 2011, during the Chinese boom, the commission might not have been appointed as far as Goa was concerned.'

7

A Solitary Tree

Well into the 1990s, a journey through Cawrem for a first-time visitor would draw the usual 'oohs' and 'aahs'. In the rains, in fact, it was nothing but magical; its beauty would have choked even the most hardened city dweller. Imagine a storybook village, cradled between the tall majesty of Devapan Dongor, the Hill Where God Lives, on the western side of the road, and the gentler slopes and valleys that fed from its own water sources on the eastern side.

Mango, jackfruit, tamarind and guava trees shaded the dwellings at the feet of Devapan Dongor. While areca nut palms towered high above the tiled roofs at the lowest point where the streams ran, giant breadfruit, clumps of banana and the odd wild fig tree grew at the back of the houses where the waste water from the kitchen flowed. Layered down the slopes, below cashew plantations, were fields growing two crops of rice a year terraced one below the other while brooks tumbled through them, racing each other to the ponds.

If you climbed further down the eastern side of the village, going to the foot of the valley, you saw an ancient community well, its granite slabs gleaming with water that brimmed all the way to the top. In the monsoons, Cawrem would have given Cherrapunji a run for its money. From October till the end of February, the days would be pleasant and the nights and early mornings as chilly as Kodaikanal in September, with mist cloaking the houses till close to eight in the morning.

During the mining seasons between 2005 and 2012, it felt like another village, turning dirty reddish brown in colour. It was as if the dust, churned daily in the wind, had formed a carefully layered coat of muddied sepia.

On this winding road through the village, we could see how mining had changed all our lives. In the old days, as you neared Devapan Dongor coming in from Maina, you would slow your vehicle to look down in awe at the sheer slope of the giant hill to your left. When you braked, the village's breath-taking eastern side would come into view.

Now you begin with a glimpse of the Fomento mine near the school, then go on to witness Alemao hacking away at Jollerancho Dongor's southern aquifers; the Magnum Mine carrying on with its assault against Paikeachi Zor's western aquifer; Dinar Tarcar's savagery on the slopes that fed the springs east of Cawrem; and immediately ahead of you, the fourth and last mining operation between Maina and Cawrem. Behind this mine, a very short south-westerly glide for a bird, was the giant aquifer of Paikeachi Zor – and indeed the spring itself.

When the rains came, welcomed as they were by a parched village, they barely washed off the accumulated dust. In fact, from the dumps and open wound of Devapan Dongor, they brought more waste down to cake the roads with sticky muck, and the rest to run off as slurry and ruin the fields on the eastern side of Cawrem.

Three quarters of Paik's Spring used to go to the Velip settlement close to the summit of Devapan Dongor. However, the water in the spring at Cawrem reduced drastically from 2009 onwards after the Magnum Mine sprung one part of the aquifer on the western slopes of this chain of hill. The water level to the east of the road also fell due to Dinar Tarcar's mine, barely 500 metres south of it. And yet, close to both water bodies were parked mining trucks owned by the same Velip community whose water sources were being destroyed.

When the water level of the spring was at its lowest ever in the summer of 2011, the women of the village finally decided to revolt. They came out of their houses, sat on the roads and blocked the trucks.

As you pass the village coming in from Maina, going towards Quepem town, you encounter three speed-breakers. A small-time mining contractor from the village, one with lesser duties and budget, would pay elderly men and women to sweep the bucketsful of dust that gathered on either side every time an overloaded truck bounced on them.

There were dwellings perched on the steep slopes of Devapan Dongor, and a government primary school whose children ate the same dust.

At either end of the village were signs that life would soon go terribly wrong for Cawrem residents who were tempted to part with their lands. There were more and more young men sitting on motorcycles, even though the air was teeming with dust. As far as one could tell from stray conversations, most of them were school dropouts, happy that there was enough money in the family to meet their aspirations of a mobile phone, a fancy haircut, jeans, tees, sneakers and dark glasses.

Cawrem's problems must have stemmed from the fact that the village is divided into two parts. On the western side, on the slopes of Devapan Dongor, one can find the original Velip inhabitants, and they had been here much before the Portuguese even made an appearance. They live in the proximity of two temples – one of them a seemingly ancient structure dedicated to Paikdev, while the other is a more recent and ornate cabin built through mining donations for a god that's as ambiguous as the place he is sheltered in.

The Velip who live here farm the fields that break below the southern slopes of Devapan Dongor, better seen as you exit the village. Most of the houses also have vegetable gardens to provide for their daily needs, protected as best as they can be against the monkeys that invaded the villages and farms of both Maina and Cawrem once the mining started. Those in the hills and slopes to the west are traditional subsistence farmers. They harvest cashews and distil feni, and practise shifting cultivation in the forest lands close by.

Many may not have had land to sell because the plots they tilled either did not belong to them, or happened to be community property. Those who had small plots of land that they did not want to sell eventually did so, taking the paltry sums offered to them and waiving their rights to their traditional livelihoods.

It helps to keep in mind that between 2005 and 2011, none of the mining companies actually thought a ban on mining would be imposed. They were here for the long haul. They did not want the fields on the eastern and southern slopes to mine ore, but to dump waste.

It is on the eastern side of the road that you notice the commerce of Cawrem – the bars, chai-shops, the provision stores and a bank. During the mining boom, new houses that were much larger and more ostentatious came up. Rumour had it that if you dug out who sold Cawrem to whom, and who then sold out to the miners, you will find a conglomerate of men from the village's eastern side.

It is also likely that many here were later settlers who usurped community lands in the mid-1960s, when the political gimmick of the government of that time was to return land to the tillers and tenants.[1] Even back then, money under the table was all one needed to get the official paperwork done.

Ironically, while these settlers went to all that trouble to own these lands and farms, their sons and grandsons, mostly school dropouts, sold all of it to the mining company, taking petty one-time payments instead of a percentage of the royalty. They didn't know better.

It was the older men and women in Cawrem that you pitied the most. Knowing only to farm, they stubbornly continued to grow onions and brinjals, dark purple-red spinach, tomatoes, lady's fingers and the small, fiercely hot chillies this area is famous for. While this was for their own use, anything extra would be taken to the Sunday market in Quepem.

From 2006, the mining lobby started hankering for a new mining bypass – a three-lane highway through forest lands – to facilitate the easy transportation of ore. It would take off east just after Cawrem and cross the Kushawati on a new bridge to become a part of the mining highway that transported the loot all the way from Collomb and Rivona to the waiting barges at Sanvordem. It would also halve the time taken, even though the thick forests to the east of Cawrem would be no more.

As you crossed the second speed-breaker, you would pass a man hired by the mining company to keep count of the trucks and regulate traffic. You could never see his face because it was always covered by a large bandana. Nearing the primary school, the forests above almost threatening to fall on you, you begin to understand the girth of Devapan Dongor – this hill that once protected Cawrem from strong monsoon winds. Right next to that speed-breaker, the Forest Department had, in 2008, put up a signpost exhorting the mining industry and its truck drivers to 'Save Forests, Save the Earth'.

As you left Cawrem, you also saw the village's dense traditional sacred grove going up to the summit, behind which, barely a stone's throw downwards, was Paikeachi Zor.

Everybody who farmed knew that when the mining operations attacking these flanks of hill systematically bled out its water, they would be dependent on the rain. Alternatively, they could hope for rejuvenated springs further east that may or may not flow towards them.

As those farmers now stood in their fields, leaning on their hoes and taking a break, they had no choice but to watch mining trucks trundle through the village in long convoys from 2005 to the summer of 2011.

The 'Devapan Dongor Mine' at Cawrem, as it was referred to by one and all (cruel as that name is), was one of the very last to start its operations.

Secrecy covered this mine too, which was said to be operated by one Xec Salim and one Sheikh Mukhtar. There were a lot of things we did not know about either of them. No one, in fact, ever saw them. Were they from an old Muslim family settled in Goa who happened to have an old colonial dispensation to mine? Were they running the operation, or was another company excavating the mine for them? Was it that the ore was being lifted by Magnum Minerals? For all the information available, the two gentlemen may have never existed.

The more you think about it, the more it seems as if Xec Salim's mine was brought into being for the express purpose of deflecting the heat from other mines in the area. It is not that hard to believe that the mine may have been given the necessary clearances so it could be closed down later, fooling the people into believing that the power in Goa was actually vested with them.[2]

It took as long as the end of December 2010 for the government to show that it had not been looking the other way while the looting was on. By then, the mine had already been operational for six months. Of course, this was the last mine to actually start work – and right next to human dwellings at that.

On that fateful day, the Goa State Pollution Board was joined at Xec Salim's mine by representatives of the departments of mines, water resources, forests and agriculture, all of whom jointly inspected the spot – showing everyone that the government could do anything or nothing. The inspection began at 10 a.m. or so, and went on past 3 p.m. without a break for lunch.

The findings were revealing. In gross violation of the clearance to dig close to 120 metres below the ground, Xec Salim and his friends had gone 167 metres and not paid royalties for six months. More importantly, they began functioning before they actually got legal consent to operate. The site visit also noted that one traditional spring was already destroyed, and another was in serious danger.

Despite these arresting findings, the mine continued to function normally for another four months, trucks entering and exiting as if there was no tomorrow.

In April, the villagers of Cawrem and some activists stormed the mine's entrance. The mining companies, sensing the heat, brought in young muscled Goan men in black tee-shirts and black jeans, usually hired as bouncers in night clubs and parties along the coast. This didn't deter them. On 21 April 2011, they blocked 300 overloaded trucks, forcing the RTO from Quepem to drive down to Cawrem and order the trucks to return to the mines and offload their ill-gotten wares. The next day, Good Friday, was a holiday at the mines. When the convoy got ready to move again on 23 April, a day after Earth Day (which, coincidentally, fell on the same day as Good Friday), the villagers of Cawrem finally woke up from their four-year-long slumber and as many as 150 women sat on the road and blocked the trucks.[3]

The government and mining companies obviously thought they had their flanks covered when they got in three busloads of riot police to move into Cawrem at 7.30 a.m. The people of Cawrem were smarter, putting themselves on the road a good half an hour earlier.

The riot police, clad in full battle gear, lathi-charged the men, hurting several, including an elderly person. Four women were aggressively manhandled, and one woman's clothes torn. The protesters, however, were undaunted. 'You can release us,' one of the women told a police inspector, 'but tomorrow morning, back we will be on the road to stop the trucks!'

The police hauled ninety-five men from Cawrem to the police station at Quepem, where they were joined by protesters from other mining-affected villages in Goa. Those men were not formally charged or even arrested, just bullied and browbeaten. They were asked to sign letters under Section 105 of the Indian Penal Code: 'Commencement and continuance of the right of private defence of property'.

The mine was only stopped when the villagers of Cawrem physically stormed the directorate of mines in Panjim and gheraoed the director and his staff until he passed an order closing it down.

In the summer months of 2010, we got a picture of Devapan Dongor that will never fade, especially now that the mining has stopped.

When I drove Aki to school, I always saw two huge dumpers and a bulldozer parked at the top of the dump – a small plateau of sorts. Behind this was a shining orange scree that held back trees further up.

The two of us were always struck by a large solitary tree with spreading branches, under which the bulldozer was invariably parked for the night. Around it all the other trees had disappeared. We wondered whether they kept this one standing to prevent the dew from falling on the bulldozer. It would cut down the time required to heat the engines the next morning and get at the hill.

As we turned the bend where the mine came into view, Aki saw it first, shouting: 'Wow!'

The tree we saw every morning had turned out to be a large laburnum, much loved by the monkeys here for its seed pods. It stood there before us, in all its blooming glory, clusters upon clusters of bright, shining yellow beads and streamers that caught the morning sun and sent it back to us.

Thanks to the Supreme Court ban, that tree is still there.

Two sharp bends out of Cawrem, the hill forests you find on both sides of the road were declared government forests and, therefore, assumed to be safe from the mining industry. But, in 2009, this road started showing telltale signs of 'prosperity' too. The tree cover on either side of the road had been cleared, and the place levelled with mining waste as villagers from Cawrem put up some thirty-five or so dwellings, virtually creating a new village. This was part of the ruling BJP's largesse to the Velip: forestland doled out with the requisite funds to put up a new house. What happens if they find ore here too, we asked ourselves. Will those who built the houses move again in exchange for money?

Not that far ahead was a forest check post, with a barrier. In the 1980s, you would have smiled to yourself, believing that our forests were in safe hands. But in the mining season, we spat in disgust while passing it. Earlier, the misdemeanours had been predictable: letting through trucks carrying illegally felled timber; a blind eye turned at someone hunting wild pig or bison; a few hundred rupees for trucks carrying smooth stones from the riverbed to landscape the lawns or gardens of a five-star hotel. Come to think of it, they were petty crimes.

In the Age of Greed, the forest officials couldn't see the forest for the ore. From 2008, they stationed a retired forester on a table at the forest check post, taking papers from truck drivers and duly returning them after they were stamped.

Twenty years back, this drive out of the hills of Cawrem, past the forest gate and the long, languorous climb, was pure pleasure. The greatest hazard on the roads would be stray cattle calmly seated on the road, chewing cud.

The climb up from the forest gate takes us past the equally scenic village of Cupar, traditionally an agricultural and pastoral settlement, but now a grimy suburb of mining operations. Up until 2000, when mining engineers were still prospecting for ore on the sly, Maina, Cawrem and Cupar were renowned for their chillies. Cawrem was a favourite among aficionados of fish curry.

When they were just a few steps away from turning orange near the stalk, these chillies dipped in a batter of gram flour and fried in hot oil could bring tears of joy to one's eyes. When picked just as the orange-red hue is just short of being deepest, and dried in the sun till they are crisp to the touch, then mixed with fresh grated coconut and wet-ground to a smooth paste, they brought orange to the curry in a way that did not need one to add turmeric to temper the stronger odours of the fresh fish, and red in a way that heightened its aromas and enticement.

On this road, before mining destroyed it, driving in and out of both Cawrem and Cupar were hundreds and hundreds of red chillies – placed in neat little carpets at the side of the road. No one ever complained about this. At Cupar and Cawrem, they were placed on either side of the two speed-breakers protecting the villages. After the rains, one or two women living close to the road would bravely bring their carpets of chillies and lay them out. When the mining resumed, the same women – mouths covered with cloth – were seen hunched over, sweeping the dust away.

In 2008, the mining contractors, truck agencies and banks generously helped locals acquire trucks, or gave them loans for motorcycles, fridges and TVs. Those just working the land as tenants were silenced with a few thousand rupees. Cupar, a tiny village in comparison to Cawrem, had just one or two motorcycles two years ago. Today, it has ten or maybe more of the two-wheelers, besides at least five trucks working for the mines. Here too forest authorities had put up a brand new signpost exhorting truck drivers and mining contractors to 'Save Forests, Save Mankind'.

Leaving Cupar and heading due north, you would part ways with the long chain of hills that has accompanied you thus far.

You headed out of the hills down a long slope, midway coming to another speed-breaker, placed there on account of a tiny government primary school at the border of the next village, Takwadi, or Takiar in local parlance. It has now been reduced to functioning with windows and doors bolted, its walls and roof covered with a fine coating of red dust.

Past Cupar's last fields and cashew orchards, there is a hillock facing the tiny school. Probably a Forest Department project, and mostly covered with shiny, locally unsuitable Australian acacia. In front of that hillock are makeshift dwellings, inventively put together with thatched coconut, discarded polythene sheeting and even bits and pieces of old billboards. These are the homes of the migrant labourers who, till a few years back, worked the laterite quarries less than a hundred metres east. Perhaps they are the happiest of all, because now with the mining stopped, the laterite quarries to the east of Takiar have all come to life. A single stone costs anything up to Rs 25 each, so now you have a regular stream of trucks groaning under the weight of overloaded laterite stone blocks.

Even some fifteen or sixteen years ago, the climb down from Cupar and up the last hill, through Ambaulim, had been depressing. Close to its summit is Takiar. At the foot of the drift below, a stream gushes in the monsoons, the hills beyond the eastern slopes of the plateau seem stationed like a pained furrow across the sky's brow. Beyond those, on the ribs of the eastern side of the Western Ghats, lie even more abandoned quarries.

Till 2005 or so, the plateau opening out to Takiar on either side was being quarried for red-orange laterite stone, which was then manually cut and shaped by an adze to make the blocks needed for building houses. While such quarrying sometimes led to natural rainwater harvesting, depending on how impervious the rock layers were, a few feet of rain is all the quarries ever held in Takiar – barely deep enough to let buffaloes wallow in when they went down on their bellies. By the end of September, there would only be a few stagnant slime-covered puddles that even the buffaloes would shun.[4]

One felt sad for Takiar in those days too, because it seemed so much like a village that owed its existence to the quarrying of laterite. On all four sides of this village, the earth was scarred.

In 2008, though, Takiar showed all the signs of becoming a small township fuelled by mining. Here too, land had been sold in bulk and procured with unbelievable haste. Barely two months after the rains of 2008, old quarries on both sides of the road had suddenly been surveyed and fenced. Brand new signage proudly proclaimed this as 'Private Property'. Was this once public property? It's at least probable.

When laterite quarrying began at Takiar in the 1960s or '70s, it was probably illegal and involved the usurping of the communidade lands by various businessmen with small cartel-like operations that translated into wealth or political power (ideally, both). The government of that time had barely a cabinet of three, and it may have been difficult for a minister, or even one of his IAS functionaries sitting in Panjim, to keep a check on what was going on in a small near-desolate village called Takiar. In those days, quarrying on the slopes of Takiar may have cost contractors only a few thousand rupees in bribes paid to small-time government officials.

It may help to look at Takiar more closely. Until recently, you could see just a cluster of ten small dwellings from the road. The orchards and dwellings on the slopes remained hidden.

However, when economic growth came a-visiting, newer buildings, with houses on the first floor and a family business like a bar or a grocery shop downstairs, cropped up. At night, you could see mining trucks parked nearby.

The illegal mining boom made its presence felt here far more blatantly. Thanks to protests from women taking their children to and from schools in the area, loaded trucks were not allowed to drive through to Quepem town when schools near the road opened or closed for the day.[5] Ironically, the husbands of the women themselves were operating quite a few of the trucks.

But even in this there was a proviso to ensure that the mining supply chain was not unduly affected by the everyday life of people in the area. In 2008, the overloaded trucks would be lined up one behind the other on the long, gently sloping road, until the very last bend, about 200 metres before a T-section crossing that took you towards the town. The trucks lined up all the way up to the crest of Takiar and down the final plunge to the plains, a good kilometre if not more, seeming like a huge dust-covered serpent sunning itself on the slopes of the hill.

The trucks barely left enough space on this road for a car to get through. What was once a lovely three-minute drive downhill now stretched to twenty or more. Everyday traffic was left with no choice but to give way to empty mining trucks rushing into Cawrem and Maina to load. If you encountered another vehicle on the stretch, you adjusted your car in the space maintained between parked trucks.

This road was used by people from northern Neturlim to go to westwards towards Bali, north to Quepem town, or Margao. And over ninety per cent of these commuters were not dependent on mining for their livelihoods. The politicians and mining companies always maintained that the Goan public must learn to 'compromise'.

The government of the day sweetly told us all that this pandemonium would continue until a mining by-pass was built. After that, everyone could breathe a sigh of relief.

Twice a day, a constable from Quepem was stationed at the foot of the plateau to make sure that the loaded trucks lined up in an orderly fashion and left enough space for the other vehicles to adjust to the inconvenience. A query posed to the constable on duty would be met with a shrug and a suggestion that complaints must be directed to the inspector at the police station. When the number of trucks began to increase exponentially from 2009 onwards, they stationed a police jeep there. It would usually have two officers snoozing in the back, and a couple of constables trying to regulate the smooth flow of trucks with whistles.

8

Recasting Ambaulim

When you followed the overloaded trucks down the plateau from Takiar, turning right at the T-junction and into Ambaulim – driving up and down two small, winding slopes – you found two more misshapen speed-breakers at the entrance of the village. Here too they paid old women to sweep the road, collect the dust, and chuck it in whatever open ground they could find. Between the speed-breakers were yet another primary school and a few government buildings, including the panchayat office and local health centre. From 2007 onwards, local papers consistently reported instances of students developing respiratory problems. Nobody gave a damn.

When you crossed the last speed-breaker, you reached that level of ground where streams straighten out to seek the plains and head towards river and sea. At least scenically your journey ought to end here, because from the time the new century broke, Ambaulim ahead showed all the signs of being converted into an extended suburb of Quepem town, barely four kilometres away.

Back in the hills between Maina and Cawrem, the problem lay with mining companies illegally foraging for ore and taking away forests and water. In Ambaulim and Quepem, rapid urbanization did precisely the same to water sources and whatever little remained of the wooded areas and fields.

This merely follows the prevailing trend in Goa. Mapusa, the main town in the north, has steadily encroached on village areas on all four sides. The fields that once separated villages have been filled with mining waste and raised, so that they can be converted into residences or shops. Choice parts of hill and plateau have been earmarked for dumping the town's garbage.[1] Mapusa draws closer to the sea off Calangute.

Panjim in the centre of the state and Margao in the south have been doing the same thing over the years.[2] Around every single one of Goa's towns, rivers and streams that once flowed freely to sea have either been blocked and turned into swamps, or reduced to becoming natural storm-water drains – full only during the rains, and then left to fester in the heat of the coming months. Residents of such areas stock up on lethal sprays to kill mosquitoes, then bolt the windows, turn on the fans and live on regurgitated air. The well-off buy air-conditioners. Goa is on the move.

Goa has the largest urban population among small states in the country. The Census 2011 data states that 62 per cent of Goa's population lives in urban areas, as compared to 38 per cent in rural areas. While the state saw an 8 per cent increase in population over the previous decade, there was a 35 per cent increase in the urban population and a negative growth of minus 18 per cent in rural areas[3]. They were reserving the land for either mining, real estate or – if the area was still scenic – hospitality projects.

So you could break your journey here to mourn the fact that in fifty years' time or sooner, all the so-called villages in Goa would have been gobbled by its towns. The towns, in turn, will graduate to becoming two-tier cities and eventually merge with each other to become yet another bloated, misshapen landscape, like the far suburbs of Mumbai.

Driving through Ambaulim in the Age of Greed, you would find yourself on a pleasantly curving road that was just like any other road in Goa – Saligao, Calangute, Benaulim, Colva or Cavellosim – the only difference being the presence of mining trucks and, of course, the dust. It helps to remember that this wasn't a mining bypass to begin with; it was an ordinary Goan village road broad enough to accommodate two buses passing each other comfortably.

With its vehicles, banks, ATMs, cold storages and shops selling durables with packaging that would add to the litter, Ambaulim too was on the move.

A few years into the new century, the large tracts of field were regularly ploughed, sowed with rice and harvested. An increasing number of perennial water bodies were infested with weed and encroached by wild shrubs, greedily bleeding them dry. The sides of the roads were lined with paper bags of garbage carelessly thrown from passing cars. Sometimes, the bags were hurled into the field below, where they burst like water bombs. Everyone just takes the trash as far away from their own houses as possible.

There were fewer fields now. There are also the sad signs of fields getting fenced, others being filled with mining waste to bring them to the level of the road, making them fit for non-agricultural use. This is a work-in-progress all over the country, the rural being made urban to bring in 'development' and privilege, predicated on the specious argument that in doing this, one is doing away with poverty.

Ambaulim was also what you would call a mining-dependent village. It boasted of at least fifty trucks, small though it was. Like everyplace else in Goa in the Age of Greed, Ambaulim had also chosen the real yet illusory benefits of the here-and-now over the more gruelling picture of trucks and dust.

It was also a village that took me back to the past in a somewhat brutal way.

Just after you crossed the second speed-breaker near Ambaulim's primary school, the road turns narrow, and bifurcates the village into rural and urban components. On the western side were the earlier Gavde settlements, much older houses and huts, and more importantly, once the site of their mands or traditional community spaces. You could tell as you drove through, almost glaringly, who on the road was Gavde and who was not. On the eastern side, you saw the newer, better-fashioned houses of the more recent settlers.

Whether that land may have been part of the Gavde communidade here in Ambaulim was probably not a concern. Nor also the fact that the Gavde in this area, predominantly Catholic tenants, was probably not made aware of their rights under the Tenancy Act that Bandodkar brought in with Goa's first government. In depriving them of their rights, the Church in Goa could have worked in the favour of upper-class Catholics, who may also have been landlords or 'bhatcars'. Ambaulim was, after all, traditionally a Gavde village.

When the narrow road broadened, if you took a right-angled turn, heading in a north-easterly direction to Quepem town, on your left is the quasi-modernist steeple and church of Ambaulim: a place of worship that dwarfed its flock.

Not that far from the church is a small bar and restaurant – the real heart of Goa some may say – set up by a man and his wife who worked in the Gulf for ten years or more, saving enough to come back and start a business. Such an establishment is almost always to be found on the ground floor, with the owner's family either living at the back, or on the first floor.

It's actually a good job to have, especially if your wife was an expert at sautéing bits of medium roast pork with onions, finely sliced green chillies and freshly dried kokum slices in stock – then lightly sprinkled with freshly ground pepper to give the accompanying sauce a piquant, spicy, totally indescribable flavour.

Between 2006 and 2011, it was my favourite watering hole. I took everyone I knew there to taste the wife's sautéed pork, or, for that matter, her serving of sliced rounds of squid tossed in garlic, butter, salt and pepper and then finished with a quick stir of a teaspoon of finely chopped fresh green coriander and de-seeded green chilly. What made matters even more interesting was that a lot of the mining truck drivers and owners and smaller mining contractors were regular customers, and provided us with enough opportunities to eavesdrop.

I liked the owner and his wife. They were polite, friendly people who always made you feel welcome. I also made my first notes on Ambaulim at this very bar, opening my laptop and keying in the terse bits I needed to add to my chronicle.

I can't remember which year the following incident occurred, and it's probably because of the number of times I stopped there. It was during the rains, though. That evening I was sitting inside because the covered thatched porch outside, under which I usually sat, was leaking. In front of me was a very large and shiny poster of Jesus Christ, a halo around his head and his right hand on his heart. The surreal picture had a stylized heart wrapped in a rosary on his chest, the cross dangling from his fingers.

The owner had just put the plate of sautéed pork in front of me. He waited for me to spear a piece and taste it, and for me to turn back and tell his wife in English, as I always did, 'Madam, it's even better than the last time.'

Usually her husband would serve me, then walk away and let each of us get back to our own morose thoughts. And then, when I ordered my second drink, he would amble over so that we could grunt at each other again. This particular evening, he seemed much more affable, and certainly desirous of conversation.

I thought I should make some small talk. 'So, you and your wife go to the church here on Sundays?' I asked, pointing at the Ambaulim church.

'Che!' he retorted, taking a small pause. 'Che' is a sound, a nuanced word used by Goans when they want to preface disapproval, surprise, wonder, awe or even disgust – depending on how they choose to stress, elongate, or emphasize this sharp, nasal expulsion of breath. There was no mistaking what the owner felt.

'I would not go to that church,' he told me in Konkani. 'It's a Gavde church ... we go to Quepem, that's our church.'

This didn't take me by surprise, although I didn't expect proof of this discrimination coming so blatantly. I pointed to the big shiny, plastic-coated poster of Christ in front of us on the wall. I could have sworn the big glistening eyes twinkled.

'But the Gavde are Catholics too,' I replied, 'It's the same God, the same Church.'

He snorted again, his mouth widening into a sneer, and laughed – a sound that was anything but nice. 'They are Gavde,' he told me. 'How can Gavde be Catholic?'

'I'm Gavde,' I told him, 'and you call me Sir.'

Now his laugh was as genuine as it could get. 'How can you be Gavde?' he asked. 'You are an educated man.'

I was blissfully unschooled till I was almost eleven, the age when I saw a classroom for the first time. At that time, we were in Mombasa, the main port of Kenya where my father, Peter, was posted when Goa's liberation took place. While I may have learned to climb a tree, do basic electrical work in the house and clean the carburettor of the car, thanks to Dora, it was Peter who opened my eyes to the other aspects of life.

When the Indian army marched through Goa and he heard the news on the BBC, he drove us to some shop at the end of Salim Road early in the morning and came out with a large box. I found out what was inside when we reached the house of the Portuguese consul in Mombasa, a Goan he detested, and took out whole bunches of firecrackers, lit them with his cigarette, and chucked them over the wall, making me shout 'Jai Hind' with him.

When I was sixteen, incensed by the chapter on India, he confiscated my history textbook *A History of the British Empire and Commonwealth*, written by two eminent Englishmen, and forced me to read Nehru's *Glimpses of World History* instead.

I had been home-schooled before I entered my first classroom ever. It was complicated. Thanks to Peter being the senior-most Goan working with the colonial government in Mombasa at that time, he was also chairman of the board of governors of the Goan High School where I studied. This was not the privileged position one would think it is, given that he had provided me with the simple instruction that were I ever to bump into him at school, I should pretend I didn't know him.

In my history period, the class-teacher, a very pleasant Goan woman who was also our singing teacher, discussed the first lesson in our textbook on India. It was on the 'caste system'. I had already read it, and frankly, it made no sense to me. Truth be told, if I had a choice between sitting in the classroom and climbing a tree, I'd have chosen the latter. Once the lesson got over, the class started talking and this was where my ears came to life.

'Teacher, what caste are you?' one of my classmates asked. 'My father says we are Brahmin.'

Before she could answer, another voice piped up: 'Yes, we are Brahmins too, my father told me.'

Before I knew what was happening, the teacher also said she was a Brahmin, and the whole class was designated into either Brahmin or Kshatriya – including, of course, Shekhar Tilak, the only Hindu student in the class, and excluding Rashid Salim, a Swahili from Mombasa who said he was Muslim. There were quite a few in the classroom who remained silent right through. One girl said she was Brahmin, and someone else in the class said she was not because her parents had told her so.

'What about the new boy?' some bright spark shouted from the back, and I squirmed in my seat because I hadn't the faintest idea. I had never heard my parents talk about caste. The class teacher came to my rescue. 'I know his father,' she told the rest of the class. 'He's Brahmin too.' I smirked because it seemed the right thing to do.

We had an hour and a half break for lunch, and school was just a ten-minute walk home. Peter was also there for lunch and a small snooze before returning to office. The dining table was the parliament of our homestead; it still is. It is where people are encouraged to speak – everything from our famous family debates to fights and reconciliations took place over the table.

'So, we're Brahmins,' I told Peter, making conversation.

He put his knife and fork down. 'What did you say?'

'I said we are Brahmins ... that's really good. Brahmins are the highest caste in India.'

I got a barrage of questions and dutifully repeated what had happened in class. I don't know what happened, but he suddenly started speaking Konkani with Dora. They did that when they didn't want us kids to follow their conversation. From what he was saying, he seemed incredibly angry.

I usually ran back to school after lunch, so I could play football with a tennis ball with the rest of the guys before class began. That afternoon, Peter drove me back. In the school car park, while I was still unsure just what I had done, Peter told me my history. Simply put, it was about a Gavde ancestor who had changed the lives of three generations of his family yet to come over a hundred years ago.

He was a toddy tapper by profession on some landlord's property, which means he probably distilled coconut toddy into the potent feni traditionally drunk by the poor. He ploughed his land, watched his wife sow and transplant the rice, then winnow it after he had harvested the crop. He gave his yearly 'tithe', one eighth of the produce from the land, to his benefactor-owner. In all likelihood, his family survived on the back of whatever feudal Catholic benevolence came his way.

However, it was this Gavde who had the vision of sending his son to study music in the church with the parish priest. The son went on to work for the band and orchestra of some maharajah in Rajasthan from where he retired as the conductor. He was known by the nickname of 'pensaokar' in the village because of a 'pension' he received from the maharajah. He bought the first bit of land, and demolished the old mud house to add two more rooms and a tiled roof. His son, Peter's father, went to study at St. Xavier's School, Bombay, after which he was sent to Kenya to work for the colonial British government. Retiring as the district clerk in Nairobi, he came back and built a bigger house in Nagoa. He bought land around the house and turned himself into a landlord.

My grandfather sent Peter to study at St. Vincent's School in Pune, a boarding school in those days, and later to Wadia College in Pune. Peter also went off to Kenya, joining the Colonial British government as a clerk, and after independence, serving the Kenyan government and retiring from the Office of the President of Kenya. On Dora's side, he told me, the story was even worse. They were so poor that they had to migrate in search of work and better prospects much earlier. Dora's mother was born in Zanzibar and married off when she was fourteen. Dora herself was born in Nairobi.

'If you see how the story of our family changed,' Peter said to me in the car, 'there is no such thing as the caste system.' The word 'Adivasi' and the terms 'Scheduled Caste/Scheduled Tribe' may not have been in his lexicon, and probably not 'Harijan' or 'Dalit' either.

'Don't think about caste,' he advised me, 'but if anyone asks you what caste you belong to say you are a Gavde.'

I got back just before the bell rang. As the class got underway, the teacher was called to the principal's office. She returned after almost fifteen minutes, and it was quite obvious that she had been crying. It is a credit to her sincerity, she never looked my way, so no one in the classroom ever knew that I was the cause of her misery. However, I always wondered if her attitude towards me changed after that.

One thing I do know, though: it was the lower-caste origin and deprived class status of Goan Catholics that made them toil abroad and turn their lives into success stories. Many, unfortunately, may have forgotten the fact that their great-grandparents and the ones before them were born at the bottom of the pile, and had to fight against adversity for over a century before they could attain their present status.

In forgetting their humble origins and eager to get either Sanskritized or whitewashed, they callously discarded an attitude of openness and a sense of modernity sorely needed by Goa in its hour of need today.

During the height of the illegal mining, a phenomenon that began as early as 2005, the Archdiocese of Goa was given ample evidence that mining was devastating parts of Quepem and Sanguem, which had a large Catholic population tracing their origin to the Scheduled Tribes.

In the Philippines, Indonesia, Burma and more than half a dozen countries in Latin America, bishops, priests and nuns have walked alongside villagers to protest the opening of new mines and fight for people's rights. In recent times, the Vatican has repeatedly stated that desecration of the environment is a strong enough offence to warrant being a 'sin'.[4]

There were some nuns in Quepem itself, probably more radical than the priests at the Archbishop's Palace in Panjim, who spoke of 'ecospirituality', which amounted to 'seeing the risen Christ in the processes of nature' and openly decrying exploitative mining operations.

Yet, in Goa, the Church remained studiously silent, sitting on the fence with its eyes wrapped tight in a surplice. In many areas of the mining hinterland, this translated into parish priests blessing new mining trucks emblazoned with exhortations that showed one and all that faith in God was alive and well. The windscreens and the metal bodies of these vehicles blared words such as 'Our Lady of Vellankani', 'Jesus, Pray for Us', 'Jesus Saves You', 'Infant Jesus', 'Mother Mary', 'St. Francis Xavier', 'Mother Mary, Light Our Way' and 'Sweet Heart of Jesus'.

It took as long as late December 2009, after more than half the hills in Quepem and Sanguem had disappeared, for the archbishop to confront the government of that time. He sat them down like errant schoolboys during the annual Christmas reception at the archbishop's 'palace', and lightly rapped their knuckles with exhortations to virtuous living.

At the height of the mining greed in Goa, the archbishop of Goa penned a letter to his flock waxing eloquent on the relationship of a God-given environment and the innate spirituality of recognizing the Holy Spirit in the natural world. It mentioned the term 'illegal mining' only once.

It was only after the Shah Commission report was made public and the Supreme Court ban came into play that the Council for Social Justice and Peace, the 'corporate social responsibility' arm of the archdiocese, became bold enough to issue a statement condemning mining.[5]

Then, intoning 'mea culpa' thrice, it conveniently forgot to mention the Rs 35,000 crore that the Shah Commission estimated was looted, and remained largely silent about bringing the guilty magnates to justice. Instead, it continued to look the other way as Goan Catholics in the government tried to find loopholes to bring back mining and line their pockets with ill-gotten wealth.

The Church in Goa, in any case, may not have shirked off its medieval allure to land, and the power and wealth this engendered. There are those who believe that it may even have played its share of games to water the agitations down.

Whether that is true or not is a moot point. The Church has yet to admit to its part in selling the island of Vanxim, extending over 500,000 square metres in the Mandovi's backwaters, to a Brahmin politician, Mahendra Gaunekar, in 2006. Gaunekar, in turn, made a killing by selling it to a major real estate player in Bangalore. This prime property will now house a resort, an exclusive golf course, spas, a jacuzzi or two, and exclusive hand-crafted marinas for yachts and boats.[6]

While it may have been easy for the Church and its many followers to later condemn the opening of a 'Playboy' club in Calangute, they were strangely silent about Vanxim turning into a similar high-end tourism venture, albeit with fewer scantily attired women and possibly less lascivious men.

Before the Church takes a position on protecting and indeed conserving the unique identity of this state that it is very much a part of, it may need to walk the talk and come clean on various factors – including allegations that it sold land in parts adjacent to Panjim, displacing or buying off the indigenous communities settled there, and bringing into being the real estate nightmare the area has become. What makes the charges graver is the fact that such land may have been donated to the Church as earlier 'indulgences' in return for a lifetime of prayer for departed souls, and therefore intended for the benefit of the larger Catholic community.

In any case, the village of Ambaulim is a case in point of how the Catholic Church in Goa may not have been catholic with all the members of its flock.

I can identify the Gavde population of Ambaulim only by counting heads at church on Sundays. It is substantial and justifies the large church and parish house it has been given. The shocking part, however, is the fact that in this entire community, there is only one graduate – John Fernandes – a practising lawyer in Quepem who continued his education while tending his livestock and family fields. He still does this, and his wife and small son bear witness to it.

John has no intentions of forgetting where he has come from, and where his roots lie. He always takes me back to Peter explaining my origins to me. John also reminded me of my great-great grandfather who gave a break to those who came after him. Dora also had a very soft corner for him, and more so because he was one of Cheryl's lawyers. We knew also that, had it not been for a stroke of good fortune that our ancestors ran into, we too may have had to start from scratch.

John's critique of the Church in an email to me is damning. He holds that not a single Catholic Gavde in the Quepem or Sanguem talukas holds land as an original owner, although most of the lands where the Gavde have traditionally resided are owned by higher-caste Catholics. He maintains that the Church in Goa does not speak up as much for tribal Catholics as it does for its higher-caste followers. He bitterly cites the recent example of a child's molestation in a school in Vasco, where the Church allegedly remained silent because the young victim was a Gavde and the culprit a higher-caste Catholic.

He alleges that Catholic priests who have tried to educate the Gavde community about their rights have been harassed by the Church's higher officials or transferred abruptly. And Joao cites how the Church steered clear of supporting a movement in 2002, when the tribals of Goa demanded that they be included in the Scheduled Tribes list, even though it was led by the Catholic Gavde.

John wrote that in the forty-three years of his life in Ambaulim, he has never seen a priest at the Ambaulim church telling the people they should educate themselves and their children; that education was the only way for them to come up in life. It has only been concerned about the spiritual development of the Gavde, not their cultural, educational, social and economic welfare. 'The Church in Goa does not propagate the idea that we should invest in education. It only preaches that we invest in God,' he stated. If the Catholic Church had propagated about twenty years ago that the Gavde should educate themselves as well as their children, the story of the community would have been different today, John writes.

He keeps his strongest critique for the last, saying that the Church was instrumental in destroying the mands, the traditional community spaces of the Gavde around which their traditions and culture revolved, in the 1990s. This community space had several functions. While it indeed served as a panchayat, where the community would come together to discuss matters of importance, it was also a space where the Gavde could celebrate (and re-affirm) their culture during the planting and harvesting seasons. Like the early slaves taken from Africa, the Gavde too could have moved seamlessly into accepting Catholicism while keeping their own links to the earth intact.

In John's own words:

'The mand was a centrally located, open meeting ground found in every ward or settlement of the Gavde. It strengthened social and cultural unity among us, as we would all gather there, irrespective of our inter-personal differences. If any case was taken up here, it was sure to have an effective result. For instance, in case of theft, the thief would speak the truth and return the stolen article.

'When paddy was harvested, the women would gather at their respective mands and perform the kannar khell or moraile, or dance the dhalo, fugdi, intruz, intrumez and zagor. Dhalos used to be performed for five, seven or nine days, and on such nights, one would hear the women singing ... Most songs during the dhalo festival are based on nature or inspired by past incidents ... Through these songs, we celebrated nature and thanked the Almighty for the harvest. Women would hold each other's hand or stand in a circle, which was a symbol of unity, while performing. This was a time all differences were put aside.

'After the sugarcane harvest, sometime during February or March, Gavde men celebrated intruz on the mand, preparations for which would begin a week in advance. During that week, it was customary to hear the beautiful sounds of the dholl, taxem, kasali, ghumot and madhali – all instruments that we learnt to play at the mand.'

In 1990, there were around nine mands in the jurisdiction of the Ambaulim parish; around six or seven in the jurisdiction of the Holy Cross Church, Quepem; another six or so in the jurisdiction of Our Lady of the Poor Church, Tilamol; and three within the jurisdiction of the church of Fatorpa. There were also mands at the Gavde hamlets in Sanguem taluka and in the villages of Ambelim and Velim in the Salcete taluka.

From the late 1980s onwards, John says, the Church orchestrated a major campaign to kill the mands. The parish priest in Ambaulim, in fact, called it 'a place of the Devil' and preached that performing the traditional arts at the mand was like worshipping a 'blind god'. Village elders responsible for performing ceremonies at the mand were threatened.

In less than a century, a village of our people – self-sustaining agriculturalists and pastoralists – was invaded by outsiders who bought land and made themselves prosperous, slowly but surely marginalizing the original inhabitants.

In the place of these traditional sites of Gavde celebration, the Church in Goa introduced the concept of a 'Small Christian

Community', an imported notion that refused to acknowledge divisions based on something as un-Christian and inhumane as 'caste'.

These days, John seems to suggest, the Church in Goa speaks about protecting the Goan daiz, or heritage, too easily – forgetting that it was the Gavde who used to protect, preserve and nurture the fragments of Goa's ancient past.

Your journey, technically speaking, ends here, just after we pass the Don Bosco High School, Quepem, and come to the cemetery of the town.

Barely half a kilometre ahead is the entrance to Quepem, a town best avoided unless you drove in on Sundays or took the road into Margao at 5.30 in the morning and came back to the farm after 8 at night.

Right through the Age of Greed, the residents of both Ambaulim and Quepem were angered by the rows of loaded trucks groaning through their narrow thoroughfares, but such annoyance was quickly squashed with promises. Such was the farce that played out, a small traffic fracas involving one of the trucks, fuelled by the heat and noise and dust was almost immediately quelled by no less than a deputy superintendent. Complaints against a mining truck for rash and dangerous driving were promptly met by requests for 'compromise', a euphemism that compels the aggrieved to take the money and shut their mouths. When Cheryl, for instance, refused to withdraw her complaints, she was told the errant drivers had been sacked by the transport contractors and could not be traced.

The most fervent protesters in Quepem were charged with causing a public disturbance by police officers as well as truck owners, who, when working in tandem, made a deadly combination allied to the enemy.

Too many, it must be said, allowed themselves to be palliated and made complicit with the evils of mining. The sheer number of houses in Ambaulim, and all along the roads to Sanvordem and Sanguem (with two or three mining trucks parked outside), bore grim testament to this.

While policemen parked their Gypsies and relaxed in the cool shade after partaking of a good lunch, the static from their wireless receivers telling everybody who rules the town, the mining companies thoughtfully provided shabbily attired security guards – with bandanas covering their mouths and uniforms coated with dust – to oversee the ebb and flow of trucks in the town. In this melancholic mess, it seemed like almost everyone had drunk from this well of poisoned water, and there was nothing to stop the rot from spreading.

9

My Family and Other Animals

It does help that Ganesha's tiny yellow blossoms came into this chronicle, almost like beautifully recurring memories. I've known this very same road since the mid-1980s and, frankly, after twelve years of mining hell, I can still afford to have some good moments from the past come and visit me again.

I remember coming to Goa by train from Delhi, and those days, driving in and out of Maina with Cheryl's late partner at that time, George, who set up the furniture business she ran in the 1990s in Varca – then the fiefdom of the Alemao family. We'd drive there in George's battered old Willy's with bucket seats, and stopped at several small bars along the way for a cold beer. Then there were the times that followed, after I came back to Goa in the early 1990s, when George and I would drive around in his upgraded post-office red Tempo Trax. Entering this area from the Forest Gate was like driving into a mist-filled dream.

I also recall our days in early March 1991, with Ujwala pregnant and the two of us blissfully in love, riding my old second-hand Yezdi to where the farm now stands. We would take off our clothes and step into the freezing water just where the water from Paik's Spring meets the Curca. After that, we would sit in the sun to dry, eating sandwiches and sipping wine.

Even later, there was the time we drove to the banks of the same river in our second-hand Premier Padmini to celebrate Zuri's first birthday, with Bobby McFerrin's Medicine Man playing on the stereo. I just can't forget the sight of Zuri feeding barbecued chicken to Virginia and Wolf, Cheryl's two giant German Shepherds, and squealing happily later, with her arms around Ujwala's neck as she got her first taste of Paik's water, her feet almost magically turning into fins. Zuri is in her early twenties now, and she has seen with her own eyes the changes that mining has wrought in Goa.

Our adventures were straight out of a book. One summer in May when I think Zuri may have been nine or ten, and Zaeen seven or eight, and I woke them just as the sun was breaking, leaving Ujwala still fast asleep. We climbed this steep hill some distance behind the farm, following the stream upwards at my suggestion that we find the source. As the birds fly, it would have been less than a kilometre from the five mines in the area.

Before the shady first ridge that we hit, thanks to Zaeen's bird-centred hiss that Zuri and I stop chattering like monkeys, we got to see a family of monitor lizards – father, mother and two kids – elegantly crawling over the rocks as if they had all the time in the world. They leisurely drank at the stream before stretching themselves at the base of the short cliff, legs moving as smoothly as their gently heaving chests. Soon, they climbed over the ledge and disappeared into forest.

Climbing higher, following the stream, we saw quite a few snakes basking in the sun and then slithering away. There was an animal swimming in a deep stretch of water that I could have sworn looked like an otter, but the kids insisted it was a mongoose. Deflecting a question on whether otters are found in Goa, I asked if mongooses can swim. They didn't know.

I turned back to see where we are. It had been a very long but gradual climb, and by my estimates, we were almost halfway up to the source. Though I did want to get there, I had badly misjudged the distance. Even worse, judging by the position of the sun, it could even be close to eleven. Zaeen looked like he had food on his mind. But on the bright side, there was lots of water to drink and the kids didn't look that worn out. We needed to climb at forty degree-angles or so to get halfway up, which – knowing these two – seemed very manageable. I also reckoned that the view would be spectacular.

Soon, all thoughts of food were forgotten.

Okay, I asked them, the creature could have been a beaver, right? Zaeen nodded excitedly, but Zuri replied with a sneer that there are no beavers in India. Still, it was two against one. We made only one brief halt, refusing to look back until we reached our spot. We did this after trudging up a good twenty minutes, maybe more, because I was pretty whacked and the kids now looked totally worn out too.

This was no beaver dam, but a lovely pool teeming with tiny brown fish with muddy yellow stripes. Above it, from a rock as big as a small elephant, we could see a ribbon of water – a couple of inches wide – flowing down from the lip of what looked like a large plate.

Beyond the rock, almost at the same angle, the hill climbed up with the rocks in the stream – now so narrow that you could barely see it – glistening in the sun, and what seemed like at least another two small trickling waterfalls like this one. We couldn't see the summit from where we stood.

There were thick forests everywhere. It did seem like we had found one of the traditional paths Pauto kept telling me about – the ones used by the old Velip people. The source could have been another forty minutes' climb away, and accorded the benefit of an even more spectacular view. I made plans in my head to climb this the next day. We could have lunch up at the source, I thought, loads of sandwiches and juice for the kids and a cold beer wrapped in newspaper for me.

The water in the pool was sweet, clear and almost icy. After we had drunk our fill and washed our faces, I showed Zaeen how to bend over and dunk his head underwater. We all did this several times.

The view below us did take our breath away. We could see the school across the road, and the hill adjacent to it. What we couldn't see was the forests behind the hill, where work had probably already started, with Fomento Resources bringing in earth-moving machinery and trucks from the eastern side by using the old road linking this area with the village of Collomb. We could see the forests beyond the highest Cawrem hill, and all the sugarcane farms stemming eastwards from Paik's valley. If you moved your eyes right, in the distance you could see the hills surrounding Collomb and Rivona. That was another part of a similar pantheon of indigenous shrines – and yet another range of hills that fell to mining in the Age of Greed.

At that time, there was just one mine that you could see – Jollerancho Dongor, which restarted its operations in 2006 but had been abandoned because the ore was of low quality. That seemed almost completely taken over by the wild. What we saw was just a rich, dense, thickly packed forest of various shades of green, bits and pieces here and there of dark blue, and in some places, where the sun didn't reach, the patches that were almost black. All of this, as far as the eyes could see, was laid out like a silk carpet shimmering in the sun.

The cool air made us a little dizzy, and we were forced to find a place where we could just sit and watch silently. The rock gave us shade, and soon enough, we had closed our eyes in sleep. I was woken up a little later by Zaeen, who seemed to be telling the world that he was really hungry.

I still remember stopping to gulp mouthfuls of water from the stream and getting hungrier by the minute as we headed back. We seemed to take longer coming down than going up, and when we finally reached, I really got it in the neck from Ujwala and the kids who willingly became turncoats. I made a six-egg omelette and a large plate of hot buttered toast at five in the evening, and we sat down for a fairly late-ish breakfast.

The kids and I made that trip when the water still flowed and the forests were teeming with life.

In 2009, armed with very dark thoughts, I made that same climb again early one morning. I took with me a couple of sandwiches, a small bottle of cold beer wrapped in two layers of newspaper, and two bottles of Paik's water to drink along the way. In hindsight, it was a good thing that I took the water because through the entire climb upstream, following the source of this stream that fed our little Curca, I could only find green, slimy ponds scattered among the rocks. The air was still, humid and sweltering, as if hung out to dry. It may help if you consider that in forest areas, acres of denuded earth do to the sun's heat what acres of concrete and tarmac do to the cities – inhaling it in the day and breathing it out at night in hunt of prey. You end up with drying forests and little moisture. Where is the possibility of life, then?

I saw no snakes, no monitor lizards, just one or two skinny frogs jumping around in the stagnant pools of water. But there were monkeys, more monkeys than I have ever seen. The ugly truth facing all of us, except the ones who did the mining and those who condoned the illegality, is that every single one of these marauding packs of simians happen to be refugees from the five threaded forests in the area that were put to the sword.

Ironically, there is beauty to be had too. Fifteen years ago, we had to spend a long time tracking the great pied hornbill before finally catching a glimpse of it returning to nest. They do this in stages, visiting several trees along the way to the nest and calling each other with sounds that are anything but bird-like. Sometimes it sounds like an irritated Pomeranian taking a sharp snap at someone's ankle, and at other times, like a chisel hitting wood. These birds are not just shy; they are deeply suspicious of human beings. And that's no surprise, because some villagers in these parts will cook them and swear that they taste better than the jungle fowl.

Now, thanks to the five mining operations of Fomento, Salgaocar, Magnum, Minescape and Xec Salim that surrounded Paik's Spring in a semi-circle, we had the great pied hornbill, an endangered species, visiting all the large wild fig trees for their fruit. In two of the vegetable gardens where the champak trees grow, we had early morning and late afternoon visits by the smaller, skinnier but equally noisy Indian grey hornbill as well as the Malabar grey hornbill.

Even better, a pair of Malabar pied hornbills, which are a smaller version of the great pied, decided to nest on the trees under which we had been growing vegetables. We got a chance to watch first-hand how the mothers push their young off the branch, then swoop after them, cajoling, nagging and inspiring them to fly. We are still in the process of deciphering their calls, which Salim Ali aptly describes as the 'raucous cackling and inane screams reminiscent of the protestations of a dak bungalow murgi seized by the cook'.

The male seems distinctly hen-pecked and speculation abounds: is the female hungry and demanding food from the male, saying, 'Hey man, I'm hungry, go get me some worms', or is the male pleading, 'Hey baby, why don't you give me some time to breathe?'

One of the vegetable gardens we tended also had a family of rat snakes in residence. Another had a cobra, which – judging from the moulted skin we found there – may have been pretty big. We saw bronzeback tree snakes by the dozen, as also the incredibly delicate green vine snake, and so many birds that we always had to keep Salim Ali's book close at hand.

When the mining was at its height, the bison came in much closer too, frightening the dogs away with their strong meaty sweat and the powerful smell of their dung. They ate up every single vegetable that Shashikala, Pauto and Anil had grown, leaving even stalks chopped in line with the mud.

The wild bison are huge, lovely, proud, majestic animals that can clear fences twelve feet high with ease. They appear to be more of a tribe than just an ordinary herd of animals. At least one villager has told me how herds of bison stay separately from each other, and have their own systems of hierarchy and order as well as adoption of those lost or orphaned.

If you sight them grazing in the grassland in the forest borders of the farm before the sun breaks, they will let you come close enough to see their powerful jaws pulling out tufts of grass (the kind that would need at least two hefty strokes of a hoe to dislodge), then chewing on it contentedly. Avoid going anywhere near the young, whom the bison appear to accord both precedence and fierce protection in equal measure. The leader who brings them to the farm is brownish-grey with a white beard, and can only be described as stately. Bison have incredibly gentle faces and even gentler eyes.

If caught in the lights of a car at night, their eyes glow a fierce red. They run away, clear the fence, and face you on the road. You are advised to lower the beam when the leader, the last to jump the six-foot fence of bougainvillaea, lands as neatly as a cat a little ahead of the car. At that distance, your parking lights are enough to see the bison, and note the shrug of annoyance at being disturbed in his night sojourn as he tosses his head and swirls his horn at you. Then, snorting in irritation, he slowly saunters off. You pay the respect owed to him, and switch all your lights off.

That year, we grew bottle gourd and cucumbers for them, stringing the vegetables on the trees in their traditional path, which we plot by finding either hoofmarks or dung, or the cashew and mango saplings that they uprooted while scratching their necks and getting their horns entangled in the branches. Like you and I picking tufts of grass.

And wonder of wonders, otters do live in Goa. In 2013, Andrea went down to the river for a swim at the very spot where Paik's water comes into the Curca. That's the deepest part now, thanks to the mining, but is still good enough to sit in and have the water circle around your neck.

Andrea came back jumping up and down; when she's excited, she speaks in non-stop exclamations of delight accompanied by whoops and shoulder-shaking. Saying she can be incoherent is putting it mildly. One can't blame her, though, given how we had all just spoken about otters and she was the first to see them. She mistook them, like my kids did, for mongoose. But they were larger, maybe even longer and taller, with sleek grey-coloured coats almost flecked with white. They came in from Paik's water, as if trying to decide whether they should explore the Curca a little more. They did not see Andrea sitting in the water, or her head of unruly hair, and as a result, she was able to see them gambolling at the edge of the water for a good five minutes. In time, perhaps thinking that the prospect of fish is better upstream, they went back in a single file. She seemed to think they were gentle creatures with fin-like feet.

But then, from 2006 onwards, when the greed was at its height and the mines were expanding like there was no tomorrow, there were casualties, lots of them. Four Rottweillers. A German Shepherd. A crazy dog who was a cross between a Dalmatian and Doberman, and another who was a cross between a Great Dane and a Doberman. In 2010, the farm lost Simone, the Rottweiler, 'Classy Rottie' as we called her, who, just when the rains were less, wandered on the forest slopes at the side of the farm

For some strange reason, Simone was obsessed with fish and frogs. She would spend hours at the edge of the Curca, patiently stalking fish the size of your small finger, before parting her jaws like a seal and going in for the kill. 'She can bite the water with great panache,' we would tease Simone as she went about her curious activity. She is the only dog I have seen who could put her complete head under the water in search of fish for a good twenty seconds, biting, missing, searching some more, and then coming up gagging for breath.

She had a very set routine. A good half an hour before the sun broke, she'd head to the river where Paik's Spring came in, or track the spring up the mountains with her snout pressed to the ground. Along the cloisters of Butterfly Alley as we called it, to where the water broke to plain, with her snout pressed to the ground and breathing like a small bellows. If it was plump hare she saw in her head, what she'd do is end up hunting fish, then give up disgustedly, and come back to prowl the ponds in search of frog, and give up there too before coming in for her morning meal.

Between the river and the farm, we found the tree against which the leopard had nailed her, the bark gouged by scratch marks of a swipe that may have missed its target. Bits and pieces of black fur and bone lay on the ground.

Old Pauto, who's born and brought up in Maina and has been working on this farm for twenty years, always told us that there were tigers in the area. They ridiculed him by saying that he drinks too much feni, and then imagines things. But then, he is no drunk. He usually knocks down three neat shots over the period of an hour, each followed by a taste of hot mango pickle on the tongue, and then he heads off for dinner. In between, he becomes your historian.

Nobody believed him about the tigers, but that didn't stop him from narrating the stories. So I dug out Aki's books from the cupboard and showed him as many photographs of leopards as I could find. He got the spotted ones right, except for a cheetah or two that I slipped in. He swore on his dead father that he saw civet cats almost every night which wasn't that common now that Maina had been put to sword by mining.

He was right about the tiger too.

He was even more insistent about tigers after Simba disappeared on one of his early morning jaunts to the river in early 2009. Simba was a Rottweiler whom Tony religiously fed cod liver oil when he was a pup, and who got a regular workout chasing stones. Everyone gave up on throwing a ball to Simba because he'd run off after it, go exactly where it landed, and bring back a stone.

We never figured out what it was – Tony swore he had never given him steroids – but Simba ended up becoming as tall as a full-sized Doberman, and a lot broader than a Labrador. He was huge. Once, he pounced on a large bull that strayed into the farm and brought it to the ground, holding on to its neck so hard that four persons were needed to prise him off and save the bovine. Cheryl and Tony gave up figuring how much they'd have to pay in compensation with Simba around, although they never had problems with cattle straying into the farm again.

We saw him chew huge bones down to a pebble that he then swallowed, giving off a healthy contented burp. Simba's sign of affection was to take your elbow in his mouth and cajole you to the door so you could throw stones for him. Knowing what he could do to bone, we all threw stones for him to fetch. He was also like the proverbial camel: you could be reading a book, and he'd put his big head on your lap to be scratched. Then he'd put one paw on your lap, then the second one, and then climb on you and slobber all over your face. Everybody scratched Simba's head.

I would agree with Pauto that Simba was not taken by a leopard. I've seen him with a bull, he was fast and he was powerful: it would have been a no-contest with both sides retreating – with Simba's back where the leopard pounced from the tree, torn and bleeding from the gashes of a paw, but the leopard too, shocked and wary and smarting from the bite Simba's tough jaws would have given him back. Kenya, in the late 1950s and early '60s, had enough stories of leopards being fought off, wounded and even killed by a big farm dog, mostly pure Ridgebacks, but also those crossed with Labradors and given full meat diets.

We found bits and pieces of Simba stretched over an area of grass just under a large branch. No scratches on the trees, no signs of the grass around being disturbed by a fight – just the blood-stained spot where he was felled. Nobody wanted to follow the trail of bloodied trampled grass that led to the hill.

Conservationists say that there is absolutely no doubt that tigers roam the eastern slopes of the Western Ghats. The larger picture for Goa, in fact, is heartening. At the northeast is the Mhadei Wildlife Sanctuary. The sanctuary is named after the Mhadei, the river that originates in the ghats further east, and supplies most of north Goa with drinking water. It travels some 30 kilometres through Karnataka, where it is now being diverted upstream, some 10 kilometres through the Mhadei Wildlife Sanctuary, and some 50-odd kilometres though Goa, where it is joined by two other smaller but important rivers, the Volvonti and Surla. Downstream, they turn into the better-known and broader Mandovi that breaks at Panjim.

Below the Mhadei Wildlife Sanctuary are two more notified areas, the Bhagwan Mahaveer Wildlife Sanctuary and the Mollem National Park, from where originates the Khandepar river and the Dudhsagar falls. Both of them feed the Opa water treatment plant, which supplies drinking water to the capital, Panjim. (It is another story, of course, that because of existing mines dotting this river system itself, water department officials have been openly admitting that there is a consistently high level of turbid, ore-infected water coming into the plant.)

The officially protected sanctuaries of Mhadei, Mahaveer and Mollem form the Western Ghats that are northeast of Maina and Cawrem. The recently notified Netravali Sanctuary, in the ghats southeast of us, adjoins this with its own forest. Close to the Netravali Sanctuary, many springs make up the Kushawati, the river that passes due east. The Curca joins Kushawati along the way, which later breaks into Zuari's backwaters at the village of Xelvona, a couple of kilometres downstream from the southern mining capital of Sanvordem.

It is from a section of the Netravali Sanctuary that the water for the Selaulim dam goes, a dam built expressly to supply drinking water to south Goa villages, towns and cities. It is also another thing that there were mines hugging the edges of the dam not even 500 metres away from the water of the Selaulim dam. Despite repeated complaints from 2006 by Rama Velip and our other friends from Collomb, they continued to make their pits around the dam till a few months before the Justice Shah Commission arrived.

More westerly but still south of us, you have the Cotigao Sanctuary that hugs the border ghats with Karnataka and from where both the rivers Talpona and Galgibaga originate. These rivers supply drinking water to the southernmost parts of Goa via the Chapoli dam. There has been no reporting or sighting of mining operations around the Chapoli dam even though the southern coastal plateaus are said to be rich in bauxite. Goa's wishy-washy Regional Plan 2021 – now made even worse by being de-notified, perhaps even re-notified to please the infrastructure industry – seems to suggest that the Talpona and Galgibaga will be colonized by the lifestyle and leisure lobby as they reach the sea.

But, for the time being, let us keep human frailties aside, and think instead of the possibilities of a better life for the poor tiger.

A vital part of Karnataka's protected Dandeli reserve creeps into Goa northwards along the ghats. This, in turn, shames notions of border when it comes to nature and wildlife with Goa's protected areas encroaching into protected areas of both Maharashtra and Karnataka. All told, this gives us something in the region of over 600-odd square kilometres of notified forest and wildlife areas and – if you ignore the somewhat tunnel vision of real estate and industrial values – arguably it is the wealthiest quarter of Goa's landmass.

Now here's the funny thing—were it not for the mining lobby and successive governments that have toadied to them—Goa could be unique in notifying its entire stretch of forests in the Western Ghats as a protected area. As all conservationists of repute have been saying, accede to the demand that the Western Ghats be declared a UNESCO Heritage Site. It would certainly improve conditions for the tigers.

In this possible reserved area with its own patch of shrunken forest, is the tiny Bondla Wildlife Sanctuary. Being the heart of the mining corridor, it has just one paw of forested stretch leading to the larger chain of sanctuaries. This, as conservationists point out, provides a vital corridor for tigers, other wild cats and all wildlife from Maharashtra to Goa to Karnataka, and if environmentalists in Kerala and Tamil Nadu win the battle against energy-fuelled growth and more industrial development, then it extends further south.

My old friend Pauto, who brings the tiger into focus in this chronicle, has been off the bottle since that night a few years ago, when he was hit by the magic of a full moon, and he felt the urge to dance his way to Pandarpur. However, back when his tongue was still susceptible to the mystique of feni, I recall his tales of tiger sighting in Maina and Cawrem.

When Pauto was a teen, he and his father wandered the forests looking for the cashew trees they had planted, collecting ripe cashew apples to distil feni from, and nuts that they would roast and then sell in the Quepem Sunday Market. He'd laugh when I'd ask him how many times he had seen a tiger. Seeing tigers from afar and spreading the word before beating a hasty retreat from the area seemed to be a fairly frequent occurrence back then. After warning everybody to keep their cattle from straying, the villagers would come back the next day in greater numbers, making loud noises and beating the ground with sticks in the hope that the hullaballoo would force the tiger to stay in the forests. They gave the tiger the rigorous scrutiny it deserved.

The only time Pauto really understood what a tiger could do was when he was eighteen, and some villagers had gone past Jollerancho Dongor to the slopes to distil feni with water from a spring that no longer exists (thanks to the Magnum mine).

Someone from the village had also brought their cattle to graze on the slopes. Suddenly, there was a mighty roar, and the next thing they saw was a full-grown cow being attacked by a tiger. The cow went down without even an exclamation of pain – and Pauto, frightened out of his wits, ran all the way down to the plains of Maina with his companions and the rest of the cattle. Till the rains ended that year and well into the next year, no one from Cawrem took their cattle to those slopes. They beat the ground, shouted and collected their cashew produce in May, the time when cattle seek higher slopes for fresher grass and tigers come closer to human habitations because they are too lazy to hunt.

I still meet Pauto even though he doesn't work on the farm anymore. He's a resident consultant now. Whenever I spot him on a road, I stop the car and give him a lift. If he's going the other way, I ask him if I can buy him a drink. But no, he waves me away before I can tempt him.

In late 2009, after Simba was killed, I told him that Tulsidas from Cawrem had seen a cow being taken by a tiger. He had also come across the carcass of a downed bison.

'Do you believe me now?' Pauto asked.

Neither of Tulsidas's sightings was followed up by the authorities. In one of the blogs on tiger protection the next year, a forest official from Sattari in Goa said that the presence of three tigers had been confirmed at the Mhadei Wildlife Sanctuary near Anjunem dam. An assistant conservator of forests had also seen the pugmarks of a tigress and a cub. Pune-based tiger conservationist Anant Zanjale visited Charavane in Sattari, where a tiger killed two buffaloes. This is what he told a blogger: 'An adult tiger requires about 80 deer in a year as food. In comparison to the tough-to-catch deer, a solitary buffalo is an easy target. The Mhadei sanctuary is the apt habitat for tigers and needs to be protected on a priority.'[1]

Situated between Verle and Salgini villages in the Netravali Wildlife Sanctuary is a hill named Vaghdongor, or tiger hill. A resident close to the area, Puti Gaonkar, told the same blog, 'Villagers of Verle and Salgini have seen tigers at Vaghdongor and even lost cattle to the big cat.' One of the Salgini panches, Narayan Gaonkar, added: 'Our villagers have seen tigers on many occasions. We respect the presence of the big cat in the jungle and try to protect it.'[2]

Now, thanks to a Supreme Court ruling in December 2004, it has been declared that there can be no mining within ten kilometres of a wildlife sanctuary. But then, this is Goa, where the greedy hold sway and the politicians are hand-in-glove with the mining industry. The secretary for forests and water, Yaduvanshi, who also happened to be the secretary for mines, noted that Goa – being such a small mineral rich state – need not have a buffer zone around its wildlife sanctuaries. As of now, it is an issue that's still being debated.

The mission of Project Tiger, which is to 'ensure the maintenance of a viable Tiger population in India, and to preserve, for all time, areas of biological importance as a national heritage' was not, quite obviously, applicable to Goa. The official figures of tiger sighting and traces in Goa seem almost haphazard: three in 1993, five in 1997, five in 2002, and five in 2005.[3] If they finally brought out their tiger census of 2010, I haven't seen it.

As some conservationists demand that animal sanctuaries be cleared of human habitations, it is important to consider that an end to mining may be mutually beneficial to both wildlife as well as agriculturists. It may even be a chance to bring the eastern parts of Goa back to what the whole of Goa was twenty-five years ago, a territory that was under active cultivation.

Goan historians, for instance, point to the existence of some fifteen shrines in Goa dedicated to the appeasement of the tiger, and etymologically linked to the word 'Vagh', or 'Tiger'. These are – barring one or two in once-forested areas close to the coast in the north that have now been laid bare – in the rib of the mining corridor.

Ironically, all earlier festivity surrounding this was neither Catholic nor Hindu, but of indigenous, distinctly local, pastoral peoples who both feared and venerated the tiger.

At least two plates in Goan temples depict Guhalladeva II, one of the Kadamba rulers of Goa as Vyagramari, or the one-who-slew-tigers. That may not have been such a bad thing in those days, given that the Indian tiger population tallied to around 80,000 in 1900. In 1972, this had fallen to around 1,800, and then in 2010, further down to around the 1,500 mark. What the maharajahs and their colonial British hunter friends couldn't finish, the successive independent Indian governments did.

The earlier agricultural practices of the people and new profit-sharing marketing structures may be the only way of keeping mining away, while yet bringing back the natural rhythms to wildlife in the forests. One should not forget in these heady days of industrialization that landless agriculturalists like Pauto and his forefathers, who lived off the land at the edges of the forest and shifted their cultivation to let the soil come back to its natural state, once welcomed the leopard and tiger to keep the deer, hare and even the bison populations in their natural, undisturbed order. More importantly, the carnivores kept most of the large herbivores away from their ripening crops and fruits.

They all know in these parts that a small herd of seven bison could finish off a chilly plantation in an early morning graze and leave you staring at stalks drying in the morning sun. Monkeys can do the same thing to an orchard of ripening chikoos or mangoes, wastefully discarding a fruit after just one bite and – displaying a particularly human trait – reaching out for some more. After they see what a wild pig can do to standing crops like ripening sugarcane and pineapple, or what deer and hare can do to spinach and beans, they wouldn't mind a leopard or two roaming the edges of the surrounding forests.

Anil, who came to the farm from Jharkhand a couple of years before my friend Pauto found his redemption, was the one who told me why he hated the crested serpent eagle for stealing his hare.

Like Pauto, you had to give him a shot of feni, and then another, to get him to talk.

'Pauto says there are tigers here,' I tell him. 'Have you seen one?'

'They are here,' he says.

'Have you seen one?'

'I have heard one.'

'What's that supposed to mean?'

'It means I have heard a tiger.'

This kind of an answer calls for another shot, some chicken. I wait for him to finish licking his fingers. If you make the second shot a little stiffer, it helps.

Anil wanted to hunt. It was a part and parcel of his life back in Jharkhand. Unlike me, he had climbed every single one of the hills around here, and that was how he spent each one of his weekends. Like anglers, hunters too have their tales, and all of Anil's finds, regardless of my political correctness on the matter, landed up in his pot for his evening meal.

'The tiger,' I remind him, 'You said you heard a tiger. How do you know it was a tiger? Maybe it was a leopard...'

'A leopard's sound is like that of a big dog's. I have heard lots of those. The tigers are not close; they are maybe two or three kilometres inside the forest (He meant beyond the Curca behind the farm). There are plenty of deer there, and where there are deer, you have to have tiger.'

'Have you been inside?'

He laughs. 'I will go inside only if there are ten other people with me.'

'Where did you hear the tiger, then?

'At the river.'

'Which river?'

'Our river.'

'When?'

He looks at me as if I am stupid. 'How can I remember that?' he asks, 'It was the day I heard the tiger.'

'So, what did you hear?'

'That's the thing,' he says. 'You will know the sound when you hear it. It doesn't come from close by ... it comes from deep in the forest. I had gone down to the river in the morning to wash when I heard it. You know how loud the sounds of the machines in the mine are when the wind blows this side? Or how sometimes, when they put their explosives in, we all hear the sound? A tiger's sound is like that. I knew it was a tiger because all the birds stopped singing. There was no sound for almost five minutes. I was frightened.'

The mining lobby's argument of doing away with or lowering the buffer zone around Goa's sanctuaries (and in one case, even de-notifying it) is not only specious but also predicated on the false premise that people living in the vicinity or even in the sanctuaries, will have to be, by law, relocated. What happens if they turn out to be better custodians of the sanctuaries than those charged with actually protecting them? Why only sell them the line that they can invest in mining trucks and make money?

In February 2009, Goan journalist, teacher and well-known conservationist Rajendra Kerkar was to find out just how subservient Goa's forestry services were to mining interests. He reported the killing of a tiger by a family of Majik, an indigenous Goan community.[4] This took place in the foothills of the forests below Vagheri, Goa's third highest mountain peak at 3,500 ft., which literally means 'abode of the tiger'. Given that the information as well as the photographs were given to him by one of his students, who wished to remain anonymous, Rajendra refused to disclose his source of information.

A year later, he was charged with abetment to poaching, later dropped because it caused a furore among environmentalists.[5] Dr Claude Alvares of the Goa Foundation openly accused the state government of wanting to cover up the tiger killing at the behest of the highly influential mining industry in Goa.[6]

He was even more incensed with the chief conservator of forests, Shashi Kumar, who he rightfully said 'was more interested in sustaining mining than the forests'.[7] He was right about that, because a few years earlier, when we took on Joaquim Alemao, minister for urban development in the recently sacked Congress government, we saw just how ineffective Shashi Kumar really was, and how, at the behest of mining interests, he politely swept a major offence under the carpet under the cover of the law.

Claude categorically told the media that Kerkar was being targeted to stifle the campaign for a tiger reserve in Goa.[8]

Ramesh Gauns, our stalwart from Bicholim, was equally forthright in reminding the media that there were nearly eighty-one mining leases in Sattari, the region where Rajendra said the tiger was trapped and shot dead. 'One of the reasons why the forest department is not interested in pursuing the tiger poaching case is because if the Sattari area is declared a tiger reserve, mining companies will have to bid goodbye to the mining leases there,' he stated.[9]

As the rains broke in 2011, at least one national TV channel and a telecom company had started a series of marketing blitzes intended to raise awareness on tiger conservation. Moreover, the mining industry in Goa was not to be left behind.

Dattaraj Salgaocar, the suave, elegant, dashing and beautifully groomed scion of a mining major in Goa, is also the chief patron of the beautifully restored Sunaparanta Centre of Arts and

Culture, Panjim, which opens into the wide expanse of the city as it slopes down the northern slopes of a hill overlooking the Mandovi.

This posh arts centre was set up in 2009, conceived by Margaret Mascarenhas, the well-known Goan novelist, art collector and curator who also manages and directs its day-to-day functioning. A large part of its funding comes from Dattaraj's generous personal endowment of Rs 25 lakh per annum as well as its own arts and cultural activities. The arts centre is housed in one of the three truly extraordinary heritage buildings Dattaraj's family has procured along the same road.

It was at this iconic arts centre that we found out that Dattaraj was also an enthusiastic wildlife photographer and specialized, no pun intended, in shooting tigers. To those who did not know of this, he duly had a photo-feature done on his exhibition by his own captive monthly magazine, Goa Today.

A young Goan, Fernando Velho, architect and avid conservationist, was quick to email the arts centre:[10] 'The current exhibition being held at Sunaparanta, to me, smacks of poor taste and bad curatorial practices. The promotion of tiger conservation is not well served by Mr Salgaocar, a person with a terrible environmental record. Furthermore, in my opinion, using a self-funded art platform to promote tiger conservation trivializes the matter.

'Mr Salgaocar, who has deeply entrenched mining interests in Goa, is part of a larger mining lobby that has used its financial and political muscle to actively dissuade the authorities from promoting the cause of the tiger in Goa. Surely the curator of the current exhibition is aware of the conflict of interest that arises when a person promotes the cause of tiger conservation in faraway Madhya Pradesh but plays a part in a movement that denies the existence of the animal in our own backyard? This, to me, is the disingenuous aspect of this exhibition.'

The director of the centre, Margaret Mascarenhas, wrote back to say there was no 'curator' for this particular exhibition, and that Dattaraj Salgaocar, in fact, was the chairman of Sunaparanta and had the right to showcase his photographs there.

'I will point out to you only this,' she wrote, adding to the insincerity a tiny pinch of pragmatism, 'If it brings money and attention to tigers, and if two major conservationists agreed to come and support the show at Raj's personal request, it can't be that bad. Here is my personal creed: What is important is what is done with the money, not where it comes from.'

The tigers themselves, of course, were to have a say in closing the chapter. In 2012, the MoEF had asked the state government to prepare a proposal for a tiger corridor. It was also predictably ignored with Manohar Parrikar, then the newly appointed chief minister of Goa, showboating and telling the media on the sidelines of a cabinet meeting that 'he was not convinced about the argument for a tiger reserve in Goa. So far, only one tiger has been spotted in the Mhadei. One sparrow does not make a summer.'[11]

Much before 2015, the media in Goa had already told us that the MoEF had confirmed the presence of five tigers.[12] In February 2015, Rajendra Kerkar was to report in the *Times of India*, Panjim, that a cow, which entered the Mhadei Wildlife Sanctuary, was attacked and killed by a tiger. This was also confirmed by officials of the forest department.

Deputy conservator of forests (wildlife division) Anil Kumar told him that, 'It (was) confirmed by our officials that the cow was killed by the tiger last week. Ponsuli area was witnessing tiger movement repeatedly on the borders of Pali and Hivre. The tiger killed the cow that entered the sanctuary while grazing.'

He further added: 'Whether it was the same tiger that killed a wild boar in Dongurli in April 2013 or a new one, our officials are still studying the collected evidence. That the Mhadei Wildlife Sanctuary accommodates tigers has been proved beyond any doubt.'

Since 2013, the forest department has been using the camera trap technique to identify the presence of tigers in Goa's forest area.[13] As per information Kerkar received from reliable sources, it was revealed that these pictures captured on a camera trap were of a new tiger.

Where the kids and I had halted, the water had stopped. There was no ribbon of water falling. The large rock that Zuri thought looked like a small elephant was just a big, hot and very sad rock – dry water marks running all the way down its sides to the bedrock, almost as if they were delicately painted tears. The pool that we dunked our heads in wasn't even a foot deep, and would never have made a good dam for beavers. Now that Andrea has given us the news of an otter sighting, others of its kind must have been gambolling here for a long time now. As if placed on one of the rocks for me to find was the splayed skeleton of a frog, the front bare and bleached, and the skin on its back dehydrated and crumpled. I dug among the stones and found nothing else. How do fish and frogs come this high anyway? What's the terror like when they know they can't get back to fresh water?

I don't look back at the forests. While I take a break, cramped in the small shadow of an overhang, I imagine I am photographing the dry watermarks. I select a few of the images, put them on my laptop and Photoshop them, heightening the contrast in some and brightening the others. Then I blow them up and showcase them at an exhibition of photographic art at a posh arts centre in Panjim, titled 'Drought'. And then, as Goa's glitterati choke on their wine and cheese, I smile.

During peak mining season, Maina and Cawrem were under siege. There was no cool breeze to dry one's sweat, just a slow heat that rose in steady waves. In the distance, keening growls and thunderous rumbles emanated from Fomento's machines.

I stand next to a rock that's as big as a posh villa belonging to one of the big mining families in Goa in Panjim or Margao or Vasco.

When I have my back to the mining pit, on my right is a path broad enough to ride a bike on. Towards its summit, the path veers left and disappears in a scraggly clump of dried grass, and above that is a rock towering a good twenty feet with very good footholds. I'd need to be a very tough monitor lizard to climb that, or maybe just ten years younger.

If I try to access the other side of the rock, on my left are thick trees merging with the rock then climbing even higher to the summit, which I still can't see. I'd have to climb the slope at fairly close to sixty degrees, and where it seems the grip will be solid enough I may just be able to climb up the eight feet that will take me to the roof of the rock. At that moment, a voice like Ujwala's comes back and says, 'Hey, don't push it, just look at the spring like you were supposed to.'

The source is worth a few tears, I reckon. Zuri would have cried for sure, which may well have got Zaeen and me started. I am left with my insides twisted and mangled, the horror frothing at my mouth. I see something sacred defiled. I pause and take a few deep breaths, but still can't rid myself of the feeling of eating dust. I spit.

I take away the newspaper wrapped around the beer. It's still cold, thanks to a trick I learned from my dad. I gulp down my beer at one go to feel the tart bitterness sear the back of my throat.

The architects who put together Goa's terribly flawed Regional Plan 2021 – the second avatar of an incredibly skewed plan first proposed by Babush Monserrate, the then Congress minister for town and country planning, and a few of his builder friends – did not pay enough attention to Goa's forests and its indigenous peoples. In fact, they paid them no attention whatsoever.

Had they even left the comfort of their conference rooms where they drew hypothetical grids and 'plans' for the rest of Goa and actually traversed these areas by car and foot, they may have come across lifestyles and cultures that could shape, alter or perhaps even cause them to reconsider their postulates. They took the easy way out by looking at the 'larger picture' that suited their own aspirations and lifestyles.

If there ever was a middle way in Goa, thanks to the mining mafia, no one really tried hard enough. They just went along for the ride because it brought them prestige.

While the Task Force for the Regional Plan identified only two 'sacred groves' in Goa, one wonders whether undergraduate students of anthropology, architecture or planning would not have done a better job of contextualising these. This would require talking to local villagers to understand the moorings of their reverence and the relationship of nature with the surrounding environment.

As I said earlier, in Goa, 'dongor', the word for hill, implies the existence of a thick forest. In fact there is no word for the almost surreal sight of a huge mound of barren waste, in either Konkani or Marathi. It is referred to by the more appropriate, almost onomatopoeic, English word 'dump'.

Around the time I had climbed this same hill with the kids, it was Pauto, a little tight with feni, who told me that all the dongors in Maina and Cawrem were now being given over to mines.

The tallest hill here, southeast of this dried spring, is known as Kollpurush – the Pot of the Spirit. Pauto didn't know what it meant or why it was called that, but Shashikala did. In fact, she knows more than Pauto about such things because she was born and raised in the ghats bordering Karnataka in the north of Goa. She was so scared when she married Pauto and moved to Maina, which was even more of a jungle than where she was born, that she needed to pray and ask other women about the shrines she could pray at.

It is out of such lived experiences that the 'sacred groves' in this area were created.

The Kollpurush shrine has just an old, empty mud pot containing a polished black stone. It is still used mostly by women praying for their family, young girls who want to find the partner of their dreams, and sometimes, men who do the same thing more secretly. They walk up the steep path carrying their slippers in one hand, while using the other to help themselves up steps made by water flowing down rocks to reach the shrine. They untie fiery orange marigolds tied to their waist and place them on rocks rich with iron, wash the mud pot and the black stone, fill the pot with water, drink from it and before beseeching the shrine with bowed head, wash the pot, drain it and place it back with the black stone in it for the next pilgrim. It is a shrine propitiated with stark spirituality.

Sitting here on a hill ten years too late, I mourn the loss of water. What ancient reverence did the mining operations defile? One could say of the simplest kind: a giant rock as old as the earth perhaps, placed at the side of this hill, such that it caps the water from an aquifer while yet giving it recourse to flow. At its base, smothered by rocks remained just a hole, big enough for a small dog to crawl through.

If I was a creature small enough, I'd go in only to test my thesis that as much as human beings may have figured out how they can map the surface areas on this planet that they see, then apportion them, or fight over them, or even lay claim to plunder them as and when they see fit, they have not yet understood that deep below the surface, where they can't see, there are sophisticated systems and patterns of water that bind hills and forests and rock and earth such that water will abound and always be present to deliver forth life.

I slither down, and put my face into the hole. There is a distinct smell of dampness, but it is not dank. Smell-wise, it gives off the fragrance of fertile earth a few days after rains. There's an essence to it; in this case one of water coming into contact with smooth stone.

I turn my face and put my ear to the hole. Try as I might, I cannot hear the echoed gurgling of a spring lying dormant while it waits for the first rains to break, the aquifer around it filled in a day or two with the pressure of water seeking space and then, suddenly breaking free.

If we are lucky, judging by the fragrance of water that still lingers, there may still be an inner stream deeper than what I can hear. The water there lies in wait for the rains so it can create another aquifer between ore and rock, building in weight until maybe it finds its way out as a spring on a lower slope south of this hill, and much further south of the mines. If we put a complete and total halt to all mining in the area, will this spring ever come back?

To my side, going downhill, the steps, the path, the little falls of rock, the entire course is discoloured with various shades and textures of dryness. We have a drought-like situation in October 2009. Barely ten years back, in hot midsummer, if the kids and I had climbed up we'd have actually seen the magic of this water spilling out at the height of the sun.

You could say that the view from the summit was spectacular. I got to see life. Like a Goan mining magnate sitting in his private helicopter, sipping French wine and surveying the sheer span of hill and forest, wilfully destroyed in the guise of being 'legal'.

I spit.

It was just before noon, the breeze cool but the sun sharp as any fire from hell. From this distance, all the mining operations were covered in giant cotton balls of red dust, each thinning as they climbed, then spreading outwards like filigree. When the morning dew fell, it would wet settled dust, which would then slowly bake in the hot sun to cast a harsh and impermeable veneer over life itself.

In the distance you could see the orange mining trucks, bumper-to-bumper, strung out like railway carriages across the wide Fomento pit, grunting and waiting their turn to load. The sounds accompanying this were muted and discordant. I spit again.

They dug pits everywhere, deep enough to suck water from all the aquifers nearby, including this stream that I traced to its source. When their pits filled with water during the rains, they pumped this water out to dig deeper, with each successive length excavating downwards, drying even more water as they let it run to the sea. Alternatively, it would mix with wasted mud from the pits to turn an otherwise fertile agricultural plot of land into a turgid swamp, or just disappear deep into the ground – probably never to return.

The buzzword for dealing with tragedy is 'closure', perversely the same word used in the mining industry to refer to an agreement (never reached in Goa), whereby a mine submits a report showing how it will stop operations and subsequently regenerate the mine.

So now, leaning back against a rock that once capped the water here and let it spurt out between the dry rocks on which I sit, and viewing a tragedy of such massive proportions, what 'closure' can one seek?

I drank one bottle of Paik's water coming up, and kept one for the way back. I unscrew the cap. Slithering back to the hole at the base of the rock, I upend the bottle and wait there, ear to the hole, listening to the very last echoes of the splashes and drops.

AFTERWORD

I began wrapping this chronicle up in Pune, on a morning in mid-June 2015. There was just a light drizzle, and every so often, clouds breaking apart to let pleasant sunshine sneak onto the balcony and into the room. On the big yellow hibiscus outside, Ujwala's daily visitor, a glossy blue-black sunbird, swung upside down.

None of this brought cheer.

Our fifteen-year-old loveable Bangalore-born stray, Monsieur Bernard Cacao aka Koko, a gentle creature who has never ever bitten anyone in his life, had just been savagely attacked by two vicious dogs, both on leashes, who broke free from their handler.

These were house-trained dogs bored with just baring their fangs at unwelcome visitors before being shepherded to a chain in the balcony, where they stood growling, eyes burning – pleading to be set free, just once, even for a few seconds, to bite into flesh and taste blood.

They hurtled at the two of us. One was an uncommonly vicious Labrador with strong teeth; the other, a dog of mixed breed, with a whippy tail, the body, strong shoulders, long snout and powerful jaws of a Doberman and a colouring that could pass for a Brindle. A dark-skinned hyena now makes more sense. This one did the most damage.

Their handler, a man hired by the dogs' owners to walk them, stood there helplessly shrieking out their names and yelling 'Arre baba, arre baba' on and on like a prayer.

I gave into instinct ten seconds too long. I kicked the Labrador under his ribs, twice, the second hard enough for him to leave Koko and stumble away dazed, letting a bystander grab his leash and haul him away. The monster got my kick flush on his testicles; and ran squealing in pain, tail between his legs fanning his burning insides.

Then I had to stand there, tears of rage in my eyes, and watch Koko bleed on the road. The owner's first words to me were: ''They have been given their rabies shots, not to worry.'

She spoke to her handler in Marathi, scolding him. 'See,' she said, 'how many times I have told you not to take the dogs for a walk together?'

She turned to me. In Hindi she told me the fault was hers, and then added in English: 'You please not to worry, just you give me the bills. I will pay all charges.'

We nursed Koko for more than three weeks. He had had his paw bitten, his tail chewed; there were deep bite marks on his fluffy neck and a three-inch tear just where his slim, elegant chest meets his haunch. He was hurting. He limped. He looked really sad. Like he was going to die – which is what I actually thought.

Beginning to think about and write this afterword having watched him being viciously attacked the way he was, only defines my despair and loss of hope further.

Was Koko being viciously attacked any different from the five mining operations between Maina and Cawrem that stripped the hills and the forests bare in that span of exponential greed that took off in 2006?

What about the mining barons who from the late 1950s have ravaged ninety kilometres or so of the eastern slopes of the Western Ghats all the way down to their skeletal remains? What about the privileged Goans who tenaciously hold on to the myth that mining is the backbone of the Goan economy?

So yes, of course I condone the two dogs that attacked Koko. I bare my fangs at the dogs' owner and others like her.

What does one do to those people who know, better than they have ever known before, that the hills and forests and water, and not just in Goa, are being pillaged by industry and government working in tandem? This is especially true of those areas in central India where the poorest in the country have their dwellings on resources badly needed to fuel higher growth rates.

Too many, all too easily appear to have bought into the idea that a big fat GDP is what the larger story is all about. Almost all eventually swallow the specious argument that the benefits of growth trickle down and will mitigate the harsh glare of poverty.

In Pune, I have seen the son of a construction worker from the time he was a tiny baby whom I could tickle and make laugh. He is Koko's friend, so we have seen him grow together. He is now eight years old, goes to school, and speaks Marathi, Hindi and the Bengali of his parents. When we bump into him playing on the road with his friends, I give him a little practice in speaking English.

He is most definitely a young Indian who has had his identities broadened. But in the last eight years, within the radius of a quarter of a kilometre, he has moved home three times – from a tiny tin-hut on a construction site where his parents once worked, to two other such tin-huts, equally small and messy, on new construction sites where they now labour.

So when are the fruits of high growth expected to fall for someone like my young friend?

Jason Hicks, an anthropologist who works out of the London School of Economics, effectively shreds the trickle-down argument of the rich and famous.[1] He writes that 'given our existing economic model, poverty eradication can't happen'. In fact, he's far more assertive. 'Not that it probably won't happen', he adds, 'but that it physically can't. It's a structural impossibility'.

If we assume, he argues, 'that we can maintain the fastest rate of income growth that the poorest 10% of the world's population have ever enjoyed over the past few decades (between 1993 and 2008), then during that period, their incomes increased at a rate of 1.29% each year'.

If we extrapolate this, how long will it take to eradicate poverty, asks Hicks. While his answer of 100 years is horrifying, it actually gets worse.

Hicks reminds us that the data he uses does not capture 'the poorest 1% of the world's population, who will still remain in poverty even at the end of this period. And that, as he pronounces, is '90 million people, more than the entire population of Germany today, who will remain in poverty forever'.

Hicks is as good a prophet of doom as you can get. The optimistic scenario of a big fat GDP, he writes, makes no mention of the fact that prices of food have 'effectively wiped out the incomes of the poor over the past few years, or the fact that climate change is already unravelling development gains across the global south'.

It is an attitude of optimism Hick suggests, that 'imagines all of this away and assumes that no further economic or ecological crises will happen in the next 100 years – which is a very big assumption indeed'.

He keeps his best for the last, mentioning that a growing number of scholars are beginning to point out that $1.25/day is not enough to survive on. 'In reality,' he writes, 'if people are to meet their most basic needs and achieve normal human life expectancy, they need closer to $5/day.'

'How long would it take to eradicate poverty at this more accurate line?' Hicks asks.

And here comes the clincher. Only 207 years.

I was back in Goa in July after Koko's wounds had healed and he was back to jumping on the bed, messing the bedspread and inviting Ujwala's wrath. The monsoon had begun to show its might.

Maina and Cawrem were as beautiful as I remembered, barring all the new dwellings that have come up in the three years since I was last here.

If there were people who really suffered because of the ban on mining in 2012, you don't see this on the same old road that kick-started this chronicle. Thanks to government doles (because Goa's indigenous people, when all is said and done, are also important vote banks), you see new dwellings come up on forestland, every house with a dish to grab 150 or whatever channels, new motorcycles and even new cars. There seems to be only prosperity afoot. There are hardly any mining trucks around.

This is as close as you will get to the days before the Age of Greed transformed Maina and Cawrem. The ground around the mines had changed miraculously. If the large fences had not been there, if you didn't know there was a mine there, you would not have seen it – taken over as all five mines were, by thick shrub and trees a good metre and a half high.

There are some who say it takes thirty years for the forest to recover from damage done to it. That's pessimistic. Seeing what happens to trees and shrub over several monsoons in Maina and Cawrem, I would say nature would be restored in an abandoned mine in half that time. The Fomento pit had become a small and very deep lake. I dreamt of stocking it with carp. Maybe I could show Aki how to build a small raft and attach a sail to it.

Cheryl's farm was lovely. I visited every single tree that I planted over the years there. The dogs were all crazier than ever. Brutus, Simba's son, is the new alpha male, and is now surrounded by a greying Kiara, a great dane, and her two daughters, born of a Doberman mate. One of them, also named Simone, has an obsession with trying to grab small frogs and tiny fish. The tiny Curca, like it did every monsoon, showed everyone how it could also run truly wild. Andrea, 27, duly introduced two other newer members of the ensemble, Katheeja Talha, 27, and Heidi Pereira, all of 19, to the joys of a natural Jacuzzi and the virtues of voice exercises that we do under water.

I did not accompany them. It was cloudy, dark, gloomy and cold, so I brooded on the dining table in Cheryl's mammoth kitchen, tasting several samples of the new season's feni dutifully stored for me.

After the Shah Commission's damning findings, I secretly hoped that the Honourable Justices of the Supreme Court would constitute a special bench and visit Goa to see with their own eyes what the mining had done.

Thanks to Justice Shah, and later a centrally empowered committee, I was sure that the earth in Goa would finally have a sincere and honest advocate. We were naïve of course. We convinced ourselves that such a visiting bench would strongly recommend that the Rs 35,000 crore said to be looted be promptly returned, with a stiff fine to boot; that the rogues, specially the politicians involved, would be awarded stiff jail sentences; that the mining barons would be forced to repair the damage they have caused over a half-century.

And, more importantly that the bench would ban mining in Goa for the next fifty years.

As all of us now know, that was just an idealistic high.

On 10 August 2015 – ironically, just a day after we commemorate 'Quit India Day' –Goa's latest chief minister, Laxmikant Parsekar, a man handpicked by the former chief minister Manohar Parrikar after he was inducted into the Central government, duly broke a coconut at a British multinational's gates and kick-started its mining operations in Goa.[2]

The other mining barons, respectful of the earth as ever, will duly wait for Ganesha to arrive with great fanfare so that he can be garlanded with hundreds of bright flowers and submerged in a mining pit that has collected the rains since 2012. A few days later, they will start pumping water out to run free down to the river, and out to sea.

Elsewhere, one can expect silence, as Goans and other Indians hide behind the argument that this much environment must go for the sake of that much 'development' to happen. Even when this is an argument as hollow as one that puts faith in new technologies to miraculously emerge to solve all the earth's problems.

It is always the earth that has the problems, never human beings.

And, now when all is said and done, even the highest authority in this country has rejected the thought that the forests and waters need to be seen as national treasures; that they be kept in custody for those yet to come.

By the time Vedanta, with great fanfare began its mining operations in Goa and promptly noted they would lobby to increase the mining cap set by the Supreme Court, I had left the village of Maina and the foothills behind and was in Assagao in north Goa with the ensemble. We were collaborating with my old friend, the jazz pianist, Steve Siqueira, and rehearsing for a forthcoming tour to Delhi.

Was it prescience that well before the Supreme Court decided to lift the ban on mining in Goa, we had collectively decided to create a new piece against mining and use for its ending the poem that ends this chronicle?

So yes, it is true: they can 'legally' take away the forests and mud and water. There are some of us left with nothing but the fading memories of a moral victory. We console ourselves knowing that our idealism was always there for the long haul.

None of what has transpired then, and now, means that we are going to calmly look the other way.

Whatever has happened after the Supreme Court lifted the ban on mining may not be as clear cut as all that.[3] When Parrikar, then still chief minister, unilaterally decided to renew twenty-seven mining leases, the Goa Foundation re-entered the fray. In an interview in *Frontline* in September 2014,[4] while he elegantly deconstructed the legal issues involved, Dr Claude Alvares was also asked a pertinent question:

'Three reports of the Shah Commission,' the interviewer asked, 'the reports of the Central Empowered Committee, and the Supreme Court judgement have thrown up many issues of alleged illegality/irregularity. What happens to all of that? Is it back to square one as some say?'

In his answer, Claude was back to his feisty best. 'I am yet to discover any aspect of the Goa mining activity of the past 10 years that is legal in any manner,' he replied. 'What is astonishing is that the Goa government feels that it can go back to the same companies involved in illegal mining to restart mining operations and to get new leases ... There is an effort made to distinguish so-called fly-by-night operators from genuine miners. This is rubbish. The principal mining companies were responsible for most of the illegal mining. The traders only deal with the small change, the leftovers.'

He added: 'The Mines Act requires the government to punish people involved in illegal mining, leases are supposed to be cancelled. People involved cannot be granted fresh leases. However, in Goa, the chief minister is now going to reward them.'

The Goa Foundation now threatens to approach the courts if the state government did not move soon to recover monies from illegal mining, which by the Foundation's own 'conservative' estimates stood at a whopping Rs 1,18,661 crore.[5]

On the night of Monday, 24 August 2015, Dr Claude Alvares addressed a meeting of some sixty or so people at the weekly event organized by People Tree, a design studio and store in Assagao, barely a hop, skip and jump away from where the ensemble were staying.

Claude was there because his wife Norma could not make her intended presentation on the ills of bringing in the American hospitality industry to Tiracol. The main feature of the evening would be Rahul Basu, a former finance executive from the ill-fated Enron project in Maharashtra who had been handpicked by the Goa Foundation to spearhead its Goenchi Mati (Goa's Mud) Permanent Fund (GMPF) launched and endorsed with great fanfare by four Goans who had been awarded the Padma Shri.[6] It argues that the people of Goa are the owners of all the ore in the state and that the money should stay with the people, not mining barons. As of now, 1.3 billion tonnes of iron ore worth Rs 404,460 crore remain, and the GMPF argues that all money from it should go to the GMPF, which will have an independent administrator.

The Goan Mud Fund doesn't excite me, though. Is it not a cynical appeal to greed? It sells the larger Goan public the idea that we can do away with land and water sources as long as the people themselves get the wealth.

Once you had Goans who pretended not to see the greed of mining, now you will have Goans who consciously take away their own hills, forests, water and mud and take coin for doing so.

Is such cynicism truly called for? Are there alternatives? In April 2013, the Supreme Court set up a 'special purpose vehicle' for mines in Karnataka, which drew revenue from fines, cancelled leases and sales proceeds. This body was directed to use the entire amount to benefit people living in Bellary, Chitradurga and Tumkur.[7] This is the alternative, the model that will better involve people there in repairing the damage.

Also, even within the GMPF model, why did Goa Foundation settle for just 10 per cent? It had pleaded with the Supreme Court that 50 per cent of the profits from mining accrue to the people to ensure 'intra generational equity'.[8]

Lastly, is the corpus of such a Mud Fund going to be the Rs 1,18,661 crore that the Goa Foundation expects the court to repatriate to the people? Or is this just a loophole the mining companies will use to continue with a clean slate?

At a meeting to promote the further eating of dust, no less a veteran ecologist than Dr Madhav Gadgil – hardly a friend of Goa when she most needed him[9] – backed another Goan Mud Fund venture. This one was launched with much lesser fanfare by the villagers of Cawrem. Since they have the trucks and know the machinery, they now propose a village co-operative that will take out the forests and water and mud.

Andrea and Heidi had already heard of the GMPF from Rahul Basu over lunch with a common friend visiting from Lahore. A very late entrant to the opposition to mining, Rahul was probably unaware that Andrea, aged all of twenty-two in 2008, without funds, dependent entirely on what we could earn through theatre, had begun extensively photographing the devastation caused by mining.

In fact, Andrea was one of the driving forces that organized the 'MTV (Mining Transport Venom) Road Trips' – getting friends her age to hire a small bus and taking them down the mining corridor. Starting off with breakfast in Margao, then through Quepem Town, past the mines at Cawrem and Maina, and onto Collomb and the beginning of the grim 90-kilometre mining corridor that goes northwards. With enough help forthcoming, she did this in the monsoon season, and even as the mining kick-started.

Andrea did not take kindly to the Goan Mud Fund the first time she heard about it. She described it as a document that was only full of numbers. Heidi, who took time off after her twelfth standard to intern with the ensemble, saw her first mine when she was fifteen.

It was a very important book that Claude edited, the iconic *Fish Curry and Rice*,[10] a copy of which was given to her when she turned seventeen, that sharpened Heidi's focus on Goa's environmental concerns.

I left the three of them to deal with Goa's ill-named Mud Fund.

The three young women came back somewhat flustered. Heidi was the most shocked. 'There were these two guys,' she said, 'that came up to me after our performance at People Tree and said how happy they were to see someone as young as me showing concern for the environment.' She seemed surprised. 'Today,' she said, 'they were viciously pro-mining!'

Andrea laughed. 'When they started talking of 'ethical greed', I knew exactly what was coming.'

The proceedings began with a CSR-like film on 'universal basic income' after which Rahul Basu made his pitch. Goa could become a model state, implementing a 'basic income' from the GMPF, and this money distributed monthly irrespective of class, caste, gender and age. The whole scheme, he added, 'reeks of equality'. Not that there was no idealism. The audience was told that this could be replicated throughout the country, cutting across narrow party lines and unite both the left and the right, the BJP and the Congress.

Andrea opened the discussion that followed, bluntly stating that the GMPF was a joke. Why talk about money, she asked, why are we not taking about the Western Ghats?

There's not even a trace of 'ecology' in the damn brochure,' Katheeja added. She was livid. 'No one seemed to care that the word "ore" is used in the document thirty times and the Western Ghats referred to just twice.'

She said the only anomaly in the brochure was a page titled 'Destruction of our Natural Wealth'.

'Somewhere in the middle of this narrative,' she said, 'rather abruptly, the page speaks of hotspots and forests and rivers, using a language that one might expect from the Goa Foundation'. This shift, Katheeja added, was chilling. 'It is like stumbling upon the Corporate Social Responsibility page of a large corporation, perhaps Vedanta or Unilever, after reading their annual report.'

The audience would listen elsewhere. As if on cue Rahul told them that the looting that had happened was a case of 'unethical greed'.

'There was this guy in his forties who interrupted,' Andrea said, 'and asked what was ethical greed. And Rahul answered that we were all greedy in some way. Don't we all desire something material?'

Heidi said that Claude took over and said that we were all idealistic, but now we have to get practical. Can anyone stop mining, he asked the young women, can any of you? There was a chorus of voices from two film-makers, a writer and assorted designers and architects asking them how they would stop the mining. Tell us how, they thundered.

Rahul Basu, not to be left out, told the gathering that it was the Goa Foundation that had stopped the mining in the first place. He asked the women not to think just about the money recovered from illegal mining, but focus on the future of mining. While Claude told them that he could not share the Foundation's plans about mining in public because the mining companies 'would get after his skin', he shrugged off all critique with the question, 'What have you done to stop mining?'

The man who had asked what 'ethical greed' meant, consoled the three women when they exchanged contact details. The woman with him shook her head. 'I don't know why there is a Plan B? We should put everything behind Plan A, which is to stop mining.'

The last word on the GMPF must rightfully go to Heidi, nineteen years old and blessed with the kindling that still takes to dreaming.

'There was something that I had to do, so I followed Claude out. He went up to Rahul and told him how tired he was of people like us, how he would love to see us take up his fight to stop mining just to watch how we end up. After seeing me, Rahul walked away so I went up to Claude.

'I told him how much of a role model he was to us students in Carmel College. He beamed. I told him I had respect for him till I heard him tonight. He got angry with me. He told me how naïve I was to miss the bigger picture, that I was fixated on something that could not be achieved. He told me he was tired of fighting for a lost cause and would much rather spend his time securing the future of us Goans. He didn't seem to care what I thought.

'I was angry too, I told him that he had given up, how could any young Goan look up to someone who doesn't stand up for what he believes in. Disgusted, he left, saying I was too young to know what I was talking about. Then he turned and said with a smirk that I was going to regret being so idealistic.'

In these chronicles I take my appointed place as the anti-hero. I tasted the bitterness and bile. The mining seasons of 2008–09 were my darkest days in Maina. All of us felt sure Paik's Spring was in serious threat of being destroyed.

I was sitting in the travesty that now passes for his temple. It was a hot afternoon in mid-April, that season of mining when you feel the heat and taste the dust in the air. We were just returning from one of our walks behind the mines to take photographs. I was angry, yet helpless. I said I'd meet the rest back at the farm later. I took Andrea's notebook and her pen.

I imagined a spring created by a divine custodian, slowly but surely dying, then the hill bereft of his forest drying in the hot noon sun, and then Paik himself, standing in the blazing mud and cursing:

Paikdev Curses

Know that I was born before your mothers spread their legs and seeded squealing children covered in the grime of birthing, washed in my waters to bring their young tender skins gleaming to life...

Know that without me all of you will only be as strong as the thickest of the branches that trembled before the whirring, gleaming axe-heads of your machines that cut through them like a hot knife through butter...

Know that I am the first-born of Devapan Dongor, this forest where God lives, where the trees were once sacred and the waters so precious people prostrated before these hills that touch the clouds, block out the sun; to know me pilgrims walk across three valleys, cross four streams, climb over rocks and touch the faces of snakes with their bare feet, insects and spiders with their hands and faces, leaves and branches with their bodies; then stooping, bending, bowing, tasting my sweetness, reaching up to touch, kiss my fern-lined mouth, stroke my moss-covered, burnt, burnished iron-rock hard face...

Know that when you hack the trees and bury the bodies under a hill of mining waste that you think no one will ever find; when you level the hills and bring monsters to dig a road deep into my heart, ripping out the mud to haul it away, sucking my waters like a leech greedily drawing blood, pumping out my sweetness mixed with dead mud to dry in the sun clogged with the dirt of life about to die; or driven away, friendless, out to the sea, never to return...

Know then that I will return in vengeance, my smile twisted, my eyes inspiring hate, my open mouth giving birth to heat, my tongue a cruel blade of fire...

Know that I will laugh in a terrible howl when you fall on your knees and pray and beg, when each one of you is the last alive, forced to watch with a terrible rage, but feeble and helpless, when your families and your children plead for water in hoarse voices even as I dry their spittle and burn their faces to spare them the shame of digging into the earth with bloodied fingernails for my waters...

My waters that you just took away...

Know before you choke on your last breaths, before you atrophy into the lifeless mud created by you, that my last smile to you will be fanned by flames a deep orange...

Pune and Goa, June–September 2015.

NOTES

A Bird's Eye View

1 Lionel Messias and I go back many moons, from the days we both were kids in Mombasa playing football. He has a solid pedigree as a journalist, and is now the editor of Goan Spirit (www.goanspirit.com) where his many articles can be found.

2 TNN, 'Citizens joins forces at Tiracol to oppose golf course project', *The Times of India*, 8 June 2015, http://timesofindia.indiatimes.com/city/goa/Citizens-joins-forces-at-Tiracol-to-oppose-golf-course-project/articleshow/47577593.cms, accessed on 6 August 2015.

3 Kenneth Bo Nielsen, 'Mopa Airport Woes: Debating the proposed airport in North Goa', *Economic and Political Weekly*, 20 June 2015, http://www.epw.in/reports-states/mopa-airport-woes.html, accessed on 6 August 2015.

4 Hartman de Souza, 'RAPE: Rapid Assessement Pauperised Environment', *HardNews*, 5 April 2010, http://www.hardnewsmedia.com/2010/04/3519, accessed on 6 August 2015.

5 Rediff.com, 'Story of Brazen Illegal Mining in Goa', 8 December 2012, http://www.rediff.com/news/report/detailed-report-story-of-brazen-illegal-mining-in-goa/20121208.htm, accessed on 6 August 2015.

6 Neshwin Almeida, 'Activists urge Margao citizens to lead uprising against Sonsoddo', *Herald*, 3 July 2015, http://www.heraldgoa.in/Goa/Citizen-Herald/Activists-urge-Margao-citizens-to-lead-uprising-against-Sonsoddo/90555.html, accessed on 6 August 2015.

7 Neshwin Almeida, 'Sonsotto Sunset?', *The Goan*, 9 November 2013, http://www.thegoan.net/Emirates-Edition/Sonsoddo-sunset/06514.html, accessed on 6 August 2015.

8 PTI, 'Goa to bring ordinance to save five-star resort', 26 February 2009, http://timesofindia.indiatimes.com/city/goa/Goa-to-bring-ordinance-to-save-five-star-resort/articleshow/4194603.cms, accessed on 6 August 2015.
See also, Sreelatha Menon, 'Goa poll heads for five-star controversy', *Business Standard*, 7 March 2009, http://www.business-standard.com/article/economy-policy/goa-polls-head-for-five-star-controversy-109030700014_1.html, accessed on 6 August 2015.
Hartman de Souza, 'Formento and Corporate Social Responsibility, my a$$', Goanet.org, 20 February 2009, https://www.mail-archive.com/goanet@lists.goanet.org/msg42542.html, accessed on 6 August 2015.

9 TNN, '12 years later, the *River Princess* saga continues', *The Times of India*, 18 December 2012, http://timesofindia.indiatimes.com/city/goa/12-years-later-the-River-Princess-saga-continues/articleshow/17659357.cms, accessed on 6 August 2015.
Also see: Pushpa Iyengar, 'At long last, Goa to bid *River Princess* goodbye', *DNA*, 25 October 2006, http://www.dnaindia.com/india/report-at-long-last-goa-to-bid-river-princess-goodbye-1060191, accessed on 6 August 2015.

10 Nisser Dias, 'The MV River Princess Saga', *targetgoa.com*, 23 September 2010, http://www.targetgoa.com/NISSER-DIAS/The-M-V-River-Princess-saga/64, accessed on 6 August 2015.

11 Joseph Zuzarte, 'Raising the dust on illegal mining in Goa', *inforchangeindia.org*, September 2011, http://infochangeindia.org/environment/features/raising-the-dust-on-illegal-mining-in-goa.html, accessed on 6 August 2015.

12 Rediff.com, 'Supreme Court bans Mining in Goa', 5 October 2012, http://www.rediff.com/news/report/supreme-court-bans-mining-in-goa/20121005.htm, accessed on 6 August 2015.

13 Government of British Columbia, 'Mining, Market Opportunity Profile, India', June 2011, http://www.britishcolumbia.ca/export/documents/india_mining.aspx, accessed on 6 August 2015.

14 Herald, 'Not DLF or Oberoi, but PE firms will be the first to hit the market', 25 August 2014, http://www.heraldgoa.in/Herald-Realty/Not-DLF-or-Oberoi-but-PE-firms-will-be-first-to-hit-the-market/77607.html, accessed on 6 August 2015.

15 Nalini Nayak and A.J. Vijayan, 'The Coasts, the Fish Resources and the Fishworkers' Movement', *National Human Rights Commission*, New Delhi, 2006, page 36, http://bhrc.bih.nic.in/Docs/Fishworkers.pdf, accessed on 6 August 2015.

16 Zeeshan Shaikh, 'Churchill Alemao: From daily wager to chief minister to jail', *The Indian Express*, 7 August 2015, http://indianexpress.com/article/india/india-others/churchill-alemao-from-daily-wager-to-chief-minister-to-jail/, accessed on 6 August 2015.

THE MINING PIT

1 TNN, 'Goa's flora and fauna rejoice as mining comes to a grinding halt', *The Times of India*, 30 December 2012, http://timesofindia.indiatimes.com/city/goa/Goas-flora-fauna-rejoice-as-mining-comes-to-grinding-halt/articleshow/17813220.cms, accessed on 6 August 2015.

2 Sreenivasan Jain, 'Goa: Land mines', *NDTV*, 8 November 2011, http://www.ndtv.com/india-news/goa-land-mines-565310, accessed on 6 August 2015.

3 Murari Shetye, 'Sesa, Formento biggest ore exporters in 2011–12', *The Times of India*, 17 November 2012, http://timesofindia.indiatimes.com/city/goa/Sesa-Fomento-biggest-ore-exporters-in-2011-12/articleshow/17249502.cms, accessed on 6 August 2015.

4 Data from the official website: http://fomento.com/sales.html.

5 Krishna N. Das, 'Top iron ore exporter Goa wants to halve fresh output', *Reuters*, 7 November 2013, http://in.reuters.com/article/2013/11/07/india-ironore-goa-idINDEE9A607N20131107, accessed on 6 August 2015.

6 Pamela D'Mello, 'Pits of Corruption', *Frontline*, 5–18 November 2011, http://www.frontline.in/static/html/fl2823/stories/20111118282304400.htm, accessed on 6 August 2015.

7 TNN, 'Goa pollution board raps 40 mines for excess production', *The Times of India*, 6 April 2012, http://timesofindia.indiatimes.com/city/goa/Goa-pollution-board-raps-40-mines-for-excess-production/articleshow/12552098.cms, accessed on 6 August 2015.

8 ENS, 'Cream of Goa politics under mining cloud', *Expressindia.com*, 3 October 2011, http://expressindia.indianexpress.com/karnatakapoll08/story_page.php?id=854722, accessed on 6 August 2015.

9 Formento Resources, 'Touching Lives', August 2011, http://fomento.com/editorial/August%202011.pdf, accessed on 6 August 2015.

10 Joaquim Fernandes, 'Government planning to build mining bypass road in South Goa', *The Times of India*, 6 December 2010, http://timesofindia.

indiatimes.com/city/goa/Govt-planning-to-build-mining-bypass-road-in-South-Goa/articleshow/7049991.cms, accessed on 6 August 2015.

11 PTI, 'Louis Berger Bribery Case: Former Goa minister Chuchill Alemao arrested, says he is innocent', *Firstpost.com*, 6 August 2015 http://www.firstpost.com/politics/louis-berger-bribery-case-former-goa-minister-churchill-alemao-arrested-says-he-is-innocent-2380962.html, accessed on 6 August 2015.

12 TNN, 'In 2007, 5 MLAs were crorepatis', *The Times of India*, 11 January 2012, http://timesofindia.indiatimes.com/city/goa/In-2007-50-MLAs-were-crorepatis/articleshow/11443580.cms, accessed on 6 August 2015.

Remembering Paik's Temple

1 Durgadas Gaonkar and Babal Gawde, 'Tribal Movements in Goa', *mandgoa.blogspot.in*, 2 July 2008, http://mandgoa.blogspot.in/2008/02/tribal-movements-in-goa.html, accessed 6 August 2015.

2 Noam Chomsky, 'Recognising the Unpeople', *In These Times*, 9 January 2012, http://inthesetimes.com/article/12501/recognizing_the_unpeople, accessed 6 August 2015.

3 Pradip Maske, 'Tribal Communities in Goa: Uncertain Future under Mafia-Minister-Police Raj', *Atharva*, Vol. 6, No. 9, 1 September 2011, http://atharvagoa.blogspot.in/2011/11/tribal-communities-in-goa-uncertain.html, accessed 6 August 2015.

4 Paul Fernandes, 'Govt studying impact of borewells in Verna Industrial Sector', *The Times of India*, 14 April 2013, http://timesofindia.indiatimes.com/city/goa/Govt-studying-impact-of-borewells-in-Verna-industrial-sector/articleshow/19540056.cms, accessed 6 August 2015.

5 TNN, 'Historic rock art included in unauthorized religious structures list', *The Times of India*, 15 March 2010, http://timesofindia.indiatimes.com/city/goa/Historical-rock-art-included-in-unauthorized-religious-structures-list/articleshow/5684085.cms?referral=PM, accessed 6 August 2015.

6 Hartman de Souza, 'The curses of Paikdev, a lament for water', *kafila.org*; 21 November 2009, http://kafila.org/2009/11/21/the-curses-of-paikdev-a-lament-for-water-hartman-de-souza/, accessed 6 August 2015.

7 Special Correspondent, '94 court arrest in Goa as anti-mining stir intensifies', *The Hindu*, 24 April 2011, http://www.thehindu.com/todays-paper/tp-national/tp-karnataka/94-court-arrest-in-goa-as-antimining-stir-intensifies/article1763420.ece, accessed 6 August 2015.

The Mining Families

1 Joseph Zuzarte, 'Raising the dust on illegal mining in Goa', *inforchangeindia.org*, September 2011, http://infochangeindia.org/environment/features/raising-the-dust-on-illegal-mining-in-goa.html, accessed on 6 August 2015.

2 Raman Kirpal, 'The Whos Who of Mining are funding Indian Political Parties', *Firstpost.com*, 11 September 2012, http://www.firstpost.com/politics/the-whos-who-of-mining-are-funding-indias-political-parties-451071.html, accessed 6 August 2015.
See also: BS Reporter, 'Black Money trail: Timblo donated nine times to BJP and thrice to Congress', *Business Standard*, 28 October 2014, http://www.business-standard.com/article/current-affairs/timblo-donated-nine-times-to-bjp-and-thrice-to-congress-114102800031_1.html, accessed 6 August 2015.

3 Rupesh Samant, 'Goa looks for political stability as election day arrives', *Rediff.com*, 1 June 2007, http://www.rediff.com/news/2007/jun/01goa.htm, accessed 6 August 2015.

4 Kiran Tare, 'Miners loot lost paradise', *India Today*, 8 October 2011, http://indiatoday.intoday.in/story/goa-illegal-mining-scam-miners-congress-leaders-digambar-kamat-margao/1/154086.html, accessed 6 August 2015.

5 Arwin Mesquita, 'Outrageous: Rich Goa made poor', *Goan Identity blog*, 29 January 2013, http://goanidentity.blogspot.in/2013/01/outrageous-rich-goa-made-poor.html, accessed 6 August 2015.

6 Mayabhushan Nagvenkar, 'Int'l investigative journos blow the lid off Goa mining families' off-shore accounts, *Target Goa*, 19 June 2013, http://www.targetgoa.com/goabuzzdet.php?bzid=5133&&id=3www.targetgoa.com/goabuzzdet.php, accessed 6 August 2015.

7 Remy Dias, 'Land Reforms in Post Liberation Goa (1961–1976)', *Radix International Journal of Research in Social Science*, August 2014, Vol. 3, Issue 8, http://rierc.org/social/paper437.pdf, accessed 6 August 2015.

8 Aarthi Sridhar, 'Eminent domain, absolute doubt: Crusade for Goa's comunidades', *infochangeindia.org*, December 2010, http://infochangeindia.org/environment/coastal-commons/eminent-domain-absolute-doubt-crusade-for-goa-s-comunidades.html, accessed 6 August 2015.

9 Government of Goa, Code of Comunidades: Legislative Enactment No. 2070, 15 April 1961, http://goaprintingpress.gov.in/uploads/Code%20of%20Comunidade.pdf, accessed 6 August 2015.

10 Nandkumar Kamat, 'Why people miss Dayanand Bandodkar', *The Navhind Times*, 10 March 2013.

11 IANS, 'Kamat was aware of illegal mining: Shah commission', *Zee News*, 8 September 2012, http://zeenews.india.com/news/goa/kamat-was-aware-of-illegal-mining-shah-commission_798463.html, accessed 6 August 2015.

Also see: Report, 'Suspended mining officials to take government to court, *goachronicle.com*, 26 September 2012, http://goachronicle.com/suspended-mining-officials-to-take-government-to-court/, accessed 6 August 2015.

12 PTI, 'Goa: Nearly 70 mines within 10 kilometers of sanctuaries: CEC to SC', *Firstpost.com*, 19 September 2013, http://www.firstpost.com/india/goa-nearly-70-mines-within-10-km-of-sanctuaries-cec-to-sc-1121079.html, accessed 6 August 2015.

13 PTI, 'Proposed buffer zone likely to eat into half of Goa's mines', *Mid-day.com*, 9 May 2012, http://www.mid-day.com/articles/proposed-buffer-zone-likely-to-eat-into-half-of-goa-mines/162018, accessed 6 August 2015.

14 Constantino Xavier, 'Commonwealth 1983', *The Goan*, 23 November 2013, http://www.thegoan.net/View-From-Afar/Commonwealth-1983/Column-Post/00371.html, accessed 6 August 2015.

15 Association for Democratic Reforms, 'Pratapsingh Rane: Candidate Profile', http://www.myneta.info/goa2012/candidate.php?candidate_id=70, accessed 6 August 2015.

16 Expose, 'Names of Goa politicians on intelligence agencies watch', *goachronicle.com*, 13 August 2011, http://goachronicle.com/names-of-goa-politicians-on-intelligence-agencies-watch/, accessed 6 August 2015.

17 Shalini Singh, 'No new mining in fragile Goa', *Hindustan Times*, 23 February 2010, http://www.hindustantimes.com/india-news/no-new-mining-in-fragile-goa/article1-511773.aspx, accessed 6 August 2015.

18 http://www.goanewsonline.com/index.php/local-news/7190-sattari-sanguem-quepem-account-for-90-of-illegal-mining-parrikar, accessed 6 August 2015.

19 Report, 'Koda has business interests in Goa as well: Goa CM', *DNA*, 6 November 2009, http://www.dnaindia.com/india/report-koda-has-business-interests-in-goa-as-well-goa-cm-1308141, accessed 6 August 2015.

20 Pamela D'Mello, 'Submerged in Illegal Mining', *Frontline*, November 5–18, Vol. 28, Issue 23

http://www.frontline.in/static/html/fl2823/stories/20111118282304600.htm, accessed 6 August 2015.

21 Gopal Krishna, 'At play in the fields of the lord', *Tehelka*, 24 November 2010, http://archive.tehelka.com/story_main47.asp?filename=Ws241110ENVIRONMENT.asp, accessed 6 August 2015.

22 Ibid.

23 Toxics Watch Alliance, 'Adverse Consequences of DMK's Regime at Environment Ministry', *Sanctuary Asia*, 26 November 2010, http://www.sanctuaryasia.com/component/content/article/81-news/3686-press-release-adverse-consequences-of-dmks-regime-at-environment-ministry.html, accessed 6 August 2015.

24 Snehal Rebello and Ketaki Ghoge, 'Raja again: Gave green nod to 169 mines in Goa', *Hindustan Times*, 23 September 2011, http://www.hindustantimes.com/india-news/raja-again-gave-green-nod-to-169-mines-in-goa/article1-749082.aspx, accessed 6 August 2015.

25 Report, 'Goa mining scam worth Rs 34,935 crore: Justice Shah Commission', *Hindustan Times*, 7 September 2012, http://www.hindustantimes.com/india-news/goa-mining-scam-worth-rs-34-935-crore-justice-shah-commission/article1-926249.aspx, accessed 6 August 2015.

26 Central Pollution Control Board, 'Comprehensive Industry Document on Iron Ore Mining', August 2007, http://cpcb.nic.in/upload/NewItems/NewItem_105_iron_ore_mining_31.07.08.pdf, accessed 6 August 2015.

27 Shibani Ghosh, 'Delhi High Court issues notice to Environment Ministry to justify its 'Experts', *The Access Initiative*, 4 May 2011, accessed 6 August 2015.
http://www.accessinitiative.org/blog/2011/05/delhi-high-court-issues-notice-environment-ministry-justify-its-%E2%80%98experts%E2%80%99, accessed 6 August 2015.
Kanchi Kohli, 'EAC's Dubious Chief', *Civil Society*, August 2010
http://www.civilsocietyonline.com/Archive/aug10/aug1014.asp, accessed 6 August 2015.

28 PTI, 'Environment impact assessments & environmental clearances on Goa mining leases highly deficient: CEE Panel', *The Economic Times*, 16 October 2013, http://articles.economictimes.indiatimes.com/2013-10-16/news/43107041_1_goa-mining-mining-firms-eias, accessed 6 August 2015.

29 Sebastian Rodrigues, 'Maina, Quepem under mining threats', *MAND*, 29 June 2008, http://mandgoa.blogspot.in/2008/06/mina-quepem-under-mining-threats.html, accessed 6 August 2015.

30 Fr. Robert Attickal, 'Goan Women up in arms against Mining Lobby', *Union of Presentation Sisters*, 12 August 2008, http://www.presentationsistersunion.org/news/view_article.cfm?id=181&loadref=16, accessed 6 August 2015.
31 Ibid.

Cheryl's Last Stand

1 Aimee Ginsberg, 'And She Wore Iron', *Outlook*, 23 May 2011, http://www.outlookindia.com/article/and-she-wore-iron/271812, accessed on 6 August 2015.
Also see: Raman Kirpal, 'She cremated her hubby on her land to thwart Goa's miners', *Firstpost.com*, 28 September 2011, http://www.firstpost.com/business/she-cremated-her-hubby-on-her-land-to-thwart-goas-miners-94384.html, accessed on 6 August 2015.
2 Report, 'Goa's first Catholic Chief Minister arrested for smuggling gold', *Ucanews.com*, 30 September 1991, http://www.ucanews.com/story-archive/?post_name=/1991/09/30/goas-first-catholic-chief-minister-arrested-for-smuggling-gold&post_id=39909, accessed on 6 August 2015.
Also see: Bhanva Vij-Aurora, 'Alemao's Gold', *Outlook*, 19 March 2007, http://www.outlookindia.com/article/alemaos-gold/234173, accessed on 6 August 2015.
3 Smita Venkateswaran, 'Goa's Ministers who are booked under criminal cases', *The Economic Times*, 16 October 2008, http://articles.economictimes.indiatimes.com/2008-10-16/news/27720372_1_goa-legislative-assembly-education-minister-churchill-alemao, accessed on 6 August 2015.
4 Report, 'Maina, Pirla locals oppose hearing of 2 proposed mines', *Herald*, 23 June 2008, http://www.heraldgoa.in/Goa/The-Sunday-Roundtable/maina-pirla-locals-oppose-hearing-of-2-proposed-mines/12107.html, accessed on 6 August 2015.

Money Drove It All

1 Statistics on Magnum Minerals Private Limited, Company Profile, *CorporateDir*, http://corporatedir.com/company/magnum-minerals-private-limited, accessed on 6 August 2015.
2 Complaint on ConsumerComplaints.in, 26 February 2011, http://www.consumercomplaints.in/complaints/magnum-minerals-c352330.html, accessed on 6 August 2015.

3 Prashant Sahu's Executive Profile on Bloomberg.com, http://www.bloomberg.com/research/stocks/people/person.asp?personId=228066070&ticker=MIL, accessed on 6 August 2015.
4 Historical Data on Investorguide.com, *MFC Industrial Ltd*, http://www.investorguide.com/stock-historical.php?ticker=MIL, accessed on 6 August 2015.
5 Pamela D'Mello, 'Goa's Mining Logjam', *Economic and Political Weekly*, 14 February 2015, http://www.epw.in/reports-states/goas-mining-logjam.html, accessed 6 August 2015.
6 MFC Indistrial Ltd's Company Profile on Reuters, http://www.reuters.com/finance/stocks/companyOfficers?symbol=MIL.N, accessed on 6 August 2015.
7 US Securities and Exchange Commission, Form 6-K, *MFC Industrial Ltd*, November 2012, http://www.sec.gov/Archives/edgar/data/16859/000120677412004622/mfc_6k.htm, accessed on 6 August 2015.
8 Report, 'Story of Brazen Illegal Mining in Goa', *Rediff.com*, 8 December 2012, http://www.rediff.com/news/report/detailed-report-story-of-brazen-illegal-mining-in-goa/20121208.htm, accessed on 6 August 2015.
9 Report, 'SIT makes second arrest in illegal mining case', *The Times of India*, 23 March 2014, http://timesofindia.indiatimes.com/city/goa/SIT-makes-second-arrest-in-illegal-mining-case/articleshow/32510921.cms, accessed on 6 August 2015.
Also see: Report, 'SIT to contest bail granted in mining scam', *Herald*, 20 October 2014, http://www.heraldgoa.in/Goa/SIT-to-contest-bail-granted-in-mining-scam-/79977.html & 'Magnum Minerals gets notice for failing to declare export proceeds', 3 June 2015, http://www.heraldgoa.in/Goa/Magnum-Minerals-gets-notice-for-failing-to-declare-export-proceeds/89270.html, accessed on 6 August 2015.
10 Report, 'SIT arrests another director of mining firm', *The Times of India*, 29 March 2014, http://timesofindia.indiatimes.com/city/goa/SIT-arrests-another-director-of-mining-firm/articleshow/32867222.cms, accessed on 6 August 2015.

Politicians, Activists, Journalists

1 Vijesh Kamath, 'The guilty, named in 2008, got away', *Deccan Herald*, 17 July 2011, http://www.deccanherald.com/content/177155/guilty-named-2008-got-away.html, accessed on 6 August 2015.

2 Justice Hedge's Report on Illegal Mining in Karnataka, *NDTV*, 28 July 2011, http://www.ndtv.com/india-news/justice-hegdes-report-on-illegal-mining-in-karnataka-463214, accessed on 6 August 2015.
3 Report, 'Somashekara Reddy and 13 others charged in mining scam', *CNN-IBN*, 4 October 2012, http://www.ibnlive.com/news/politics/somashekara-reddy-13-others-charged-in-mining-scam-514082.html, accessed on 6 August 2015.
4 Report, 'Hegde cites times constraint in nailing Bellary mining culprits', *The Economic Times*, 25 September 2011, http://articles.economictimes.indiatimes.com/2011-09-25/news/30200868_1_lokayukta-santosh-hegde-today-illegal-mining-bellary, accessed on 6 August 2015.
5 Prince Matthew Thomas, 'U.V. Singh: On a mission to end illegal mining', *Forbes India*, 30 August 2012, http://forbesindia.com/printcontent/33630, accessed on 6 August 2015.
6 Arun Prabhudesai, '2013 Update: Per Capita Income of various Indian States', *Trak.in*, 17 December 2013, http://trak.in/tags/business/2012/03/30/average-per-capita-income-indian-states/, accessed on 6 August 2015.
7 Details of The Goa Foundation's legal work against mining can be found on their website, http://www.goafoundation.org/mining/, accessed on 6 August 2015.
8 More on the Goa Foundation's petition: http://www.goafoundation.org/pages/public_interest_files/91-92.html, accessed on 6 August 2015.
9 Hartman de Souza, 'The Reason for Locking Up Cheryl', *Mand*, 2 November 2008, http://mandgoa.blogspot.in/2008/11/reason-for-locking-up-cheryl.html, accessed on 6 August 2015.
10 Kurush Canteenwala's documentary, *Goa Goa Gone* can be viewed here: http://infochangeindia.org/videos/goa-goa-gone.html, accessed on 6 August 2015.
11 Sebastian Rodrigues' anti-mining blog can be found here: http://mandgoa.blogspot.in/, accessed on 6 August 2015.
12 Report, 'Govertment Servants Own Majority of Mining Trucks', *Goacom.com*, 16 November 2012, http://www.goacom.com/goa-news-highlights/2711-govt-servants-own-majority-mining-trucks, accessed on 6 August 2015.
13 Stefan Geens, 'Hunting Illegal Mining in Goa', *Ogle Earth*, 9 October 2011, http://ogleearth.com/2011/10/hunting-illegal-mining-in-goa/, accessed on 6 August 2015.

14 Krishna Kumar, 'Assembly Line 2012: Never mind that India's political economy is on a downslide – Goa is among the best for growth recorded in the world', *Daily Mail*, 2 March 2012, http://www.dailymail.co.uk/indiahome/indianews/article-2108918/Indias-political-economy-downslide-overall--BUT-Goa-best-growth-recorded-world.html, accessed on 6 August 2015.

15 Report, '2012 Goa elections: 3 of four rich contestants are mining contractors', *Pravasi Today*, 23 February 2013, http://www.pravasitoday.com/2012-goa-elections-3-of-top-four-rich-contestants-are-mining-contractors, accessed on 6 August 2015.

16 See Chapter 1, note ii.

17 Report, 'Babush took 24.75 crore from builders in Goa: IT', *The Times of India*, 1 February 2012, http://timesofindia.indiatimes.com/city/goa/Babush-took-24-75-crore-from-builders-in-Goa-I-T/articleshow/11708655.cms, accessed on 6 August 2015.

18 Cecil, 'Wendell confronts Sujay, and sends him packing!', *Mand*, 24 May 2009, http://mandgoa.blogspot.in/2009/05/wendell-confronts-sujay-and-sends-him.html, accessed on 6 August 2015.

19 Claude Alvares, 'Mining Blues and its Many Hues', *Goanet.org*, 24 February 2011, http://permalink.gmane.org/gmane.culture.region.india.goa/120442, accessed on 6 August 2015.

20 Report, 'Drop Suit against Seby, greens scream', *Gomantak Times*, 13 January 2009, http://mandgoa.blogspot.in/2009/01/drop-suit-against-seby-greens-scream.html, accessed on 6 August 2015.

21 See A Bird's Eye View, note vii.

22 Auduth Timblo, 'Mineral farming brings health and employment', *Herald*, 16 January 2009, http://www.heraldgoa.in/Edit/Editorial/mineral-farming-brings-health-and-employment/21713.html, accessed on 6 August 2015.

23 State Level Committee for RGP-21, Regional Plan for Goa 2021, https://www.goa.gov.in/pdf/RPG21.pdf.

24 Venita Coelho, 'Strip Mining is not Farming, Mr Timblo', *Herald*, 21 January 2009, http://mandgoa.blogspot.in/2009/01/strip-mining-is-not-farming-mr-timblo.html, accessed on 6 August 2015.

25 Hartman de Souza, 'A vote of disgust', *Outlook*, 7 March 2012, http://www.outlookindia.com/article/a-vote-of-disgust/280185, accessed 6 August 2015.

A Solitary Tree

1 See Chapter 3, 'The Mining Families', note 1.
2 Report, 'Joint inspection confirmed illegalities at Devapan Mine', *Mand*, 22 December 2010, http://mandgoa.blogspot.in/2010/12/joint-inspection-confirmed-illegalities.html, accessed on 6 August 2015.
3 Hartman de Souza, 'It Has Finally Happened', *Target Goa*, 23 April 2011, http://www.targetgoa.com/goabuzzdet.php?bzid=2234&&id=3, accessed on 6 August 2015.
4 An example of the kind of laterite quarrying that was carried out in Goa: http://www.teriin.org/teri-wr/projects/laterite.htm#image, accessed on 6 August 2015.
5 John Fernandes, 'People–police clash over mining transport in Ambaulim, Quepem', *Mand*, 28 November 2008, http://mandgoa.blogspot.in/2008/11/people-police-clash-over-mining.html, accessed on 6 August 2015.

Recasting Ambaulim

1 Report, 'Mapusa Garbage Dumped on Assagao Communidade Land set on fire yet again', *Goacom.com*, 28 January 2013, http://www.goacom.com/goa-scan/5514-mapusa-garbage-dumped-on-assagao-communidade-land-set-on-fire-yet-again, accessed on 6 August 2015.
Also see: Report, 'GSPCB issues ultimatum to Mapusa Municipal Council on city's garbage management', *Herald*, 2 January 2012, http://indiaenvironmentportal.org.in/content/345388/gspcb-issues-ultimatum-to-mapusa-municipal-council-on-citys-garbage-management/, accessed on 6 August 2015. Report, 'Mapusa–Siolom road reeks of garbage', *The Times of India*, 30 August 2013, http://timesofindia.indiatimes.com/city/goa/Mapusa-Siolim-road-reeks-of-garbage/articleshow/22150505.cms, accessed on 6 August 2015.
2 Basuri Desai, 'That sinking feeling in Panjim', *The Goan*, 20 September 2014, http://www.thegoan.net/Goa//That-stinking-feeling-in-Panjim/08611.html, accessed on 6 August 2015.
3 Goa Population Census Data 2011, http://www.census2011.co.in/census/state/goa.html, accessed on 6 August 2015.
4 Thomas Collins, 'Laudato Si: Sin is at the root of the desecration of the environment', *Spero News*, 18 June 2015, http://www.speroforum.com/a/

WGTUWUTZUB39/76079-Laudato-si-Sin-is-at-the-root-of-the-desecration-of-the-environment#.VaFb0vmqqko, accessed on 6 August 2015.
Also see: James Hookway,' Church Efforts Slows Phillippines Mining', *The Wall Street Journal*, 13 February 2009, http://www.wsj.com/articles/SB123449556539081061, accessed on 6 August 2015.
Report, 'The Church supports the campaign against mining exploitations in Flores', *Agenzia Fides*, 24 October 2014, http://www.fides.org/en/news/36619-ASIA_INDONESIA_The_Church_supports_the_campaign_against_mining_exploitation_in_Flores, accessed on 6 August 2015.
Austin Ivereigh, 'The great reformer', *Democracy Now*, 31 December 2014, http://www.democracynow.org/2014/12/31/the_great_reformer_pope_francis_biographer, accessed on 6 August 2015.

5 Press release, 'A Reflection for Social Apostolate Day', *Council for Social Justice and Peace*, 3 October 2010, http://www.csjpgoa.org/press-releases/, accessed on 6 August 2015.

6 Vanxim belonged to the Santa Monica convent in Old Goa, and its original inhabitants were converts to Catholicism, very probably Gavde, who looked after a piggery that supplied various priests with pork – a Goan Catholic delicacy, if not an imperative. The island of Vanxim was sold on behalf of the present archbishop by the then procurator Fr. Arlino De Mello at a rate that started at Rs 6 and did not exceed Rs 20 a square metre. The total amount officially received by the church was in the region of just Rs 55 lakh. The accusation is that the island of Vanxim was sold by the church without consulting the tenants who lived there, and precautions were taken to ensure the secrecy of the land transaction. They must have known that if the deed was not challenged in a court of law, future recourse to action would become time-barred.
See also: Report, 'Goa Church under cloud for selling island to resort company', *Thaindian.com*, 8 December 2010, http://www.thaindian.com/newsportal/uncategorized/goa-church-under-cloud-for-selling-island-to-resort-company_100410920.html#ixzz0wOgmr0oK, accessed on 6 August 2015.

My Family and Other Animals

1 Rajendra Kerkar, 'Dire need to save Goa's Tigers', *The Times of India*, 20 February 2011, http://timesofindia.indiatimes.com/city/goa/Dire-need-

to-save-Goas-tiger-woods/articleshow/7530844.cms, accessed on 6 August 2015.

2 Ibid.

3 Steve Connor, 'Is it time to give up on Tigers and Pandas?', *The Independent*, 9 November 2011, http://www.independent.co.uk/news/science/is-it-time-to-give-up-on-tigers-and-pandas-6259146.html
See also: Report, 'Wildlife Census Points to Presence of Tigers in Goa', *The Hindu*, 13 May 2010, http://www.thehindu.com/sci-tech/energy-and-environment/wildlife-census-points-to-presence-of-tigers-in-goa/article429002.ece, accessed on 6 August 2015.

4 Report, '4 Detained for Tiger Poaching', *The Times of India*, 26 May 2009, http://timesofindia.indiatimes.com/city/goa/4-detained-for-tiger-poaching/articleshow/4577237.cms, accessed on 6 August 2015.

5 Report, 'Wildlife Kerkar named as abettor in tiger killing', *Daijiworld.com* 9 February 2010, http://www.daijiworld.com/news/news_disp.asp?n_id=71967, accessed on 6 August 2015.

6 Shalini Singh, 'Now, Goa may contribute to the national tiger count?', *Ruralindiaonline.org*, 10 June 2014, http://www.ruralindiaonline.org/articles/now-goa-may-contribute-to-the-national-tiger-count/, accessed on 6 August 2015.

7 Armstrong Vaz, 'Tiger killing in Goa haunts green journalist from Goa', *Digital Journal*, 23 February 2010, http://www.digitaljournal.com/article/287985, accessed on 6 August 2015.

8 Ibid.

9 Report, 'Tiger, tiger burning bright in Goa's forests', *The New Indian Express*, 6 February 2011, http://www.newindianexpress.com/nation/article393538.ece?service=print, accessed on 6 August 2015.

10 Personal communication with Fernando Velho.

11 Report, 'One sparrow doesn't make a summer: CM on tiger proof', *Goacom.com*, 2 October 2013, http://www.goacom.com/goa-news-highlights/14038-one-sparrow-doesn-t-make-a-summer-cm-on-tiger-proof, accessed on 6 August 2015.

12 Report, 'Goa is home to 5 tigers: Census', *Herald*, 21 January 2015, http://www.heraldgoa.in/Goa/Goa-is-home-to-5-tigers-Census/83787.html, accessed on 6 August 2015.

13 Report, 'Hi-tech cameras prove presence of tigers in Goa', *The Times of India*, 16 April 2015, http://timesofindia.indiatimes.com/city/goa/Hi-tech-cameras-prove-presence-of-tigers-in-Goa/articleshow/46937930.cms, accessed on 6 August 2015.

AFTERWORD

1 Jason Kicks, 'It will take 100 years for the world's poorest to earn $1.25 a day', *The Guardian*, 30 March 2015, http://www.theguardian.com/global-development-professionals-network/2015/mar/30/it-will-take-100-years-for-the-worlds-poorest-people-to-earn-125-a-day, accessed 6 August 2015.

2 See these reports: PTI, '60 Goa Mines would be able to work once ban is lifted: CM', *Moneycontrol.com*, 24 April 2013, http://www.moneycontrol.com/news/business/60-goa-mines-would-be-able-to-work-once-ban-is-lifted-cm_858273.html
Tara Cunningham, 'Vedanta Resources soar as iron ore mining reopens in Goa', *The Telegraph*, 10 August 2015
http://www.telegraph.co.uk/finance/markets/marketreport/11794968/Vedanta-Resources-soars-as-iron-ore-mine-reopens-in-Goa.html

3 Pamela D'Mello, 'Goa's mining logjam', *Economic and Political Weekly*, 14 February 2015, Vol. L, No. 7, http://www.epw.in/reports-states/goas-mining-logjam.html, accessed 6 August 2015.

4 Interview with Claude Alvares, 'Goa must appeal against High Court ruling', *Frontline*, 19 September 2014, http://www.frontline.in/the-nation/goa-must-appeal-against-high-court-ruling/article6364814.ece, accessed 6 August 2015.

5 TNN, 'Goa must recover illegal mining money', *The Times of India*, 11 December 2014, http://timesofindia.indiatimes.com/city/goa/Goa-must-recover-illegal-mining-money/articleshow/45481863.cms, accessed 6 August 2015.

6 Report, 'Goa Foundation and 4 Goan Padma Shris launch Goenchi Mati Permanent Fund campaign', *Target Goa*, 12 July 2014, http://www.targetgoa.com/goabuzzdet.php?bzid=6195&&id=3D3, accessed 6 August 2015.
See also: News alert, 'Ethical mining: Permanent funds and Inter-generational equity', *Inclusive Media for Change*, undated, http://www.im4change.org/news-alerts/ethical-mining-permanent-funds-inter-generational-equity-4675354.html, accessed 6 August 2015.

7 Mridula Chari, 'In a first, Supreme Court order on Goa mining aims to use natural wealth for public good', *Scroll*, http://scroll.in/article/662583/why-the-activists-who-demanded-a-halt-on-mining-in-goa-welcome-decision-to-lift-the-ban, accessed 6 August 2015.

8 Ibid.

9 Hartman de Souza, 'Who will save Goa?', *d-sector.org: Making Sense of Development,* http://www.d-sector.com/article-det.asp?id=1379&idFor=1379, accessed 6 August 2015.

10 'A note on Fish Curry and Rice', *India Environmental Portal: Knowledge for Change,* http://www.indiaenvironmentportal.org.in/content/260140/fish-curry-and-rice-a-source-book-on-goa-its-ecology-and-life-style/, accessed 6 August 2015.

Acknowledgements

This is long, but I have to do it.

My most thanks must go to Ujwala Samarth who gave my first draft shape in her own inimitable way, and placed the idea (and edited-out material!) for a possible sequel on Goa in my head; and also for suggesting the title.

As strong thanks must go to the editors at Harper Collins and in particular, Ajitha G.S., who pared and pruned the manuscript to give it a better flow, and politely poured water on the fire and brimstone. Thanks to Ujwala and Ajitha, I learnt a lot about writing. And many thanks to Antony Thomas for the meticulousness of his proof-reading. If there are blemishes, they must surely be mine.

Also equally big thanks to Zuri and Zaeen for reading the first draft, Zuri for getting me the right cover and Andrea, for the many photographs to choose from.

While writing this book and later readying it for press, I worked as artistic director with the Space Theatre Ensemble and thanks must go out to them and indeed, their mother body, the Society for Promoting the Arts, Culture and Education (SPACE), Goa, and in particular, Lisa Dias-Noronha, its founding member.

Lisa, her husband Alwyn, and their children Anjora and Amir also played very welcoming and gracious hosts to me while I wrote sections of this book, and were also at the Aguada jail with the other crazy Dias sisters to welcome Dora and Cheryl when they walked out. Thanks also for reading the draft, Alwyn!

Grateful thanks also to the Rector and staff at the Papal Seminary in Pune who let me live there like a monk for three weeks, listening to jazz and taking this book ahead; equally grateful thanks to Thomas Louis, amazing potter, who gave me his beautiful studio in Soccoro, Goa, to finish my final chapters.

There were many who worked with the Space Theatre Ensemble at the farm, volunteering their labour on the land in exchange for Cheryl's hospitality, my culinary skills, and a forest clearing where we could work on our Anti-Mining, pro-environment performance repertoire. We did this till the Mining Ban of 2012.

This body of people comprises the 'We' that I consistently use in the text.

So many thanks to Terence Jorge, Arman Motamedi, Natasha Agarwal, Raghav Malik, Nieta Bruto da Costa, Ria De, Pankhuri Singh, Shymala Kittane, Stephie Madurel, Roweena Lobo, Shashank Chander, Evi Soors, Annapoorna Narayan and Rachana Rajan for their labour and conviction. Big thanks also to Phoebe Pereira and Jarryd Parsekar. In that collective 'We' are also all those activists from Jharkhand, Chhattisgarh, Odisha and Kerala who took the trouble to visit us on the farm and see with their own eyes what the mining was doing to Goa. So special thanks to Xavier Dias, BIRSA, Ranchi; activist grandmother, Carmen Miranda; 'Green' writer, Suprabha Seshan, Sudhirendar Sharma and A. Latha. Their sincerity, solidarity and support were invaluable to all of us. Thanks also to Rama Velip, Shankar Jog, Ramesh Gauns, John Fernandes, Krishnendu Mukherjee and Samir Kelekar whose opposition to mining in Goa was unstinting. Our collective struggle of course, is only beginning...

Many thanks also to Kurush Canteenwala, filmmaker, for the searing documentary on mining that he made at our behest. Very special thanks to my old friend from Mumbai, Uma Narayan, who now teaches philosophy at Vassar College in the US, and whose brilliant poetry on the environment is now very much a part of the ensemble's repertoire.

I am most indebted to Andrea Pereira, the incoming artistic director of the Space Theatre Ensemble, who first suggested that I write about what the mining was doing in Goa; who took hoe in hand with Terence, Stephie, Roweena and I when we farmed the land for three good years and let the land shape our theatre.

Andrea must be joined by the current members of the ensemble, Katheeja Talha, Heidi Pereira and Sugita Thangavelu who performed beyond the call of duty and gave me enough time to do my final edits while on our performance tour. Very special thanks to Katheeja for using her skills to provide me all the footnotes I needed while closing things in Assagao, Goa. Thanks for years of encouragement to old Goan friends, Devika Sequeira, Charudutta Prabhudesai and Lui Godinho. Also new friend, Aritra Bhattarcharya, whose long, silky hair is the envy of all women east of the Suez Canal.

For their financial support to the Space Theatre Ensemble, very grateful thanks to Deepak and Carol Pathania, Sandra D'Souza, Arundhati Ghosh, Joyce Gonsalves, Dean D'Cruz, Reboni Saha, Amita Kanekar, Dr James Albert, Maja Daruwalla and her colleagues at HRI, Satish Padmanabhan and his colleagues at *Outlook*, Meenakshi Subramaniam, Ayesha Kagal. Sunalini Kumar, Anjora Noronha, Amir Noronha, Brinda Singh and our student friends at Lady Shri Ram College, Delhi, who passed the hat around.

In Goa, the ensemble would like to thank Sr Rita Paes of the Nirmala Institute of Education. And for their help and hospitality in Gujarat, many thanks to Fr Cedric Prakash, Gopika Jadeja, and to Hasmukh Baradi and Manvita Baradi of the Garage Theatre; in Bangalore grateful thanks to Gitanjali Sarangan and her team at the Snehadhara Foundation, Poorna Learning Centre, Yohan Chandy and Priya, Tasqeen Macchiwalla and Asad Hajeebhoy, the team of Maraa, Deepika Sarma, Chetana Ajit and Karthik Ranganathan; and in Chennai, thanks to Na Muthuswamy and Natesh Muthuswamy of the Koothu-p-Pattarai theatre group, and Jeny Dolly and Nityanand Jayaraman (and the collective); in Hyderabad, Deepa Kilambi (and her late sister, Sputnik) and Vijay Marur; In Thiruvannamalai to the Marudam Farm School and community and specially to Maitreyi and Ajay and their wonderful kids, and Gayatri Gamuz and Ananda; and in Salem, to Piyush Manush and the workers at the farming collective.

On tour in Delhi when the final edits were being done, the Space Theatre Ensemble was given so much warmth and hospitality, the names of every single person would run to at least two pages. But they are in our heart where they belong. Special thanks in Delhi though to my old friend, the dancer, Bharat Sharma, for opening his heart and teaching us to add new kind of movement to our repertoire.

In Delhi, special thanks must go to my old friend Vibodh Parthasarathi, who kindly allowed us to take over his warm, gracious flat. For hosting this nomadic theatre group, thanks also to Ekta Mittal and Susan Koshy of the Maraa Delhi office, Shriya Singh and Rashmi Sawhney. It was a joy reintroducing the ensemble to my old friends in Delhi, John Dayal, Dilip Simeon, Juliet Reynolds, Ayesha Kagal, Ananda Swaroop, Nivedita Menon, Eddie Rodrigues, Jamal Kidwai, Raman

Kirpal and Amit Sengupta, and meet new friends of the theatre, Brinda Singh, Britta Ohm, Sunalini Kumar, Neel Chaudhuri, Kanav Gupta, Sachin Narayanan, Payal Agarwal and Sahana Manjesh, all of whom we feel we have known for years.

Rahul Sharma, our young handyman and resident cynic from Jammu, with his banjo and Idaho redneck accent, is a connosieur of beef kababs available between Lajpat Nagar and Nizamuddin and brings invaluable skills with him. He also introduced the ensemble to the joys and hazards of busking in Delhi, and it must be officially put on record therefore, that he is the best roadie and musical sidekick the ensemble has ever had.

In Assagao, Goa, many thanks to Fr Oswald, Fr Johnson, Fr Anand and Fr Pakiam of the Palloti Mission who gave us a beautiful space to rehearse, and Edwin and Ida Fonseca and their family at the Hotel Astoria in this beautiful village, for their hospitality and warmth; also Nilankur Das and Chan Yangya (and baby Neziah) and the family that is the People Tree Design Studio and Store, and its twin sibling, the iconic Gunpowder restaurant. So big thanks to Satish Warrier and his family too. Both these people-friendly establishments allowed us their space as a secretariat while finalizing this for press.

And last, but certainly not least, editors at the *Herald*, *Hindustan Times*, *The Hindu*, *Hardnews*, *Outlook*, *Himal* and *Kafila* that used Andrea's photographs and let me write about the mining in Goa.